USER INSTRUCTION
in Academic Libraries

A Century of Selected Readings

Compiled by

Larry L. Hardesty
John P. Schmitt
John Mark Tucker

The Scarecrow Press, Inc.
Metuchen, N.J., and London
1986

Library of Congress Cataloging-in-Publication Data
Main entry under title:

User instruction in academic libraries.

Includes bibliographies and index.
1. Libraries, University and college--Addresses,
essays, lectures. 2. College students--Library
orientation--Addresses, essays, lectures.
3. Libraries and students--Addresses, essays,
lectures. I. Hardesty, Larry L. II. Schmitt,
John P., 1948- . III. Tucker, John Mark.

Z675.U5U84   1986   025.5   86-960
ISBN 0-8108-1881-7

251547

To

James A. Martindale

and

Donald E. Thompson

for

wise and generous counsel

TABLE OF CONTENTS

v

For many academic librarians, and especially for those who have entered the profession in the last ten or so years, bibliographic instruction is almost a given. Even though it may have been barely mentioned in library school, the number of times one encounters it in the professional literature and in a profusion of workshops and conferences indicates that it's firmly established in the profession. And it is probably not much of an exaggeration to assert that academic librarians in any area of public services today either have something to do with bibliographic instruction or have given some thought to why they don't. One hardly sees an advertisement for a public services position in an academic library that does not include bibliographic instruction as part of the job description.

It's hard to realize that it was not always so--indeed, it's been so only a relatively short time. Perhaps that newness is sufficient reason for calling attention to its history now, but there are more compelling reasons.

Those who are actively involved with bibliographic instruction programs know what a busy, immediate process it is. That activity necessitates focusing on the practicalities-- on methods and materials, on comparisons of experiences--all with the intent of making our own work more effective. We haven't had the time or the inclination to look at our history or roots. And yet that history can be useful, even if looking to history for "lessons" is always an uncertain pursuit and sometimes an illusory one. On the other hand, while history may not obviate the need for asking some of the same questions again and again, it can at least help us make our questions more critical and permit us to make more sense out of our experience.

A personal case in point.

Some years ago, after I'd been working in bibliographic instruction for almost a decade, I was asked to teach a course in academic libraries. One of the books I read to prepare for that course was Harvie Branscomb's Teaching With Books. Very quickly I realized--with both surprise and satisfaction-- that Branscomb had asked thirty years before many of the questions I'd been asking, and drawing some of the same inferences I'd made. I'm sure I encountered Branscomb at some point while I was in library school, but he didn't mean much to me then. Now, however, what he had to say not only had meaning for me, but gave me new insights and sparked ideas that became an important part of our program's theoretical foundation.

But an even more important reason for delving into the history of bibliographic instruction, it seems to me, is that it can give us a better sense of our intellectual and practical heritage. That, I think, is most desirable, and not simply because establishing historical connections conveys academic respectability. Nor is it because bibliographic instruction librarians feel unaccepted, or that they have to establish their professional legitimacy.

I found it enormously satisfying, for example, to read Otis H. Robinson saying more than a century ago that "the chief duty of a librarian" is no longer "to collect books and preserve them." Rather, it is "to get them used most extensively, most intelligently, and at the same time, carefully." Or to know that only a few years after that, Melvil Dewey commented that "every reputable college owes it to its students to give them not only experience in a laboratory library, but also instruction in the use of bibliographical apparatus." I'd known those principles were the correct ones, and my work had in large part been based on them. But to realize that my efforts were part of a long and honorable tradition gave my work an added luster--a patina, as it were.

Reading these essays, and the editors' introductions about the men and women who wrote them, may remind us of our goals, our high calling, and help give us new insights and perspectives to enhance our effectiveness in working toward those goals.

Evan Ira Farber
January 4, 1985

INTRODUCTION

More than one hundred years ago Harvard librarian Justin Winsor wrote that "new interest" had been "awakened in libraries as educational agencies" and that the academic library had embarked on a "new career." That career would, much more firmly than in the past, establish instruction as one of the major purposes of college and university libraries. With rapid change and growth in the academic community in the latter part of the nineteenth century, the appearance of various library-oriented publications issued by the U.S. Bureau of Education, and the birth of Library Journal in 1876, there arose a significant body of literature devoted to librarianship. The value of teaching students how to use libraries took its place in this literature as a topic of frequent discussion.

Our purpose in drawing from this material, in arranging and reprinting the articles for this collection, is to illustrate the historical development of user instruction in American academic libraries from 1880 to 1980. It would be impossible to compile an anthology of the "Greatest Hits of Library Instruction" nor is it our intent to do so. Of the numerous books, articles, and reports on user instruction and related topics in academic librarianship, we selected twenty that help identify some of the significant trends and concepts that have emerged since Winsor's recognition of the "new career."

Several factors were brought into play in establishing the scope of this collection. We focused on the academic library since its history generally parallels that of American colleges and universities, and because, as academic librarians, we are most familiar with this portion of the professional literature. The collection also focuses on undergraduates rather than than graduate students, reflecting to some degree the emphasis expressed in the literature as a whole.

xi

The nature and scope of the publications about user instruction are suggested, in part, by the bibliographies that identify disparate items in periodicals and collected works.

Some of the more extensive lists are the following:

- Bonn, George S. Training Laymen in Use of the Library. New Brunswick, New Jersey: Rutgers University, Graduate School of Library Service, 1960.

- Givens, Johnnie. "The Use of Resources in the Learning Experience." In Advances in Librarianship, vol. 4, edited by Melvin J. Voigt, 149-174. New York: Academic Press, 1974.

- Krier, Maureen. "Bibliographic Instruction: A Checklist of the Literature, 1931-1975." Reference Services Review 4 (January-March 1976): 7-31.

- Lockwood, Deborah L., comp. Library Instruction: A Bibliography. Westport, Connecticut: Greenwood Press, 1979.

- Millis, Charlotte. "Toward a Philosophy of Academic Librarianship: A Library-College Bibliography." Library-College Journal 3 (Summer 1970): 49-56; 4 (Winter 1971): 56-58; and 4 (Summer 1971): 48-56.

- Tucker, John Mark. Articles on Library Instruction in Colleges and Universities, 1876-1932. University of Illinois, Occasional Papers, no. 143. Urbana: Graduate School of Library Science, 1980.

- Young, Arthur P. "And Gladly Teach: Bibliographic Instruction and the Library." In Advances in Librarianship, vol. 10, edited by Michael H. Harris, 63-88. New York: Academic Press, 1980.

When we add to these the volumes edited by John Lubans, the published proceedings of conferences such as those at Eastern Michigan University, and the annual bibliographies compiled by Hannelore Rader for Reference Services Review,

xii

we can begin to appreciate the phenomenal growth of the literature.

The bibliographies devoted to library use instruction, representing hundreds of items, frequently call attention to much that is repetitive and unenlightening. In that sense, publications about user instruction resemble the literature of librarianship in general. However, just as in belles lettres there is much that has lasting value, so in bibliographic instruction, that subset of academic librarianship, we find a number of contributions that should be preserved and pondered or that at least merit a fresh reading. It has been our fortunate task to sort through some of these articles in search of enduring concepts and major trends that can inform novice and veteran practitioner alike.

What is needed, then, is a historical anthology, a collection that preserves the classics, resurrects forgotten but provocative notions, and challenges ill-formed assumptions that are based on an inadequate knowledge of earlier ideas and programs. These selections have been made from our own varied (and at times in-depth) involvement in library use instruction, historical research, and numerous discussions with colleagues in the field. Despite our efforts, it is inevitable that we have overlooked an important essay or a reader's favorite. We welcome the opportunity to discuss your suggestions and, thereby, to broaden the dialogue about the nature of the literature. Finally, we hope this compilation can be of value in moving library use instruction forward into the next century, based on a firm understanding of its historical foundations in the past century.

Larry L. Hardesty
John P. Schmitt
John Mark Tucker

Part I

THE BEGINNINGS OF A DIALOGUE

1880–1900

Significant growth in library use instruction during the 1880s
and 1890s followed naturally from the dramatic changes occurring in higher education in the same period. Although reports on instruction about the library's "most rare and valuable works"[1] date from the 1820s, substantial, continuous
course offerings and course-related lectures came about only
as a result of major developments in the library's academic
environment in the latter part of the nineteenth century.
Among these trends were the adoption of original research as
a necessary function of academia, the introduction of the seminar method of instruction featuring student presentations,
and the birth of new curricula in the social sciences and in
professional and technical education. Consciously imitating
their German counterparts, American universities created doc-
toral programs designed to make graduate-level research the
capstone of higher learning.

New graduate departments in the various disciplines
employed increasingly rigorous methods of scholarship and,
thus, made greater demands than ever before on the services
and collections of academic libraries. The libraries, in turn,
were able to increase their administrative support and they
constructed new buildings, oversaw rapidly growing collections,
and extended their hours of service. For example, between
1875 and 1891, Cornell University increased its book collection from 10,000 volumes to 111,000 volumes and between 1876
and 1896 Columbia increased its hours of opening from 12 to
98 per week. This aggressive, bustling, unprecedented
growth created an environment in which library use instruction was the subject of discussion and experimentation.

The optional credit course in bibliography was an important feature of user instruction during this period. More
often than not, the course stressed descriptive bibliography,

the history of books and printing, or even the history of libraries, but it also invariably contained a solid library-use component. Usually taught by the college librarian, it included intellectual or enumerative bibliography designed to show students how to determine the intellectual contents of books. It introduced undergraduates to indexes, bibliographies, and reference works of a general nature and, occasionally, sources in specialized subjects. Assignments necessitated an orientation to the library's physical arrangement, exposure to the card catalog and the classification system used by the library, and knowledge of the bibliographical apparatus underlying disciplines in the humanities and social sciences.

Academic librarians in the latter part of the nineteenth century attempted methods other than the credit course. They gave book talks, bibliographical lectures, and orientation tours. Their experimentation did not produce any established structure or even a generally accepted method for effective instruction. The quality and style of their approaches varied widely from librarian to librarian and from institution to institution. They were sometimes confused about the differences between user instruction and education for library service, also in formative stages during the same period. They did, however, begin the dialogue about the nature and purposes of user instruction. They called for clearly stated objectives for their instructional programs, they sought conceptual models for the library (referring to it as the "heart of the university" or the "laboratory of the liberal arts") and, of perhaps greatest significance, they caught a vision of the educational potential of the library in the academic community.

NOTE

1. Keyes D. Metcalf, "The Undergraduate and the Harvard Library, 1765-1877," Harvard Library Bulletin 1 (Winter 1947): 49.

College Libraries as Aids to Instruction: The College Library

Justin Winsor

Winsor is aptly remembered as first president of the American Library Association and prototypical scholar-librarian. A prolific historian, he was also president of the American Historical Association in addition to duties as head of the Boston Public Library (1868-1877) and the Harvard University Library (1877-1897). At Harvard he championed President Charles W. Eliot's curricular innovations and provided the leadership under which library use, user instruction, and open stack arrangements could emerge. His achievements are assessed by Robert E. Brundin in "Justin Winsor of Harvard and the Liberalizing of the College Library," Journal of Library History 10 (January 1975): 57-70 and John Y. Cole, "Storehouses and Workshops: American Libraries and the Uses of Knowledge," in Alexandra Oleson and John Voss, eds. The Organization of Knowledge in Modern America, 1860-1920 (Baltimore: Johns Hopkins University Press, 1979), pp. 364-385.

This selection illustrates Winsor's conception of the librarian as educator and claims the library as the "central agency in our college methods." The librarian becomes a teacher, not one who hears recitations, but one whose classroom is a "world of books." Aware of newer methods of teaching and research due to the emerging social sciences and expanding graduate programs in the latter part of the nineteenth century, Winsor saw libraries as natural rivals to textbook teaching methods. This essay was reprinted by Wayne Cutler and Michael Harris in Justin Winsor, Scholar-Librarian (Littleton, Colorado: Libraries Unlimited, 1980), pp. 151-155. Along with the following essay by Otis Hall Robinson, it was reviewed by Charles Ammi Cutter in Library Journal 5 (June 1880): 179-182.

[In Circulars of Information of the Bureau of Education; No.
1--1880, pp. 7-14. Washington, D.C.: United States Government Printing Office, 1880.]

•   •   •

President Eliot, in writing of the Harvard Library in a recent
report, spoke of its "having a profound effect upon the instruction given at the university, as regards both substance
and method: it teaches the teachers." And yet, I fear, we
have not discovered what the full functions of a college library should be; we have not reached its ripest effects; we
have not organized that instruction which teaches how to work
its collections as a placer of treasures. To fulfil its rightful
destiny, the library should become the central agency of our
college methods, and not remain a subordinate one, which it
too often is. It is too often thought of last in developing efficiency and awarding appropriations; committed very likely
to the charge of an overworked professor, who values it as
a help to his income rather than an instrumentality for genuine
college work; equipped with few, or even without any, proper
appliances for bibliographical scrutiny; and wanting in all
those administrative provisions that make it serviceable to-
day and keep it so to-morrow.

There is often a feeling that books are, or ought to be,
sensible enough to maintain their own ranks, without the need
of a drill sergeant. A good deal of the librarian's work is
doubtless that of the drill sergeant; but the genuine custodian
of a library knows that his best work is a general's, who has
campaigns to plan and territory to overrun; in other words,
he has got to force his ranks into action, and make each book
do the work for which it was made. Books skulk. Few are
aggressive and compel attention, unless the librarian puts each
on its own vantage ground.

In all this the librarian becomes a teacher, not that
mock substitute who is recited to; a teacher, not with a text
book, but with a world of books. The man is but half grown
who thinks a book is of no use unless it is read through and
would confine his acquaintance to the few score or hundreds
of volumes that he can conscientiously read from beginning
to end in a lifetime. One may indeed have a few books that

remain a constant wellspring to him; but these should be very
few, unless he wishes to have his conceptions dangerously
narrowed. There is nothing so broadening as an acquaintance
with many books, and nothing so improving as acquiring the
art of tasting a book, as the geologist takes in the condition
of a landscape at a glance. Let your few bosom books qualify
your intellectual nature; and then give yourself the food you
will grow upon by the widest discursiveness. The way to
avoid being appalled at the world of books is what the library
of the college is commissioned to point out. Nothing is more
certain than that the so called text book is really more the
author's predilections of a subject than a true exposition of
it. I would not certainly underrate the advantage often to
come from any subject being passed into the alembic of an author's individuality; but it is not all: the subject as a virgin
creation still attracts us. We must often get it from many
angles, and it is the many books that give us this.

I will not now stop to discuss the thraldom or, if you
choose, the practical necessity of the class system. It is
quite true, however, that the arguments for it have resulted
in the text book--something that hits an average, with a void
on either side of it.

I will not say that the library is the antagonist of the
text book; but it is, I claim, its generous rival and abettor,
helping where it fails and leading where it falters. If this
is so, it follows that we must build our libraries with class
rooms annexed, and we must learn our ways through the wilderness of books until we have the instinct that serves the
red man when he knows the north by the thickness of the
moss on the tree-boles.

I do not write this as a piece of idealism. I know it
to be practical. It needs indeed time, money, industry, skill,
patience, but it can be done. You may count the time and
doubt the expediency; you may reckon the money and ask
where it is to come from; you can promise industry; you hope
for skill; you may question if your patience will hold out;
but, with all these saved or acquired, it can be done.

The proposition then is to make the library the grand
rendezvous of the college for teacher and pupil alike, and to
do in it as much of the teaching as is convenient and practicable. This cannot be done with a meagre collection of books

indiscriminately selected, with an untidy, ill lighted, uncomfortable apartment. The library should be to the college
much what the dining room is to the house--the place to
invigorate the system under cheerful conditions with a generous fare and a good digestion. It may require some
sacrifices in other directions to secure this, but even under
unfavorable conditions the librarian can do much to make
his domain attractive. As he needs the coöperation of his
colleagues of the faculty, his first aim is to make everything
agreeable to them, and himself indispensable, if possible.
College faculties are made up much as other bodies are--the
responsive and sympathetic with those that repel and are
self-contained. A librarian shows his tact in adapting himself to each; he fosters their tastes; encourages their
predilections; offers help directly where it is safe, accom-
plishes it by flank movements when necessary; does a
thousand little kindnesses in notifying the professors of
books arrived and treasures unearthed. In this way suavity
and sacrifice will compel the condition of brotherhood which
is necessary and is worth the effort.

With the student also the librarian cannot be too close
a friend. He should be his counsellor in research, supplementing but not gainsaying the professor's advice. It
would be a good plan to take the students by sections, and
make them acquainted with the bibliographical apparatus,
those books that the librarian finds his necessary companions,
telling the peculiar value of each, how this assists in such
cases, that in others; how this may lead to that, until with
practice the student finds that for his work he has almost a
new sense.

I am afraid few librarians not brought up amid an af-
fluence of such reference books understand all that they can
accomplish. It is too much to expect more than a very few
college libraries to be equipped with such books by the
thousands--twenty thousand would not be too many for per-
fection--but there is much that is bought for libraries that
would be best postponed until the librarian can offer such
instruction to the students with a well balanced if not large
bibliographical and reference collection at his hand.

Let me enumerate a few of the books that every librarian will cite among those of chiefest importance to him, and
such as it is a pity every student has not a working knowledge of.

When we consider the broad field of all languages and
all subjects, we must probably give the first place to
Brunet's Manuel du Libraire, the last edition of which (Paris,
1860-1865) is now being completed with some supplemental
volumes. A book must have a certain prominence before
Brunet chronicles it. This work is in its main body alphabetical by authors, but there is a classified topical key in
the last volume. In some respects there is a more ample
record in Graesse's Trésor de livres rares et précieux, but
it is without subject clews.

If we deal with foreign languages and literatures, we
must know also how to use Quérard's various bibliographies--
his La France littéraire and La litterature française contem-
poraine, which with Lorenz's Catalogue général, 1840-1865,
make a record covering 1700-1865. In German the chief
help is Heinsius's Allgemeines Bücher-Lexikon, beginning
1700; but its many supplements make it inconvenient in use.
Kayser's Vollständiges Bücher-Lexikon, beginning 1750, has
the preference for those who wish to use a subject index.
Notice of other languages is hardly called for with the
present purpose.

On the English helps I must be fuller. Watt's
Bibliotheca Britannica is arranged by authors and by subjects, but contains nothing later than 1820. Its topical
arrangement gives it often advantages over Lowndes, who
cannot in all ways be said to supersede it. Bohn's edition
of Lowndes's Bibliographer's Manual is the best to have,
with all its faults; but it is an arrangement by authors only.
Its eleven parts as issued are sometimes bound in six volumes.
Lowndes published the work originally in 1834, and Bohn began the new edition intending simply to revise and add to
Lowndes's entries; but as the work went on, Bohn extended
his scheme, and the later volumes are much fuller than the
first, and they contain the record of various writers whom
Lowndes had ignored. In this way it is a pretty good regis-
ter of authors who appeared before 1834, chronicling for
about thirty years later their newer publications and editions
of older works. The article on Shakespeare, for instance,
is much elaborated, and is one of the best of the Shake-
spearian bibliographies, and it extends into other languages.
The eleventh part of Bohn, in his sixth volume, is the only
convenient record we have of the publications of societies
and printing clubs, of private presses, and of similar excep-
tional issues.

Allibone's Critical Dictionary of English Literature is
indispensable. It is useful biographically as well as bibliographically, but as there was an interruption in the printing
the user must bear in mind that up to the letter O the
record is not later than 1858, while after that it is in some
parts as late as 1870. The author frequently gives under
another writer, whom he may be treating of, sometimes with
appositeness and sometimes with hardly any, addenda to
articles which had already passed in the printing. Though
a large part of the third volume is made up of indexes,
which nobody uses, no index is given to these continuations,
and they are lost unless the user makes his own index to
them. They are of this kind: Under Syntax, the pseudonym
of Combe, the record of his publications is continued, and as
John Camden Hotten chanced to edit an edition of Dr. Syntax's
Tour occasion is taken to introduce a long list of Hotten's
editions, to supply a deficiency under H.

These two books, Allibone and Bohn, are those chiefly
to be commended; but for the publications of the day they
need to be supplemented with Whitaker's Reference Catalogue
of Current Literature for English books and with Leypoldt's
Uniform Trade List Annual for American ones.

For books distinctively American in text or print, and
which were still in the market in 1876, the American Catalogue
is as nearly a complete guide as it is practicable to make.
This catalogue will have, when completed, a topical index.
Such a subject aid is at present found to a much less extent,
but for small libraries quite sufficient, in F. B. Perkins's
Best Reading. For older English books, particularly for
those of too transitory an interest to find place in the bibliographies, there may be occasion to consult the various
publications known as the London, English and British Catalogues; also, such similar publications as Low's Index and
the Bibliotheca Londinensis; and even the lists of current
books printed from month to month in the Gentleman's and
the London Magazines in the last century. So, for the older
American books, one has to consult the last giving those
back of 1776, appended to the last edition of Thomas's
History of Printing, Trübner's Biographical Guide, and
Roorback's Bibliotheca Americana, 1820-1860, continued by
Kelly in his American Catalogue.

The skilled librarian sees that I have given but the

rudimental sources for research, and that the foreign languages admit in some cases of even finer details than the
English. I have mentioned such, however, as it were well
everybody having to do with books should know something
of.

It is further true that there is generally a great lack
of knowledge of the most common books of reference, with
little understanding of the help they can be in literary research for the sources of knowledge. I always know a man
who has learned to work in a great library by the aptness
of his choice of books of reference in any emergency. All
things considered, the most useful of these books, and the
surest to respond to one's wants, is Larouse's Grand dic-
tionnaire universel du XIXe siècle. It is an immense con-
glomeration of matter, and its fine but legible printing
occupies sixteen large quarto volumes. Its cost may shut it
out from the smaller libraries, but it is worth some sacrifice
to get. The Encyclopaedia Britannica can be much more
easily dispensed with, and, notwithstanding the authoritative
character and fulness of its articles, it will not compare with
Larousse for genuine encyclopaedic value.

I can hardly conceive a college library in fit trim that
has not one or more of the principal encyclopaedias now
current, like Appleton's New American Cyclopaedia, Chambers's Encyclopaedia, and Johnson's New Universal Cyclo-
paedia--each good in its way. Appleton is naturally prefer-
able for many American topics and is better supplied with
illustrations. Chambers is better on British subjects.
Johnson, however, gives you more for your money than
either of the others, and is an excellent working reference
book. Of those in foreign languages, after Larousse, the
great German Conversations-Lexikon of Brockhaus, which is
in some sense the parent of the modern cyclopaedia, is the
first choice. There are various other cyclopaedias which
are desirable companions, and some of them have a distinctive value. It is perhaps not of so much consequence which
one we use as it is to use some one constantly. They often
help one by their references to the best literature on a subject. For instance, in all matters appertaining thereto we
shall find very full and well assorted references in
McClintock and Strong's Cyclopaedia of Biblical, Theological,
and Ecclesiastical Literature; a chief use of Allibone's
Dictionary of Authors is for its references. For a compact

general dictionary of biography and mythology, Thomas's
Biographical Dictionary has no superior, and he guides you
to the sources of his information. Haefer's Nourelle biogra-
phie générale has ample notes for further inquiry.

  The indexes of the important periodicals should always
be kept in mind. There are two convenient lists of such
indexes, one in the initial publication of the new Index Society, Wheatley's What Is an Index? and the other in the
little Handbook for Readers, issued by the Boston Public
Library. Poole's Index to Periodical Literature, though
nearly thirty years old, is a necessary adjunct to the reference shelves, and the new edition, now in progress under
the joint action of American and British librarians, will add
a new resource for the inquirer.

  Of the great mass of library catalogues, a few principal ones stand out as distinctively and characteristically
useful, and experience soon discloses them. As a general
rule the subject catalogue of a large collection is a peculiarly
American product; though some of the principal European
libraries are giving signs of efforts in a like direction.
Meanwhile in Britain, the Advocates' Library at Edinburgh,
the Bodleian at Oxford, and several sectional publications of
the British Museum are of constant use in a well equipped
catalogue room. The publications of the latter institution
include their catalogue for the letter A, which Panizzi put a
stop to forty years ago; the catalogues of the King's and of
the Grenville collections; and the very useful list of twenty
thousand volumes which form the handy reference collection
of their great reading room.

  Of the continental libraries it is enough for our present
purpose to name the chronological and classified catalogue of
French history and biography, prepared at the great library
in Paris.

  Of the American library catalogues I can be more particular. Those of the Public Library of Boston are probably
the best known, beginning with the Bates Hall Indexes, two
volumes, and including those of the Ticknor and Prince Collections and of the Barton Collection, still unfinished. This
library has also issued for more general use annotated Class
Lists of History, Biography and Travel, and Fiction, making,
with their critical, descriptive, and advisory notes, the

earliest examples of what has since been called the Educational Catalogue.

For assistance to scholars, however, we can hardly boast anything better than the great Catalogue of the Boston Athenaeum, of which three volumes, bringing it to the letter M, are now published, and into which Mr. Cutter, an exemplar in such work, is putting his careful and discriminating scholarship.

The Subject Catalogue of the Library of Congress, 2 volumes, 1869, and later authors' lists with subject indexes disclose the assiduous care which Mr. Spofford is bestowing upon the national collection.

The student, however, will rarely find for his ordinary work any catalogue to stand him in better stead than Mr. Noyes's classified Catalogue of the Brooklyn Library, and he will regret its present incompleteness, which, it is to be hoped, will not long continue. The Brooklyn Library will not rank with our larger libraries, but it is a good one, and this catalogue forms a better key to it than belongs, in print, to any other of our collections. It follows the Boston catalogues in giving annotations, though not to the same extent; but its references to periodical articles are more systematic, and in this respect it constitutes much the best single continuation of Poole's Index. It can be supplemented in some ways by the Catalogue of the Public Library of Quincy, Mass., which has other features to warrant its taking a place on our nearest reference shelf. I should not pass from this topic without mentioning the Catalogue of the Astor Library, 4 vols., 1857-1861, with a supplement in 1866, an authors' list, with a condensed index of subjects; the Catalogue of the Philadelphia Library, 3 vols., 1856, which is well indexed.

There is no occasion now for my mapping out the limits of the science of bibliography, but I simply give a reference to the article upon it in the Encyclopaedia Britannica, 9th ed., vol. iii. It is the key to all knowledge and the sparer of unfruitful pains. Can there be any instruction fitter for our colleges? There is scarcely any department of learning so little attended to. There is nothing to indicate its scope later than Dr. Petzholdt's Bibliotheca Bibliographica, 1866, and an examination of this thoroughly German specimen of erudition will teach one what it is to be a bibliographer.

Dr. Petzholdt divides his subject into eight heads, covering all languages:

1. General literature.
2. Anonymous and pseudonymous works.
3. Incunabula.
4. Works prohibited by censors.
5. Works on or by particular persons.
6. Engraved portraits.
7. National literature.
8. Classed literature.

There are two minor lists of classed bibliographies, sufficient for most purposes, in Nichol's Handbook for Readers at the British Museum and in the Boston Public Library Handbook already referred to. Supplementing these, the librarian will do well to watch the Bulletins and other Bibliographical Contributions of Harvard College Library, the Boston Public Library, the Boston Athenaeum, and the Lenox Library. Nor can the librarian fully keep abreast of the literary progress without a file of the Publishers' Weekly of New York, the London Bookseller, the Bibliographie de la France, and similar publications of the other modern languages.

I have dwelt upon these extraneous helps because they are something that care and money can procure at the outset. The librarian's great labor, however, the ever accumulating evidence of his devotedness, is something that money will not buy off-hand, but comes, after much pains and never ending assiduity, in the catalogue of his own library. I can hardly here fully indicate the variations of the vexed question of the catalogue, which librarians will always discuss and rarely come to conclusions upon. It may be desirable that some determinations should be reached, but it is by no means necessary to the end in view. All catalogues, if there is a reasonable application of common sense in their construction, are fitted to do good work, and there is no doubt that a good catalogue thoroughly understood is better than a superior one whose principles have not been mastered. That comprehensive Report on American Libraries, issued by the Bureau of Education at Washington in 1876, contains a paper on catalogues by Mr. Cutter, and a code of rules for cataloguing, admirably exemplified by the same authority. This code, which is so thoroughly fashioned that it has become an

authority everywhere, will disclose to anyone who examines
it a new field of intricate knowledge, and it will broaden the
conceptions of any one who is destined to a life of mental
action.

If the librarian and his coadjutors, the instructors of
the college, are to work for a common end effectually, the
collection gathered about them must be catalogued. This
means no rough work of the auctioneer's kind, but scholarly
and faithful inquiry embodied in a fixed and comprehensive
method. Every book must be questioned persistently as to
its author, its kind, its scope, its relations to all knowledge.
Answers to all these questions must be made record of, once
for all. Let not the cost frighten; a library without such an
index is no library, but a mob of books.

My own preference is to have the authors and subjects
catalogued in one alphabetical arrangement, on what is called
the dictionary system, of which the best examples are found
in the printed catalogues of the Boston Athenaeum and of the
Boston Public Library. The plan doubtless has disadvantages;
but for the general user it presents clews that are most easily
followed, and carries in large part its own key. For the
skilled and habitual user, classed catalogues, especially those
in which related subjects stand in close propinquity, may be
more satisfactory; but such users are always rare. Both
kinds, in fact, need a complemental index to restore the
balance lost in the light of the other. In this way the two
are put on planes of substantial equality, and the matter of
choice between them becomes largely a question of predispo-
sition. For the dictionary catalogue the key should be a
tabular classification, showing the relations of allied topics,
with an index of synonymous terms. For the classed catalogue the key should be an alphabetical list of topics,
entered under every conceivable synonym.

There is a kind of indexing too seldom done in libraries, and yet it represents a present need, constantly emphasized. Live questions of the day, and literary questions
brought into prominence by passing events, are matters that
recur to students in their outside reading, and they constitute some of the more profitable subjects for themes and
forensics. Articles and chapters bearing on such questions
are usually buried in periodicals or books of miscellanea,
sufficiently gone by to be not easily recalled. The librarian

who has pursued a habit of indexing such articles as the
numbers pass by, is always much better prepared for all
such questions than he who lets the memoranda pass into dim
corners of his unassisted memory.

I here leave the question of the relations which the
college library should bear to the general conduct of the
academic instruction, commending it to the serious attention
of all whose lot has brought them to undergo the yoked labors of our colleges. The new interest that has of late been
awakened in libraries as educational agencies does not, I feel
sure, leave out of consideration that kind of library which
seems so peculiarly fitted for sharing largely in the general
appreciation. The college library, I trust, is starting on a
new career.

College Libraries as Aids to Instruction:
Rochester University Library--Administration and Use

Otis Hall Robinson

Robinson taught at the University of Rochester from 1864 until his retirement in 1903. He was appointed Professor of Mathematics in 1869; at various times he also taught astronomy and natural philosophy, occupying the chair of natural philosophy from 1891 to 1903. In addition to these duties he was appointed Assistant Librarian in 1866 and Librarian in 1868, serving in the latter capacity until 1889. His place in the history of academic librarianship has been established by Edward G. Holley in "Academic Libraries in 1876," College and Research Libraries 37 (January 1976): 15-47 and "Robinson, Otis Hall (1835-1912)," Dictionary of American Library Biography (Littleton, Colorado: Libraries Unlimited, 1978), pp. 439-440.

Writing for the DALB, Holley claims that Robinson did "as much as anyone in the American library profession to push the idea of the educational role of the college library." A major reason for this legacy is the body of cogent, well-reasoned literature produced by Robinson that described library instruction at Rochester and defined the purposes of academic libraries in general. His articles include "College Library Administration," in Public Libraries in the United States of America: Their History, Condition, and Management (Washington, D.C.: United States Government Printing Office, 1876), pp. 505-525 and "The Relation of Libraries to College Work," Library Journal 6 (April 1881): 97-104.

In the selection included here, Robinson described student library use. "Curiosity begets inquiry; inquiry leads to research. With notebook and pencil in hand,

reading and investigation are planned, based not wholly on
the opinions of others, but also upon personal examination
of the books to be used." Thus, Robinson affirmed the importance of independent inquiry in broad scholarship. He
also underscored the significance of the teacher's role, urg-
ing that professors offer voluntary personal assistance to
students in the library in order to help them make intelligent
choices about books and articles appropriate to their subject
interests. Robinson added that this kind of activity was
much more productive of educational objectives than "any
amount of class lecturing."

[In Circulars of Information of the Bureau of Education;
No. 1--1880, pp. 15-27. Washington, D.C.: United States
Government Printing Office, 1880.]

                    .   .   .

In an institution of learning the transition from a small library to a large one is like the transition in a household from
poverty to wealth: with new powers come new duties. It is
fortunate in one case as in the other if with larger means
there come also enlarged views, if new plans are devised
which embrace the economical use of large and increasing resources. How to use a library is, therefore, a question of
great and growing importance to nearly every college in the
country. It is due to those liberal patrons of learning who
are erecting library buildings and filling them with books
that this question be carefully studied. It is due to officers
of instruction that such a system be adopted that all the departments may increase symmetrically and be used in due
proportion, without collision and without omission. It is due
to students that with the use of larger libraries courses of
study should be enlarged, and that special instruction should
be given in methods of investigation. It is due to the public,
in an age when libraries are exerting so great an intellectual
and moral influence, that young men should come from the
colleges thoroughly trained in their nature and their use.

There is evidence that a reform in this matter has already been begun. The old method, or rather lack of method,
is passing away under the influence of the Library Association,

the Library Journal, and the reports of the Commissioner of
Education. The idea that a college librarian may serve the
classes as an instructor quite as successfully as the professor of Latin or of mathematics is beginning to take root. It
is beginning to be understood also that teachers can make
an important use of the library in giving their regular instruction. In many places the libraries are becoming so
large that careful attention must be given by readers to
selection. The time has passed when a smart reader could
exhaust the resources of the library on a given subject in
a few weeks. Time is lacking now, not books. The question now is, what is up to date in science, vigorous in
literature, and pertinent to one's wants--what on the whole
is best? In answering this, teachers, as well as librarians,
begin to see how great an influence for good may be exerted.
The time is passing also when the chief duty of a librarian
was to collect books and preserve them. How to get them
used most extensively, most intelligently, and at the same
time carefully, is becoming his chief concern.

The object of this paper is to describe clearly, yet
briefly, the methods adopted in the Library of the University
of Rochester, hoping thereby to contribute somewhat to the
reform which we believe to be steadily going on.[1] In doing
this it will be proper to state the opinions which underlie
our library administration, and some of the results of it
which have become clear and definite. We wish to do this
without pretension, claiming nothing except that we have
given our attention to the subject. We have adopted some
methods which we were not ourselves taught, and we think
they have been successful. In some respects we are conscious that our library facilities are inferior to those of many
other institutions, but we yield to none in the desire and
the earnest effort to make the best use of what we have.

Statistics of the Library

For convenience of reference we give at the outset the principal statistics of the library:
    1. The library building is fire-proof and contains:
       (a) A public room for the library, 112 feet long,
          46 feet wide, and 22 feet high.
       (b) A commodious room for art books and such
          others as require special care.

   (c) A reading room.
   (d) A librarian's private working room.
   (e) A lecture room.[2]
2. The number of volumes is (December, 1879) 16,430.
3. Endowment for increase of the library, $25,000.
   (A definite promise has been made to double this
   fund.)[3]
4. Average yearly increase for the last three years,
   1,325.
5. Reviews and magazines taken regularly, 29.
6. The classification is in 42 departments.
7. The officers are:
   (a) A library committee for general management and
   purchase of books.
   (b) A librarian (one of the professors of the university).
   (c) One assistant librarian. (Other competent assistants are sometimes employed for special
   work.)
8. The library is open two and a half to three hours
   every day and two hours extra on Saturdays.
9. Everybody, without distinction, is invited to use
   the books at the building during library hours.
10. The readers who are allowed to borrow books to
   be used out of the library are:
   (a) All officers, students, and resident graduates
   of the university.
   (b) All officers and students of the Rochester
   Theological Seminary.[4]
   (c) Resident clergymen.

   Books are also sometimes lent, on special application,
to other persons of known character and responsibility.

I. Preparation of the Library

Let us consider first the arrangements for making the use
of the library easy and attractive. To those who have acquired the habit of reading and consulting, it will be
attractive if easy; but very few of our readers come to us
with such a habit. We are reminded every year by students
about to leave that at first the library was to them little
more than a blank; indeed, some of our best library workers
have told us this. We are thus made to feel the importance
of creating such an atmosphere in our library as shall
attract those who, never having enjoyed the use of one, are
not prepared to appreciate it. Whatever we fail to do, it is

our purpose to make every student a reading man for life.
The preparation of our library has this end constantly in
view.

In the first place, all our cyclopaedias and dictionaries,
in fact all books that are used chiefly for reference, are kept
in open cases in the central portion of the main room, always
freely accessible to every one. There is no lack of room
around them for work. As getting up and down is inconvenient while consulting large volumes, a long desk, to be
used standing, is placed near these cases. Chairs, settees,
and low tables are also at hand. Huge windows admit a
flood of light over the whole. This is the students' working
area. It is immediately under the eyes of the librarian and
assistant at their desks, and yet there is absolutely no re-
straint except what is necessary for good order. It does
not take long for the most inexperienced to begin to prize
the free use every day of cases full of dictionaries and
cyclopaedias, including not only the general miscellaneous
works of this class, but also those of history, biography,
mechanics, chemistry, statistics, every thing, indeed, that
is published with that methodical arrangement which fits it
for reference.

Next after the works of reference comes the general
catalogue of the library. This is on cards, complete, always
up to date, two or three cards for a book--authors, subjects,
and titles mixed in one alphabetical arrangement like a dictionary. Classed catalogues are good for experienced
readers, but for the student with little or no experience we
believe every obstacle should be removed. We assume that
he comes to the library with a knowledge of the alphabet
and the Arabic numerals, and, requiring only these, try
to put every thing within his reach. He has an opportunity
to study classification at the cases, as will appear hereafter.
By the use of numbers at one corner of the card, reference
is made to the department and place of the book sought.
These numbers are in the form of a fraction, the denominator
denoting the department and the numerator the place in the
department. A label on the back of the book contains the
same fraction. The attention of every freshman class is
called to a little printed card which hangs near the catalogue,
containing directions in perhaps a hundred words for using
the catalogue. When this has been done it very seldom

happens that anything further has to be said. The work is
so simple that it goes right on.[5]

The use of a catalogue suggests the importance of an
index. All that class of books whose titles are so general
that they do not suggest to an inexperienced reader the
nature of their contents require an index. This is true
not only of periodical literature, but of collections of essays on miscellaneous subjects, reports, and transactions
of learned societies, &c.

While the cataloguing is going on a memorandum is
made of every volume of this class in a book kept for the
purpose. During each summer vacation the books so entered, together with the volumes of periodicals of the
preceding year, are carefully indexed by subjects. The
arrangement of the indexes is alphabetical.

Great care is taken to find out the word or words
under which each article would be likely to be sought, the
printed titles very commonly being ignored altogether. We
have thus all of our periodical literature since the date of
Poole's Index and nearly all our other books of a miscellaneous nature thoroughly indexed. The mode of keeping these
indexes always in alphabetical order, up to date, and without
supplements, is fully described in the Government report on
libraries, and need not be given here.[6] We shall probably
discontinue this manuscript index of periodical literature, as
the Library Association has undertaken the work of making
a printed one. But the index to miscellaneous literature,
fortunately kept separate, has become an essential part
of the growth of our library. It could not, either in its
present or its prospective condition, be replaced by anything
else.

There is no device which puts a student on the track
of an investigation like these indexes. Very few subjects
arise on which they do not contain something. And everybody knows how much of suggestion for further reading is
often contained in a well written article which may be read
in three hours. There is some advantage in keeping them
just as we have done, so that they shall be exactly coex-
tensive with the miscellaneous works in our own library,
though the method is attended with much labor and expense.
The printed indexes, in separate volumes, of the Atlantic

Monthly, Harper's Magazine, and others, are seldom touched,
while Poole's Index, for periodicals published before 1852,
and our own, for everything else that we have, are in constant and most vigorous use.

Before leaving the subject of indexing it may be well
to mention the mode of taking care of our pamphlets. We
bind everything that we save, assuming that if a pamphlet
is worth saving at all, a pile of them an inch and a half
thick is worth a cheap binding. As they accumulate they
are classified and numbered with the numbers of the general departments of the library, precisely like the books.
They are then kept in a case prepared for the purpose,
where the classes may be distributed in separate numbered
boxes. When there are enough of them to do so advantageously the contents of the boxes are subclassified and volumes
are made up under general titles. The more valuable of them
are put into good bindings, and, when completed, are indexed like other volumes of miscellanies; those of less value
are bound in the cheapest way. A table of contents, pasted
on the cover inside, completes the volume in all cases where
the pamphlets are not of a serial nature. We believe that
pamphlets are quite as easily referred to in the library,
and much less likely to be lost in the circulation, when thus
classified, bound, and indexed, than when kept separate.

II. Privileges Allowed Students

When all these means have been provided--cyclopaedias and
dictionaries in abundance, catalogues and indexes in the
most perfect order, and all the appointments of the library
convenient and attractive--we have but opened the door and
made the access easy. It remains to awaken and direct an
interest in the books, for very few students will become
regular and systematic readers merely from a sense of duty,
whatever may be their facilities for finding the best reading
when they want it. The trouble is, in many cases, that
they do not want it. The want must first be created and
then supplied. How is this to be done? We believe that it
cannot be done well by shutting up the cases and requiring
the student to stop with the cyclopaedia, catalogue, and index,
and depend on an assistant librarian for the rest. This
would be paving the road to the library, and forbidding any
one to travel it. Education is best when it stimulates inquiry,

gives it the right direction, and answers it. It is not idle
curiosity which prompts a young man to take down books
and turn them over. If he is a student, it is the curiosity
which he ought to have and to indulge. There is danger
in it. This no one will deny. We have often seen books
worth fifty or a hundred dollars taken down from the shelves,
turned over for half an hour, and put up again, with no
more care than would be given to those which could be replaced for fifty cents. It has cost us a shudder. But then
we have remembered that those costly books were here to be
used, and that the student was here to use them, and if it
were not for his curiosity and his freedom to gratify it both
these ends would very likely be defeated. And we have remembered also that that student may be one of the scholars
of the next generation, and that he may be beginning here
a life work among books, and that the whole course of a
distinguished life may be determined by the opportunity
given in those alcoves. If he fails to appreciate the rare
old volumes, to understand their place in the history of
science or literature, it is likely to be the fault of his
teachers and his opportunities quite as much as his own.

And then we may have misjudged. Not unfrequently
do we find, in our intercourse with students in the alcoves,
that the best things in the library are known as such. The
costly books are usually known, and the reason why they
are costly. Indeed, in many respects, we find ourselves
anticipated by students in the course of our instruction on
the library and its uses. This is a kind of knowledge that
propagates itself. Free, on certain days, to roam among the
cases, the strong become the leaders of the weak. In the
student society, as elsewhere, there is mutual dependence.
A bright man whose early advantages have been superior,
who is quick to see and ready to communicate, soon becomes
a centre of influence. We have no fears for the tendency of
such influence. Here the best opinions inevitably prevail.
The library becomes a school of itself. What is taught by
professors or found out by consultation is talked over with
friends, and handed down from class to class, till there is
a considerable body of facts and opinions which is the common property of all the readers. All the while the new men,
inexperienced in libraries, are acquiring methods which will
be of incalculable value for life. All this mutual assistance
among the students themselves is a clear addition to that
which is rendered by teachers.

Our library is thrown open in this way one day in the week. On Saturdays the students are all required to attend chapel and one lecture. At about ten these are over, and they have no further duties for the day. Then comes the time for the library. At least half the faculty and a large percentage of the students make it regularly a rendezvous. The best work of the week is often done here during the next three hours. Curiosity begets inquiry; inquiry leads to research. With notebook and pencil in hand, courses of reading and investigation are planned. These courses are based not wholly upon the opinions of others, but also upon personal examination of the books to be used. Statements of teachers or others, regarding books and authors, are made to be purchased by those who are soon to graduate and leave. And then the endless variety of themes for essays and orations and debates are all brought in at this time for personal investigation. Scarcely a Saturday passes but every department in the library is ransacked for its best material on many subjects. It is not claimed that such investigation leads to the discovery of new truth; but, properly directed, it cannot fail to give the student much valuable knowledge of books, and, what is better, to develop a method without which no one can acquire broad scholarship. Add to this that a real interest is awakened in books as they appear in a library. In this age of libraries no course of education can be called complete which does not provide in some way for an exercise of the kind we have described.

III. Instructions on the Library Given in the Class Room

So important do we regard a good library education, that special instruction is given on libraries and the method of using them. It is a common saying, and a true one, that next to the acquisition of knowledge itself is the learning where and how it may be acquired. The range of knowledge is rapidly increasing. New sciences are springing up and new and diverse applications of science are rapidly multiplying. And in every department of learning new outlooks are taken, giving rise to new forms of thought. All these demand a place in a curriculum of study. But the student period of a young man's life cannot be indefinitely increased. We believe, therefore, that the demand can be met best, not by making the curriculum cover everything, but by giving

special attention to the where and the how of acquisition.
A young man, diploma in hand, equipped with a good method,
is far more likely to become a real scholar than one who has
attempted a much wider range of study under instructors,
but has not learned to instruct himself.

Attention is given to this subject by the faculty, both
in the class room and in the library. The writer is accustomed, as librarian, to give familiar lectures from time to
time to freshman and sophomore classes, to make them understand the great advantage of the use of a library, to explain
in general terms the nature and use of the devices for finding what one wants, to show how they may supplement their
course of study at every point by reading the authors and
subjects studied, and, in general, to awaken as far as possible an interest in library work. Some facts are also given
relative to the growth of libraries, especially in this country.
These lectures or talks occur as opportunity offers, filling
gaps when other professors are absent, or taking part of an
hour now and then from his own regular class work. Professor Gilmore also, in connection with his lectures on English
literature, gives special emphasis to the importance of becoming familiar with the library; and, besides, the mode of
giving his instruction and the work he requires of students
make such familiarity, in some departments at least, necessary, as will appear hereafter.

IV. Instruction and Assistance Given in the Library

But it is in the library itself that most of this kind of instruction is given. During the free hours on Saturday the
professor of English, the professor of history, and the librarian are always present. President Anderson and other
members of the faculty spend more or less time there. The
work there is face to face with the student. Professors
come, not with a lecture prepared, but ready in a semi-
official way to take up any subject which may be presented
and show the inquirer how to chase it down. They understand well that they do this at some risk. It is one thing
to appear always before classes on carefully studied subjects
in one department of learning. It is quite another thing to
go into a library for several hours every week where scores
of students are at work, take off your professional gown, and
offer yourself for assistance on everything that comes to you.

Of course, each officer is likely to do most in his own special field. This division of the work is facilitated by the classification of the library, which is based, as far as practicable, on the division of the curriculum of study into departments usual in colleges.

We believe that this voluntary personal work does more to encourage broad scholarship and to make men independent in their investigations than any amount of class lecturing. First of all, it prevents the teacher himself from falling into ruts. No greater curse can come to an institution than the habit of repeating instruction unchanged year after year. In this work new fields of thought and action constantly demand attention. Old questions often come up in a new light and with fresh interest. Moreover, instruction so given is not given at random. The experience of a lifetime of study and reflection can here be brought to bear with peculiar emphasis upon those special needs which are felt and expressed. There is an opportunity to find out what has been read, and starting with that, to show what may best be done and how. It is often expedient to take down the books for those who are inclined to ask questions but have not learned how to question a book, and open them at the chapters which should be read.

The intimate personal acquaintance and the natural influence of a teacher will enable him to do what a public librarian could not do. He may urge the use of good books where the tendency is to worthless ones. He may so direct the student that the freedom of the cases shall not lead to the dissipating habit of merely browsing among books, but to that of regular and systematic work. He may teach him how to take the measure of a book in an hour's examination so as to set it down in his note book for what it is worth. Sometimes a class lecture on the use of the library may be profitably followed up by taking a subject and showing how the various departments can be made to contribute to a thorough study of it. No description of this work can be complete, nor can the results of it be fully stated. It is sufficient to say, first, that those teachers who engage in it most heartily find themselves amply repaid by the increased interest taken in the work of their class rooms, and, secondly, that the students who are thus encouraged and assisted almost invariably become our best scholars while here, and after graduating

look back to their work in the library as one of the most
beneficial exercises of their college course.

While on this subject it may not be impertinent to suggest that possibly the new demand which we often hear for
library professorships can be met best, in all but the largest
institutions, by a plan in some respects similar to what we
have described. Let it be somewhat more complete and systematic, but not compulsory. Every officer of instruction
knows his own department better than the most learned librarian could be expected to know it. Let every one have a
regular hour, one that shall be convenient for students,
when he can be found in the library to encourage, direct,
and assist all who are reading or making special references
in his department. Let the official relation of the professor
be replaced for the time, as far as possible, by that of a
literary or scientific friend, and the interviews, thus made
pleasant and profitable, will soon become attractive. The
work could thus be well done which now, we suspect, many
a librarian, from no fault of his own, is doing but poorly.
The labor for each would not be great; the results, if we
may judge from our experience, would be most beneficial.

V.   Use of the Library by Professors
     in Giving Their Regular Instruction

From all that has been said it will be evident that the use
of our library influences very largely the character of the
instruction given in the class rooms throughout the university. Our library is to us all what a laboratory is to a
teacher of physics or a cabinet to a teacher of geology.
The narrowest view of education that can be taken is that
of mere text book learning. But from a good text book
as standing ground, an outlook may be taken as broad as
may be desired. It is customary, we believe, to accomplish
this by means of supplementary lectures by professors.
This is our custom in part; but we have for several years
added to it, and that we think successfully, an outlook by
the students themselves through the use of the library.
The system so involves the administration of the library
that it should be given here.

In nearly every department, in addition to the text
studied and to the professor's lectures, oral dissertations

are required on subjects assigned. These are not usually
written, but carefully prepared and delivered to the class
from notes. The subjects are assigned by the professor
early in the term: they are made so that, all together,
they shall cover the principal points, historical, biographical,
&c., suggested by the term's work. References to books
are given with the subjects. When the term is well advanced
the dissertations are given from time to time, as is found convenient. The student assumes for the time the functions of
the teacher. No exercises are prepared with greater care
and no instruction receives better attention from the classes
than this which is given by the members themselves. The
professor is present to correct or to supplement wherever
he sees the need of it.

These dissertations have in general nothing to do with
the work of English composition as taught by the professor
of rhetoric and English. And still it is in this department
that they probably have their highest value. The nature
of the subjects assigned, the reading done in investigation,
and the presentation to the class, all have a direct and
manifest bearing on the work of that department. For this
reason Professor Gilmore has made a specialty of this exercise. He keeps in the library for the use of students a
book of subjects, with references, from which selections are
made for these dissertations. The references are constantly
undergoing revision as the library increases. He keeps also
in the library an extensive printed list of themes, with
references, from which students may make their own selections as essays are required. In connection with these
themes he gives explicit printed directions for finding material in the library, and says, in addition: "The professor
of rhetoric will be in the library every Saturday morning to
assist students in finding material for essays, dissertations,
&c." Other professors find it expedient to follow their
classes to the library for the same purpose.

We give as specimens a few subjects which have been
used, taken from several of the departments. It will be
seen that the whole scheme requires a vast amount of work
in the library. It cannot fail to be noticed also that thirty
or forty of these subjects, carefully prepared and presented
to a class during a term's work in any department, must
enlarge the view and broaden the scholarship immeasurably,
as compared with mere text book work. And while doing

this a method is acquired which is worth more than all the
rest.

1. History of the use of the term "idea."
2. Influence of Cartesianism on English thought.
3. Savings banks, their history and safeguards.
4. The place of Adam Smith in political economy.
5. History and uses of bills of exchange.
6. Carbon, native forms and compounds; uses in the
   arts; functions in animals and plants.
7. Sugar, principal kinds; sketch of the history of
   beet root sugar.
8. Bread, manufacture, kinds, adulterations.
9. The Puritan literature of Britain.
10. The great English orators.
11. English translations of Homer.
12. The invention of logarithms and the origin of
    logarithmic tables.
13. The methods of Galileo and Descartes in physical
    science compared.
14. Newton's experiments in light, and his explanations
    of the phenomena of light on the emission theory.
15. The commerce of the Phoenicians.
16. Description of the pyramids of Egypt.
17. The organization of the Persian Empire under
    Darius the Great.

VI. Extra Curriculum Work Growing Out of the Use of the
    Library

Besides the extension of the course growing out of these
class room dissertations, we encourage and provide for a
large amount of extra curriculum work which depends almost
wholly upon the use of the library. There are, we believe,
in every institution two classes of students, the text book
men and the reading men. Lack of natural ability, sickness,
poverty, and disinclination to study limit many to the mere
work of learning lessons assigned. An easy subject may be
prepared now and then for presentation in the class room,
but their ability or their ambition does not extend beyond
this. They pass examinations from year to year, and receive
their bachelor's degree, with no special marks of distinction.
It often happens, however, in after life, when the disabilities
are removed, that these men acquire a scholarship beyond the

promise of their college days. The other class, more fortunate and more ambitious, the reading men, are always looking
for more work. This demand might be met by extra text
books and lectures, but this method, besides imposing an
additional burden on teachers, would fail to develop the
very powers which these men are likely to possess. We have
chosen, because better for the students themselves, to give
them subjects for investigation requiring wide and careful
reading.

These subjects form a clear addition to our course.
They constitute a variable element, which adapts itself to
the ever changing demands of the times and tastes of the
students.

We select and present as specimens a few of the subjects which our students have studied during the last two
or three years. No mention is made here, however, of the
extra curriculum work done in classical and mathematical
reading, for which they can easily provide their own books,
as this has no special relation to the library.

1. The place of Edmund Burke in literature and
     politics.
2. The political character and aims of Julius Caesar.
3. The political characteristics of the Greek colonial
     system.
4. The ethical and economical bearings of modern
     socialism.
5. The national school of political economy in Germany.
6. The spread of the Greek language and literature
     through the conquests of Alexander.
7. The educational system of Rome during the classical
     period.
8. The causes of obscurity in Tennyson's poetry.
9. The theory and uses of the pendulum.
10. The principles involved in the construction of the
     telescopo and its uses in astronomical investigation.

On subjects like these about one-fourth of our students
are always engaged. A college year is spent on a subject.
The library is, of course, the principal source of information,
and that it may be well supplied for this work purchases are
made every year with special reference to the subjects announced for the year. The assistance given by professors to

the students in the library tends to save students from
wasting time by reading at a disadvantage. The excellence
of their work is tested by requiring either written answers
to questions set by the faculty or general written dissertations on the subjects. By this system we believe it is
practicable, with suitable attention on the part of the officers
of instruction, to preserve the time honored curriculum of
disciplinary study substantially intact and at the same time
to meet the modern demand for a greater range and variety
of elective studies.

VII. Post Graduate Studies Encouraged

By proper administration a college library may prolong its
usefulness to students after the regular course of study is
finished. We believe there is truth in the saying that "the
library is the best university"; but the university course
implied by this saying should follow the ordinary college
course of America. It is our aim to fit men to pursue such
a course independently and successfully. Having acquired
such library habits as we have described very few young
men will lay them aside on graduating. We give to our
alumni the same library privileges as to students, and the
number of post graduate readers is constantly increasing.
We have but two regular post graduate courses endowed.
These are of such a nature that they are not likely ever to
be taken except by men of reading habits. For them the
library is a constant resource. Many others who become
teachers, or who pursue professional studies in the vicinity,
continue their investigations in the alcoves of our library
almost as regularly as when they were students.

VIII. Dangers to Be Avoided

There are some tendencies in the use of a library, as we
have described it, which cannot be commended. First of
all, there is danger that some will make it merely a place to
find answers to questions or to study particular questions
previously determined upon. Doubtless a library should be
used in this way very largely, but it may be overdone.
There are books which should be read through leisurely as
a whole, not for the sake of finding out what they say on
some narrow question, but for the sake of the books them-

selves. Some may be read in this way several times with
profit. Courses of reading should be pursued where one
brings to the best authors regularly at his leisure hour a
mind free to receive an impression from their learning and
their style. The minds of the young will be enlarged by
such contact with the masters in literature and science as
they could not be by merely running over books for a
chapter here and an article there on the subject they are at
work on. We do not say that this is incompatible with our
library management, but it must be admitted that there is
a slight tendency, in the rush of work on subjects, to neglect this kind of reading. Culture demands that it should
not be neglected, and the professors, as well as the librarian, should keep it steadily in view.

Another tendency which has to be guarded against is
that of indifference to the pecuniary value of books. We
believe in using our books, and not in shutting them up,
though we are well aware that young persons who are allowed
to use freely what costs them nothing are likely to use it
without sufficient care. Of course, this is a matter which
can be met only by constant watchfulness. It should be said,
however, to the credit of our students, that during the
thirteen years that they have had the freedom of the cases
every week we have hardly lost books enough to be worth
mentioning, and the handling of those used has seldom been
censurable. We have trusted them freely, appealing to their
honor, and we have not appealed in vain.

We may add, as another possible evil, that there will
always be students who will be ready to justify a neglect
of the regular work of the course for the sake of reading.
It seldom happens, however, that such students are regular
and systematic readers. They are usually vagabonds in the
library as well as in the classes. No library administration
would give them fixed purposes and steady habits. If the
officers of instruction are able in any way to turn their
willingness to read to good account, it may be the best thing
that can be done for them.

We recognize these as apparent objections, or dangers,
in a system which gives so great freedom in the library and
requires so constant use of it in the study of subjects. We
know of no case, however, where they have led to serious
evils. With the eyes of nearly all the faculty continually on

the work done in the library it is not easy for an evil tendency there to escape observation.   ·

NOTES

1.   If in some parts of this paper the writer has repeated, in another form, opinions already expressed by him
in the Government report on libraries, it is because he could
not otherwise perform well the task imposed upon him of
describing our own library administration.
2.   Besides the rooms enumerated here, the building
contains another of the same size as the large public library
room and directly over it.   This is to be used for our geo-
logical and mineralogical cabinets till the library is large
enough to require it.
3.   Since the above was written this promise has been
fulfilled.
4.   This is a courtesy extended by each institution to
the other.
5.   It may be remarked that after much careful study
we have adopted, with some modifications, the system of
classification known as the "combined system," devised by
Mr. Schwartz, of the Apprentices' Library of New York.   As
much has been said and written on classification, and as
Mr. Schwartz's plan has been pretty fully explained in the
Library Journal, it need not be given here.
6.   Indexing periodical and miscellaneous literature,
in Public Libraries in the United States, Washington, 1876,
part I, page 663.

Teaching Bibliography in Colleges

Raymond C. Davis

Davis was a librarian at the University of Michigan from 1877
to 1905 and Librarian Emeritus and Professor of Bibliography
from 1905 until his death in 1914. He presented this paper
at the ALA conference in Milwaukee in 1886. Davis had been
giving library lectures since 1879 and in 1881 he won approval
from the Michigan Board of Regents to offer a credit course.

Similar to other bibliographical courses of this period,
his course emphasized historical and descriptive bibliography,
but it also included "intellectual" bibliography which he
defined as the classification of literature and the contents of
books. He taught the use of the card catalog, reference
works, and the important books in disciplines such as history,
philosophy, and literature. He claimed that each year since
initiating this program his students had improved "both in
their ability to use books and in their appreciation of books."

Davis has been hailed by contemporaries and historians
alike as an influential leader in the offering of credit courses
in bibliography. His contributions were recognized by Henry
Evans in "Library Instruction in Universities, Colleges, and
Normal Schools," U.S. Bureau of Education Bulletin no. 34
(1914): 3; George S. Bonn, Training Laymen in Use of the
Library (New Brunswick, N.J.: Rutgers University
Graduate School of Library Service, 1960), p. 28; and John
Mark Tucker, "The Origins of Bibliographic Instruction in
Academic Libraries, 1876-1914," in Robert D. Stueart and
Richard Johnson, eds. New Horizons for Academic Libraries
(New York: K. G. Saur, 1979), p. 270. Arthur T. Hamlin
describes Davis as teaching the first course in bibliography
offered by an American university in The University Library

in the United States: Its Origins and Development (Philadelphia: University of Pennsylvania Press, 1981), p. 144.
The most comprehensive study of Davis's teaching is the
chapter, "The Professor of Books and Bibliography," in
John C. Abbott, "Raymond Cazallis Davis and the University of Michigan General Library 1877-1905," (Ph.D. diss.,
University of Michigan, 1957), pp. 177-195. Excerpts of
this particular selection appeared in American Library Institute Papers and Proceedings (Chicago: American Library
Association, 1916), pp. 100-108.

·   ·   ·

I had not performed the duties of a librarian long before it
became evident to me that many of my readers were working
at a disadvantage. Their knowledge of books of common
reference was very limited; they did not know of the
existence of special bibliographies, and of indexes to serial
publications; that they could help themselves in these matters by an intelligent exercise of their reasoning powers
never occurred to them. They were, in short, running in
a rut out of which it seemed impossible for them to get. In
addition to this they made no effort, on coming into the
library building for the first time, to learn what they might
expect, or what was expected of them, or the whereabouts
of anything. They were willing to leave all to chance.

As one effort to remedy these evils I decided to give
a few lectures on the library in general, and on library aids
in particular, at the opening of each college year. This I
did first in 1879, and have continued to do since. One lecture (the first) has reference to the use of the library. I
endeavor to show the student what his obligations are as a
user of the library, and also what his rights are. I also
describe the card catalogue, showing how it is constructed,
and how it should be handled, with a mention of the printed
catalogues of other libraries in our possession, and how they
may be helpful. I give a list of the books of reference, with

explanations of their scope and value. Particular attention
is called to the special bibliographies which are becoming so
numerous. And, lastly, I endeavor to teach that mental
process which is available everywhere, and under all circumstances, in which the present knowledge of the inquirer is
interrogated, and made to indicate the direction in which
further knowledge is to be sought.

This lecture is followed by a second, on "The Books
of the Year," and a third, on "Reading--Why we Do it, and
How we Should Do it."

These lectures, delivered, as I have said, at the
opening of the college year, are sometimes well attended,
and sometimes not. I shall continue them, because I have
evidence every year that some individuals are helped by
them both in their ability to use books and in their appreciation of books.

In the year 1881 I submitted to the Faculty of the University an outline of a systematic course of instruction in
Bibliography, which they were desired to consider, and, if
it met with their approval, to recommend to the Board of
Regents for incorporation in the curriculum. The scheme
was approved by the Faculty, recommended by them as desired, and, at the next meeting of the Board of Regents,
the course was established. It is an elective, lecture course,
of one hour per week, extending through the second semester.
Those who take it, and pass a satisfactory examination, receive a credit of one-fifth.

Before proceeding to give an outline of this course of
study I will make a few explanatory remarks.

I hardly need to say in this presence that, although
Bibliography is not a new subject, and although it has been
the specialty of a number of eminent scholars, its boundaries
are not quite settled yet. While generally agreeing that it
is the "Science of Books," writers differ more or less as to
the extent of the field it may cover.

Some of the most distinguished of the French and
English bibliographers have included in it the study of ancient MSS., as well as the study of printed books. The
writer of the article on the subject in the 9th edition of the

"Encyclopaedia Britannica" confines it to a consideration of
printed books, and applies to a consideration of ancient
MSS. the term Palaeography. There is no need of controversy here. Bibliography properly covers ancient as well
as modern books; it includes Palaeography. If it is sometimes desirable to consider modern books alone, so it is
sometimes desirable to consider ancient and modern books in
connection,--the modern as a development of the ancient;
and it is sometimes desirable to consider ancient books alone.
In neither case should the use of the term Bibliography be
prohibited as inapplicable.

This is undoubtedly a bibliographical association, yet
the line dividing between types and pens, between paper,
and parchment and papyrus, is never crossed in the papers
that are read at its meetings, or in the discussions that
follow the readings. If there is a bibliographical journal
published in the country it is the Library Journal; and yet
I think only one article of an antiquarian character has ever
appeared in it, and that was followed by a note stating that
it was an exception to the rule of the Journal, which "confines it to topics that concern the librarian as an administrator rather than as a scholar."

I think the language of the announcement of the
School of Library Economy to be opened at Columbia College
at the beginning of the coming year is that "the principles
of library management" only will be taught. Of the wisdom
of the founders of the Association, and of the Journal, and
of the School of Library Economy, in thus confining study
and discussion to the utilitarian side of Bibliography there
can be no doubt. Time and use, which test the wisdom of
all courses of action, attest the wisdom of this course as
regards the Association and the Journal.

But the case is altered when the subject is to be
taught to college students not for a specific purpose but
rather as a part of liberal education. The antiquarian, or
historical, side is important then. The student should become familiar with that portion of the subject in all of its
aspects. If art contributes to it--as it does--he should know
what it contributes. If history contributes to it--as it does--
he should know what is gained from history. If literature
contributes to it--as it does, largely, of course, he should
know what literature gives.

In the course given at the University, therefore, all
these contributions from art and history and literature are
collected and arranged in that order which seems the most
natural, and to the two divisions of Bibliography which
are generally recognized, viz.: Material, or Practical, and
Intellectual, another is added, which I term Historical
Bibliography, and place first as introductory. We have,
then, three main divisions of the general subject:--

I. Historical Bibliography

This comprises a description of the writing materials of the
different ages; of MSS.; of the preservation of ancient literature; of the revival of learning in the fourteenth century,
and that almost simultaneous event, the beginning of modern
literature; of the invention of printing and the improvements
in the art; of the early printers and their works; of libraries, and of the copyright.

2. Material Bibliography

This has reference to the denominations and sizes of books,
and their mechanical execution; to bibliographical nomenclature, to editions, to catalogues, to buying and caring for
books, etc.

3. Intellectual Bibliography

This has to do with the classification of literature, and the
contents of books.

In order to convey as clear an idea as possible of what
is taught I will give a synopsis of the twenty lectures which
at present constitute the course.

On Historical Bibliography there are seven lectures:

I. WRITING MATERIALS

The origin of writing growing out of the desire of man to
give expression to his thoughts and perpetuity to his
achievements; Rock inscriptions; Tables of stone, ivory,
metal, and wood; The use of coloring matter, making available the barks and leaves of trees, and the skins and

intestines of animals; Clay tablets; Papyrus; Parchment;
Wax tablets; Palm leaf of the Cingalese, and other Eastern
nations; Origin of modern paper, and when and how a
knowledge of its manufacture was introduced into Europe;
Minor materials, as pens and inks.

2.   CLASSICAL MSS.

Forms assumed by MSS.; The characters in which they were
written; How they were multiplied, and to what extent, in
the times of greatest literary activity in Greece and Rome;
The subject illustrated by a view of books and reading in
Rome in the first century; The nomenclature of the subject;
Dangers to which classical MSS. were exposed; Their preservation through the Dark Ages; Part of the Monks in the
matter.

3.   THE REVIVAL OF LEARNING

What this revival was; "Through 700 years," said Lionardo
Bruni, "no one in all Italy has been master of Greek letters;"
Petrarch; Boccaccio; John of Ravenna, the itinerant profes-
sor of Latin; Emanuel Chrysoloras, the Greek; Filelfo;
Poggio, and the MSS. found and transcribed by him;
Nicholas V., and the Vatican library; Vespasiano, first of
modern booksellers; Vittorino da Feltre, the model educator;
Aldus Manutius, the first printer of critical texts; Decadence
of classical learning in Italy in the 16th century, and its
rise in Northern Europe from the labors of Grocyn, Linacre,
Reuchlin, Erasmus, and others.

4.   MSS. OF THE MIDDLE AGES AND THE
BEGINNINGS OF MODERN LITERATURE

Ulphilas and the Gothic language in the 4th century; Cyril
and the Sclavonic language in the 9th century; Celtic MSS.,
and Celtic learning in the 7th and 8th centuries; Arabian
MSS., and Arabian learning in the 9th and 10th centuries;
What the MSS. of the Middle Ages contained that still finds
appreciation in its entirety, or has been worked over and
finds appreciation in other forms of literature.

5. THE INVENTION OF PRINTING

The arts of the first part of the 15th century; Wood en-
graving; Playing cards; Block books; Political and social
condition of Europe in the 15th century; The invention
typography, not printing; The claimants to the honor of
the invention; Warmth of the controversy over these al-
leged inventors; The older writers on the subject bibliographers rather than practical printers; Their conclusions
unsatisfactory on this account; Elimination of all from the
list of claimants except Coster and Gutenburg; A consideration of the claims of each; The phenomenal books, the
"Biblia Pauperum," the "Ars Moriendi," the "Speculum,"
the "Donatuses," and others; How were they printed, and
who printed them? Why the ancient nations did not print;
The conditions that made the art possible in the 15th century.

6. THE EARLY PRINTERS

Fust and Schoeffer; Their "Offices of Cicero," the first
classic printed (1465); Sweynheim and Panwartz at Subiaco
and at Rome; Their "Lactantius;" Roman type first used
by them in their edition of Cicero's Letters (1467);
Nicholas Jensen; The Manutii; Their editions of the Greek
classics; The Aldine, or Italic type; Ulric Gering, the first
printer of France; Antoine Verard, and the new school of
printing founded by him; The Estiennes, or Stephenses;
John Amerbach and his editions of the Christian Fathers;
Jean Froben, Amerbach's successor, and the friend and
publisher of Erasmus; The Elzeviers; William Caxton;
Wynkin de Worde; Richard Pynson.

7. LIBRARIES

Ancient libraries; Libraries of the Middle Ages; The classi-
fication of libraries; The Library of the British Museum;
The National Library of France; The Library of the Vatican;
The Imperial Library of St. Petersburg; Harvard College
Library.

On Material Bibliography there are five lectures:

1. DENOMINATIONS AND SIZES OF BOOKS

Anonymous, pseudonymous, posthumous, and other names
of books resulting from circumstances of authorship; Eso-
teric and exoteric books; Classics; Sizes of books, as folios,
quartos, etc.; How the sizes are produced; This method of
designating books unsatisfactory; Efforts of librarians to
change it; Methods of the American Library Association and
the United Kingdom Library Association.

2. THE MECHANICAL EXECUTION OF BOOKS

Paper; Type; Illustrations; Bindings, etc.

3. EDITIONS

What editions are; How they are multiplied; Wherein editions
differ; Books of which there are many editions; The choice
in editions.

4. CATALOGUES

Catalogues of authors; Catalogues of subjects; Classified
catalogues; The dictionary system; General catalogues, as
Brunet's and Lownde's; Catalogues of libraries; Catalogues
of collections for sale; Written and printed catalogues; The
card system; Special bibliographies; Poole's index of periodical literature; The cooperative index: Bulletins.

5. THE CARE OF BOOKS

The enemies of books enumerated by Mr. Blades, viz.:
"fire, water, gas and heat, dust and neglect, ignorance,
the bookworm, other vermin, bookbinders, and book col-
lectors;" How improvements in the construction of library
buildings preserves from some of these enemies; In what
ways ignorance is inimical to books; What the bookbinder
does that is disastrous; The book collector, or bibliomanic:
his idiosyncrasies; How to pack books.

On Intellectual Bibliography there are eight lectures:

1. THE CLASSIFICATION OF KNOWLEDGE

Schemes of Bacon, Bentham, Coleridge, and others, relating particularly to philosophy; Systems for the classification of books in libraries, notably Bouillaud's, Ersch's, Horne's, Brunet's, Edwards', and later ones.

In the seven remaining lectures the main classes into which literature is divided are subdivided to as great an extent as possible, and an endeavor is made to name the best books in each of the subdivisions.

The reasons for the course that existed in my mind, and by which I justified the request for its establishment, may be formulated thus: The book is the student's chief tool,--his sine qua non.   Has he mastered the Literae humaniores, if on the day of his graduation he knows little or nothing about this tool with which he has wrought--either its history or its workmanship?   It has been necessary for him to become familiar with the theory of the evolution of man from a primordial cell.   Should he not also become familiar with the fact of the evolution of the modern book from a rock inscrip tion, or, more remotely, from a grove of trees, or a pile of stones?   Why should not the college student be taught bibliography as well as philosophy, or art, or literature? It may be said that a knowledge of books, as books, is of less importance than a knowledge of philosophy, or of art, or of a particular literature.   I cannot admit it.   I wish to be understood aright.   I am not considering the relative importance of the subjects abstractly,--weighing them,--but their importance to the student in general.   The exigencies of life will make a demand on that student for bibliographical knowledge twice where they will make one demand for the other more special knowledge.   I appeal confidently to the experience of college-bred men for confirmation of what I affirm.

Again, it may be said that a knowledge of Bibliography is gained from a study of other subjects.   Yes; something about the MSS. of certain ancient classical writers will be imparted by the professors of the ancient languages.   Something about the various editions of the modern classical writers will be received from the professors of the modern languages.   But all this is incidental; the facts

are few and disconnected, and the impressions made will not
be permanent. For instance, if the student is reading the
Correspondence of Cicero, he will probably be told that the
sole authority for the letters "ad Familiares" is a MS. discovered by the poet Petrarch at Vercelli. He will wonder,
momentarily, how this happened to the sentimental Italian,
with whose name he has always associated that of Laura, the
woman who was the source of his inspiration, and then he
will probably forget the fact altogether.

Now give this fact to the student, with the associated
facts, in a chain of interesting events. He beholds Petrarch
in a new character; as a student of Cicero, and a lover of
the old Roman literature, art, life, and philosophy. Laura
does not appear upon the scene. Petrarch's utterances are
those of a practical, earnest man. "I detested," he said,
as he turned from what was about him back to the past,--"I
detested the frivolities and senseless chatter of the moderns.
. . . I was the first, in Italy at least, to bring back the
style of our forefathers." The student will not forget the
fact in this company, nor the associated facts. He will be
taught not only that the poet was the apostle of the Renaissance, but also what that great movement was, and what
was accomplished by the actors in it.

Again, the teacher of Italian literature will dwell upon
the piquant style of Boccaccio, upon his wit and his elo-
quence, and will remark probably that it is a pity that his
masterpiece, the "Decamerone," is too indecent to be read.
His association with Petrarch, and his participation in the
revival of learning may be mentioned incidentally, but his
earnest and successful labors in the interests of learning
will not be given sufficient prominence to make him live in
the mind as any other than the author of a fascinating, but
licentious, book. But the page of Boccaccio's life that is
open to the bibliographical student does not tell him about
the "Decamerone," but describes his indefatigable pursuit of
the relics of ancient literature. What lives in the memory is
not a tale penned to delight an immoral court, but his noble
and indignant protest against the mutilation of books as he
looked tearfully over the neglected library at Monte Casino.

While, therefore, bibliographical knowledge is obtained
by the study of literature as commonly pursued, and by the
study of other subjects, it is only at those points where the

subjects dovetail into each other, and it is consequently inadequate. In the study of a literature, the end of the study
is a knowledge of that literature pure and simple. The instructor, at the moment that he says, "Here is an interesting
fact, but not altogether relevant," calls attention away from
it again. It can only be something "by the way."

Now a practical consideration: A college education is
supposed to, and generally does, make books a necessity.
Should not a part of that education that makes books necessary include instruction in the arts of acquiring and caring
for them? The existence of a School of Library Economy at
Columbia may be taken as a justification of this instruction
for librarians. I need only to call attention to the fact that
any man who collects books in large numbers has to meet
many of the responsibilities of a librarian.

The results of the experiment may be given briefly.
During the four years that the lectures have been delivered
there has been an annual average attendance of twenty-four
persons, regularly enrolled. Others are present, but are
not members of the class. About ten percent of those regularly enrolled take the work for some other reason than a
desire to be benefited by it, and they are not benefited by
it particularly. They fail at examination. About twenty-five
percent both grasp the subject as a whole and enter into its
details with intelligence and enthusiasm. They speak often,
with gratification, of finding links that bind together frag-
ments of knowledge already possessed by them, but of
which they had not before perceived the connection. And
they find much that is suggestive in the matter brought to
their notice,--much that provokes them to profitable research
in this direction and in that. Also they find that, as an immediate result of their study, their grasp of all the accumu-
lations they have made is rendered more comprehensive. Of
the remaining sixty-five percent it may be said that they do
their work fairly well, and are helped by it.

I think these results justify the establishment of the
course, and I consider that part of the matter as practically
settled; but that it may be so modified and so changed as to
produce far better results is certain in the nature of things,
and I shall not only welcome suggestions but I shall also endeavor to take criticism in that spirit which makes it profitable.

The Relation of the Colleges to the Modern Library Movement

Melvil Dewey

The achievements of Melvil Dewey overshadow those of any other American librarian. He created the Dewey Decimal Classification and founded the first library school in America; he also played key roles in establishing the Library Journal and the American Library Association. He was Assistant Librarian at Amherst College (1874-83), Librarian at Columbia (1883-88), establishing the library school in 1887, and New York State Librarian (1888-1905).

In the inaugural issue of American Library Journal, Dewey had christened librarians as educators: "The time is when a library is a school, and the librarian is in the highest sense a teacher." See "The Profession," American Library Journal 1 (September 1876):5-6. A decade later he observed the dramatic increase in professional interest in using libraries and in teaching students how to use them in "Libraries the True Universities for Scholars as Well as People," Library Notes 1 (June 1886):49-50.

In his speech to the Middle States Association of Colleges and Secondary Schools, Dewey envisioned an ideal academic library as a "laboratory" essential for college level study. The purpose of a college education was to provide tools for further study, "the most essential [tool] of all being the ability to use libraries effectively." The library functions of acquiring and maintaining collections should be secondary to the functions involved in using those collections. This speech was reprinted in Sarah K. Vann, ed. Melvil Dewey; His Enduring Presence in Librarianship (Littleton, Colorado: Libraries Unlimited, 1978), pp. 78-83.

Reprinted by permission of the Middle States Association of
Colleges and Schools from the Proceedings of the Second Annual Convention of the College Association of the Middle
States and Maryland, pp. 78-83. Philadelphia: Globe Printing Co., 1891.

•   •   •

In the fifteen minutes allotted me I can only give the texts
on which, if I ever get the opportunity, I should like to
preach to this body the sermons.

First, what is the modern library movement? Libraries
are of three kinds--storage, recreation and laboratory libraries. Of course, every library must have its function as a
reservoir for storing literature. Certainly it is a proper
function for public and many other libraries to furnish the
highest kind of recreation. The conception of the library
as a laboratory is comparatively new, and is an essential part
of the modern library idea. There was a time when only
chemists considered a laboratory as essential to their college
work. Then we found the necessity of laboratories for
physics, mineralogy, geology, biology, botany, zoology, etc.,
and Professor Stoddard just now voiced the feeling of every
first-class instructor with the modern spirit when he demanded
for his department an English literature laboratory.

As we glance over the field of philosophy, theology,
political and social sciences, philology, art, literature and
history, we find that for everyone the library is the laboratory, and that even in science where certain apparatus is
necessary the library is also the laboratory in supplying in
books and serials the result of the world's experiments.

The functions of all libraries are threefold--to get, to
keep, and to use. The old librarian had the miserly instinct
of getting as many books and pamphlets as possible, usually
also of keeping them safely; but it is a large item in the
modern library idea to use this material to the fullest extent.
To get, to keep and to use, but the greatest of these is to
use.

The modern librarian is proud to show how much his

books have been worn by legitimate use. The old librarian
was distressed to see his books show signs of wear. Indeed
I knew of one case in which a college librarian sent a request for the president to read in chapel, that the students
should abstain from reading a certain article in the Encyclopaedia Britannica which a professor had commended, because
those leaves showed signs of special wear and detracted
from the beauty of the volume.

Most libraries have also the threefold departments for
reference, the news-room for serials, and the circulating
department for home use.

As the next text, note--without exact chronological
order or anything more than suggestion--how marked and
universal has been the movement in developing the scope of
education. It was once for the rich alone; now for the poor
as well. It was for the nobility; now for the common
people, so that often the education of a modern bootblack
would put to shame that of a mediaeval knight. The old
education was for males only; to-day some of the best higher
work at home and abroad is being done by women and
women's colleges. The old was for the bright; the new also
builds schools specially for the feeble-minded. The old was
for those with all their faculties and senses; the new includes
the blind and the deaf, and astonishes the world with the
results attained in spite of what once seemed insuperable obstacles. The old was for natives only; the new concerns
itself with immigrants, the Chinese, etc. The old was for
the white; the new is doing famous work for blacks and
Indians. The old conceived of only elementary education for
the masses; the notion is now abroad that something higher
belongs to every citizen, regardless of nativity, color or sex.

Now mark the two distinctions that are most modern,
for all these that I have named have been already generally
received. The old education was for the young; the new
will provide for education all through life. Last, the old
education was thought of as confined to schools and colleges,
and when students left them the idiom of the language had
it that education is not for the young only, but is to last
all through life, and that it is to be given not alone in the
schools, which furnish the best tools for carrying on an
education, but that it is to be given at the home and in connection with the regular work of life.

We find circumstances exactly adapted to these new ideas, for there is a growing difficulty in keeping students and colleges long enough to complete satisfactory courses; but at the same time there is growing opportunity for out-of-school education because of shortened hours of labor.

The modern library idea recognizing all these conditions would provide, with the library as the central and most important part of the institution, what we call the people's college in every community of any size. If this idea were housed in a building in the form of a Greek cross, one wing should be devoted to the library, another to the reading-room, a third to the museum of science, and the fourth to the museum of fine art; for our conception is clear that with the library in the people's college should go the museum, including not only science and art, but historical and other museum collections which help to educate by exhibition. When we take a book from the library we learn by holding the printed page before the eye and taking in new ideas; when we stand before the picture or marble, or case of scientific specimens, we are simply taking in ideas through the eye by reading not from the printer's book, but from the book of nature or art. The second story of our building would provide lecture and seminar rooms for university extension courses, classes and other agencies essential in completing the work of the people's college. To illustrate the growth of this idea, I mention that Milwaukee hopes in its new library, for which plans are now being drawn, to include in its upper rooms a feature, as yet untried, as a part of their musical library in which texts of the best music will be provided. Remote from the reading-room they hope to have a piano, violin, guitar, flute and other instruments, so that musicians consulting the musical library may have an opportunity to read the music they are consulting, each by aid of the instrument which he plays.

The work to be done by an ideal library is threefold. First, it should make more readers than ever before, inducing those to read who have not acquired that priceless habit. Second, it should teach its readers better methods, in order that they may obtain more from their reading, learning how to get the most out of a book in the shortest time. Third, it should teach them to read better books. The ideal will only be attained when a librarian may closely approximate to giving to each reader at each visit to the library the book that then and there, and to him, will be most useful.

The duty of the college. You should first make your
own library include the modern and most important functions--
to be in the best sense a laboratory. The college as well as
the university is responsible for this work which some at
first thought consider as belonging wholly to the university.
But college training is to give tools for getting further education, the most essential of all being the ability to use libraries effectively. Every reputable college owes it to its students to give them not only experience in a laboratory library, but also instruction in the use of bibliographical
apparatus. To make your libraries what they ought to be,
you must, of course, provide the best books and serials.
Will each of you think for a moment of your own library, and
estimate what per cent of the books now in it you would buy
as the best, if beginning anew to-day? You will be astonished
to see how small a percentage of the volumes which you report
you would dare call the best existing for your purpose.

The college library should be like the college well, open
to the students whenever they are in the mood to use it, and
not at fixed and limited hours. From eight in the morning
until ten at night, including holidays, the doors should be
open for all who wish to come. Too many are as I found the
New York State Library two years ago--it was carefully locked
till the hour when every officer and clerk in the capitol must
be at his desk, and was as promptly locked again when they
were released, so that throughout the year it was ingeniously
arranged that they never had access to the books. It is now
open for twice as many hours, including all holidays and va-
cations.

Another important feature for which the scholarly mind
is in danger of feeling too little respect is the provision of
physical facilities. Library rooms in light, heat and ventila-
tion, in tables, chairs and all conveniences for work, should
be carefully arranged to avoid distracting the attention of
the busy worker. A man cannot do his best work in an uncomfortable chair or in a bad light or in an unventilated
room.

Your students should have more liberal access to the
shelves. It will cause some confusion and make extra labor
for your librarian. You may even sometimes lose a book, but
suppose you lose twenty or fifty or one hundred dollars'
worth (which experience proves you will not), the privilege

is worth tenfold that cost to the body of students in whose general education it will play so large a part to be able to handle the books for themselves whenever they can command a leisure hour.

The books and physical facilities must be supplemented by bibliographical aids, by the best catalogues, classifications and indexes, by shelf-labels, guides and by notes and ample cross-references. Stop and think what this means, and you may avoid a common and grave mistake of expecting too much in too short a time. It takes time, money and sympathy with this great work for even the best librarian to get his collection in complete working order. We have seen repeatedly, when some college or board of trustees were a little stirred on this question and determined to do something to improve the library, the most ridiculous expectations as to early results. It is a great undertaking to so arrange and administer a collection of 100,000 volumes that to any man it will be possible, within a few moments, to give from that collection not only the book or pamphlet, but the article hidden away in some volume of transactions, or in some periodical, which to him, then and there, is the thing he most needs. It requires almost infinite labor, but it is well worth the cost. Think of this, and do not, after a new librarian with the modern spirit has undertaken this herculean work, expect in a few months or even years that he can transform a great collection as if by magic, properly catalogue and prepare all the new material received, and also go back and do the work that has been left undone perhaps for fifty years. It is as foolish as is a family living in tents should begin to build a splendid hall of stone, and before the foundations had fairly risen above the surface of the ground should pass judgment, saying this new plan that promised such extravagant things is a failure, for it is no warmer or more comfortable than in the old tents.

That the colleges are turning their attention in this direction is evident when we look about and see that nearly all the leading institutions have, within the last few years, built new and greatly improved library buildings, and yet hardly one of them has by any means realized the ideal. Harvard, Yale, Columbia, Cornell, Amherst, Dartmouth, Williams, the Universities of Michigan, Vermont and Pennsylvania, Syracuse and Colgate are among those that occur to me on the spur of the moment.

But the colleges have a responsibility beyond making their own libraries what they should be and showing their students how much can be accomplished in liberal education in a well-administered library without other aids. You ought to send your graduates out with such an appreciation of what it is possible for a library to do as will make each a missionary in the town where he may live, earnest and active in seeing that it is provided with what the modern librarian calls the people's college. I see here a graduate of Amherst, whom I have not seen for fifteen years, who recalls a classmate who wrote me this week that he had remembered the seed sown in one of my lectures before his class in 1875; that he was now a lawyer in an inland town and trustee of its academy; that he had contributed largely himself and succeeded in raising from others sufficient money to make a creditable beginning on a library which they meant to make something near the ideal which I had set before him so many years ago. This illustrates my point, that if the subject is properly presented, sooner or later the seed sown will bear fruit. The colleges owe it to the public in every way to aid this great educational movement.

As pointed out yesterday, university extension work, which is an essential part of the modern library movement, is revolutionizing the face of England, bringing old Oxford and Cambridge into relations with the general public such as have never existed before. With us, we are giving great privileges to our colleges. In New York we have repealed the old laws limiting the power of holding property to $ 000 [sic] for academies, and to 40,000 bushels of wheat for colleges, and raised the limit to $250,000 of annual income. We have freed them from taxation. We last year freed them from the five per cent collateral inheritance tax, and are constantly, by law, giving them great powers and privileges. To them much has been given, and of them much will be required. The colleges cannot, in justice or with safety, much longer neglect the higher education of all the citizens, and confine their efforts to the favored few able to bear the cost of four years' residence.

To accomplish these results two things are needed. First, money for buildings, books and equipment. If the right brain guides its expenditure this will accomplish much, but it is not the most important factor or the one most difficult to-day to secure. However fine your library and its

equipment, it will never be more than a half success unless
there is behind it a large, strong, earnest human soul
which will supply the vital force that makes all the plant efficient. It is as if every building on this campus was
equipped most splendidly with chandeliers and electric lamps,
beautiful in form, perfect in model, and lacking nothing but
the dynamo. Without that connection they are cold, dark
and useless, in fact as well as technically "dead." The librarian holds a similar relation to even the best equipment.
To spend money on the plant without securing the man is as
unwise as to build the finest and largest cathedral organ and
then put on the bench a young girl who can only pump out
Moody and Sankey hymns. You will never know the almost
divine possibilities of the instrument until there sits down to
it a master of every stop and pedal.

Realizing all this for many years, we who had most at
heart this modern library idea four years ago established a
school for training librarians for their peculiar work. It
started with a twelve weeks' course which rapidly developed,
as it only partially met the demand, to six months, a year,
and after one season to two years.

It has drawn candidates from Maine to California. Its
standard has been raised each year. We have to-day thirty
pupils at Albany, coming from some fifteen different States
and representing many of our best colleges, but yet we have
not enough of the best material to meet the demand which is
increasing all over our land. The duty that I wish most
strongly to urge upon the colleges to-day is that you should
present or allow some of us who are interested to present to
every class the unequalled opportunities of usefulness offered by the librarian's profession at just this critical time
when it is developing so rapidly. We probably do not want
one out of a hundred of your graduates. We reject each year
scores of candidates. We have no place for the men that will
probably not succeed in law, or medicine, or in the pulpit,
but we do wish above all things to secure the occasional man
whom nature has fitted for the highest success in this peculiar and inspiring work; a man with capacity that would
command success in business or in the learned professions
and who will welcome this great opportunity. If you can
send us such men you will not only do them the greatest
service in finding for them an ideal life-work, but in the

end, in the far-reaching influences, in the work accomplished
for higher education by their agency, all that it has cost you
will come back ten, or twenty or a hundredfold.

Part II

THE SHAPING OF THE RESEARCH LIBRARY

AND ITS INSTRUCTIONAL FEATURES

1901-1917

THE SHAPING OF THE RESEARCH LIBRARY
AND ITS INSTRUCTIONAL FEATURES, 1901-1917

With the coming of the Progressive Era in the nation at large, higher education began to solidify the gains it had made in the previous century. Arthur E. Bestor described the period of 1875 to 1917 as witnessing the transformation of American scholarship; after the turn of the century the ideals of research, technical training, and liberal education became fully operative, achieving intellectual and bureaucratic stability.[1] Universities also were seen as much more useful to society and the nation than previously and, thus, the social and scholarly pressures on academic libraries to succeed in their support of research and service reached new heights.

Libraries became at once more bureaucratic and more service oriented. Samuel Rothstein defined the period from 1896 to 1916 as the decades when reference services were being integrated into the permanent administrative structure of research libraries.[2]

Librarians committed to user instruction took courage from both the burgeoning new collections and the stronger service ethic. Vast and complicated library resources offered tacit testimony to the student's need of instruction and assistance. The appointment of full-time reference librarians was a source of moral support, but it should be noted that while instruction in library use became as visible as reference work, it did not become as enduring. It failed in its attempts to obtain widespread or long-term curricular acceptance of credit courses and in its efforts at full integration into the personnel, service, and bureaucratic structures of academic libraries.

Undaunted, librarians looked backward and forward, in

57

both retrospectively examining their craft and in planning for the future by conducting regional and national surveys of instructional programs. In a speech presented at an ALA council meeting in 1915, Ernest C. Richardson of Princeton described as a "classic event" the appointment of Justin Winsor nearly four decades earlier as "professor of books" at Harvard, thereby initiating the practice of offering credit courses and invited lectures on library use.[3] Joseph Schneider credited Raymond C. Davis at Michigan as having given more "impetus to this movement" than anyone else.[4] In their surveys, librarians discovered a considerable amount of experimentation with instructional methods. Willard Austen's 1913 survey for the New York State Library Association found that 49 percent of 165 respondents engaged in some type of instructional program. An ALA survey conducted a year earlier had found that 57 percent of 149 institutions offered required or elective courses and, in 1914, Henry Evans reported that 20 percent of 446 colleges and universities and 56 percent of 166 normal schools offered instruction in library use.[5]

NOTES

1. Arthur E. Bestor, Jr. "The Transformation of American Scholarship, 1875-1917," Library Quarterly 23 (July 1953): 164-179.
2. Samuel Rothstein, The Development of Reference Service Through Academic Traditions, Public Library Practice and Special Librarianship (Chicago: Association of College and Reference Libraries, 1955), pp. 34-36.
3. Ernest C. Richardson, "Extracts from a Paper on the Place of the Library in a University," in American Library Institute Papers and Proceedings (Chicago: American Library Association, 1916), p. 176.
4. Joseph Schneider, "A College Course in Bibliography," Catholic Educational Review 3 (March 1912): 217.
5. Mary E. Ahern, "Library Activities During 1912-13," in Report of the Commissioner of Education for the Year Ended June 30, 1913 (Washington, D.C.: United States Government Printing Office, 1914), vol. 1, p. 327; John D. Wolcott, "Recent Aspects of Library Development," in Report of the Commissioner of Education for the Year Ended June 30, 1912 (Washington, D.C.: United States Government Printing Office, 1913), vol. 1, pp. 381-382; and Henry

R. Evans, comp. "Library Instruction in Universities, Colleges, and Normal Schools," U.S. Bureau of Education Bulletin no. 34 (1914): 3.

A College Course in Bibliography

Joseph Schneider

Educated at Ecole Libre in Paris, Schneider was Assistant
Librarian at Georgetown University (1893-1899) and Reference
Librarian at the Library of Congress from 1899 to 1908 when
he was appointed library director at Catholic University of
America. In 1924 he published Library Science, a book de-
signed to aid the user of small libraries.

Schneider defined "literary" or "intellectual" bibliography as the study of the contents of books. In this
selection he urged institutions of higher education to offer
courses in intellectual bibliography to teach students the
"common books of reference" including special bibliographies
and indexes to serial publications.

He was inspired by the earlier appeals of Ralph Waldo
Emerson and William Frederick Poole on behalf of course instruction in the methods of book use and he applauded the
leadership provided by Raymond C. Davis and his credit
course at the University of Michigan. Schneider's article
is a rare contribution, indeed, given its attempts to place
bibliographical instruction in the context of international
developments in general and the work of the International
Institute of Bibliography (IIB) in particular. Boyd Rayward
discusses the historical significance of the IIB in "The Evolution of an International Library Community," Journal of
Library History 16 (Spring 1981): 449-462.

Reprinted by permission of The Catholic University of America
Press from the Catholic Educational Review 3 (March 1912):
215-22.

•   •   •

It is the general opinion that books are the principal source
and means of culture. Directly or indirectly, they are almost the sole means, since the personal element, which often
is so great a feature in education itself, must depend upon
this source for its development.

It is therefore to the library that we must go for the
systematic improvement of our minds or for our mental cul-
tivation.

In former days it happened too often that the library
was only an incidental feature of the college or university.
This, however, is no longer true. Notable changes in
methods of instruction, the multiplication of lecture courses,
the organization of debating societies, have had an excellent
influence in bringing students in closer touch with the college or university library. The authorities of educational
institutions recognize the real relation between the library
and the college, the need of a large amount of library material in the work of instruction and the necessity of special
training in the one appointed to organize and to care for
this material and to make it speedily accessible to both professors and students. But notwithstanding the careful
training of the librarian, it would be impossible for him to
keep informed on the enormous output of the world's printing press, were it not for numerous bibliographies giving
lists of books published on almost every subject.

Search has been made with some care for a short and
satisfactory definition of the word bibliography, but without
complete success in ascertaining what it means to librarians
and to the world at large. Some enthusiasts maintain that
it is a science which comprehends all the other sciences and
arts. Others, more modest, are content to define it briefly
as the science which treats of the description, cataloging
and preservation of books. Two main divisions underline
the general study of bibliography, viz., material and literary, according as books are regarded with reference to their
form or to their content. The former concerns the book collector and the bookseller who value books on the basis of
their material finish, their elegant type, ample margins, fine
illustrations and artistic binding; the latter interests the

literary man, the scholar. In this short paper we propose
to treat only of the literary, or, as it is sometimes called,
intellectual bibliography, which treats of books with reference to their contents, and their connection in a literary
point of view. We shall try to show the necessity of making
the study of bibliography a part of the curriculum in our
colleges and universities.

Emerson, in his essay on books, demanded that every
college should have a professorship of books and reading.
Dr. Poole stated that the study of bibliography and scientific methods of using books should have an assured place
in the university curriculum and that a wise and professional bibliographer should be a member of the faculty and
have a part in the training of all the students. No one
realizes better than the librarian himself the importance of
the bibliographer's work. In the performance of his duties
in the reading room, he sees every day that the great
majority of his patrons are working at a disadvantage. To
the general student the knowledge of books of common reference is very limited, and very few indeed know of the
existence of special bibliographies and of indexes to serial
publications and periodicals. In his search for information,
the student leaves everything to chance, and as a rule,
it is only after having lost a good deal of precious time in
his fruitless search that he comes to the librarian for help.
This is always cheerfully given, and in most of these cases,
if time permits, the librarian tries to give a few general
directions in the use of reference books and bibliographies.
By practical experience one may get acquainted with a number of reference books and bibliographical works, but experience has shown that nothing can fill the place, in this
matter, as in many others, of a regular course of study.

To Mr. R. C. Davis, librarian emeritus of the university of Michigan, we owe more than to any one else for
giving an impetus to this movement. As far back as the
year 1881, he succeeded in having a course of bibliography
and reference works made part of the curriculum at Ann
Arbor. This example has been followed since by Brown
University, Dartmouth College and many other educational
institutions. At Yale University, a course in bibliography
of history is required of all students before further courses
in history can be taken. The course has proved to be an
excellent training for later college work. It develops the

habit of work, and gives a training in the independent use
of books; in one word, the student receives good mental
equipment for the proper treatment of any subject. During
the connection of the Library School with Columbia College
a complete library education was obtainable in connection
with the college course.

It is singular that universities should have neglected
this growing demand for library knowledge, since the
requisites for such instruction were practically already supplied; and while in certain ways the training of librarians
verges on the technical, yet in others it is far more academic
than many of the branches taught in universities. That professors are in favor of such a movement, there can be no
doubt. For a number of years back, in nearly every college
and university they have had appended to their courses of
lectures on various subjects, more or less bibliographical
information; they realized that without suggestions of this
sort the student would be puzzled to know how he should
go about the work prescribed by the professor.

If the study of bibliography is of comparatively recent
date, it has, however, already made rapid progress. Most
books published within the last few years contain a bibliography of the treatises consulted in the preparation of the
work. Today, an encyclopaedia without a full bibliography
accompanying each article is considered of little value. A
number of editorials in magazines have highly praised this
feature in the Catholic Encyclopaedia. Owing to these
excellent bibliographies in books and encyclopaedias the
reader finds, not only the facts, but also the sources from
which the facts are drawn. He can go back to the sources
which he may perhaps interpret in a different way, or at
least consult them to confirm or upset the conclusions of the
author.

Enough has been said to show that bibliography ought
to be made part of the curriculum in every college and university not only as an important factor in research work, but
also as being part of a liberal education. It is not necessary
that the student should learn the contents of the most useful
books, but he should know their existence and what they
treat of. He should know what are the most important reference books which will answer not only his own questions,

but also the many inquiries put to him by less favored associates who regard him as an educated man.

The interest shown by the literary world at large for
bibliography is another proof of its importance. National
and international societies have been formed all over the
world for the advancement of bibliography. The Société
Bibliografique of Paris deserves here special notice for
having been the first to enter the field. It was founded in
1861, and aside from its regular bulletin, it publishes a universal bibliography--Le Polybiblion. Of this publication, two
parts appear each month, one literary and one technical.
The latter includes a bibliography of new works published
not only in France, but also in foreign countries, summaries
of the principal periodicals, French and foreign, and of the
publications of learned societies. But even societies, if
private, seem hardly equal to the task of bibliography making. For this reason, those interested in the progress of
bibliography have looked to the state for assistance. Thus
national and even international bibliographical societies have
been organized within the last quarter of a century. The
foundation of the "Institut international de bibliographie" at
Brussels in 1895, is the most important step in this direction.

An excellent idea of the work done by this institute
can be formed from the proceedings of its second meeting in
1897, when the following resolutions were adopted:

1. The International Bibliographical Conference recognizes the necessity of giving the work of bibliography an
international organization...
2. It congratulates the Belgian government on the
valuable encouragement which it has given to bibliographical
science during these last two years. It associates in these
congratulations the following Swiss authorities: the Federal
School Board, the governing council of the Canton of Zurich
and the Town Council of the City of Zurich...
3. The Conference adopts the principle of special and
critical bibliographies as supplementary to the Universal Bibliographical Index;
4. Recognizes the usefulness of forming national
branches within the International Institute of Bibliography;
5. Urges learned societies and editors of periodicals
to send every month on separate slips to the national

secretaries of the International Institute of Bibliography a
table of contents of the periodicals published under their
editorship, for the purpose of rapidly compiling the Universal Bibliographical Index.

    6. Expresses the wish that in advanced courses of
study greater weight should be laid upon bibliography.

    7. Expresses the desire that an agreement should be
reached in the several countries between the associations of
publishers, booksellers, librarians and the International
Institute of Bibliography or its national sections for founding
Library Schools;

    8. Commissions the officers of the International Insti-
tute of Bibliography to appoint a committee of specialists in
various countries for the purpose of establishing an international code of rules to be followed in compiling bibliographical notices;

    9. Commissions the officers of the International Insti-
tute of Bibliography to form a committee for the purpose of
studying the most practical and economical methods of printing bibliographical cards.

    10. The assembly continues the officers of the Inter-
national Institute of Bibliography in their functions until the
next conference.

    During the few years which have elapsed since these
resolutions have been adopted, most of the wishes expressed
in these resolutions have been realized. To mention only
our own country, we may well be proud of the number and
high standard of our library schools. The plan suggested
by J. Thomson in 1902, for a bibliographical society of
America, has also been realized.

    The division of bibliography in the Library of Congress,
cannot be too highly praised for the work done during the
last fifteen years. Were it not that everybody in the library
world understands the importance of bibliography, such progress could not have been made within a few years.

    But the reader may ask what is to be the scope of a
practical course of bibliography for the college man. Such
a course having passed its experimental state in universities
where it has been given for a number of years, it will be
sufficient to mention here the topics which may make up a
course of about 30 hours a year. Two or three lectures on
reference books may be followed by a short history of printing

and the material side of the book as well as on the history
of libraries.

As for the description of bibliographical works, the
following division may be adopted:

1. Bibliographical history.
2. Bibliography of bibliographies.
3. Universal bibliographies (general catalogues, encyclopaedias, incunabula, anonyms and pseudonyms).
4. National bibliographies (trade bibliographies).
5. Bibliographies of special subjects or authors.
6. Indexes to periodicals and serial publications.

In the study of these six classes of bibliographies,
the professor of books, as Emerson calls him, will:

1. Introduce the student to the principal bibliographers
from the earliest one, Richard de Bury (1381-1445) to those
of the present day.
2. Among the many bibliographies of bibliography he
will point out the different features of each and indicate those
which may be consulted with profit in preference to others.
3. Concerning universal bibliographies, the student
will become familiar with the best printed catalogues such as
those of the British Museum, the national library of France,
the Peabody Institute in Baltimore, the Surgeon General's in
Washington, etc. He also will be given instruction on the use
and relative value of encyclopaedias containing bibliographical
references. For rare books and incunabula a description will
be given of Brunet's Manuel du Libraire ... Hain's Repertori-
um Bibliographicum ... Panzer's Annales Typographici ... etc.
A study of Barbier, Quérard, Weller, Cushing, etc., will
teach him to find the real author of anonymous books and of
books signed by pseudonyms.
4. As for national bibliographies, they will be described by countries. Trade bibliographies, which are the
best guides for finding author, title, place and date of publication and price of books, will be carefully studied.
5. In the study of bibliographies of special authors
or subjects the student will be especially taught how to make
such bibliographies in connection with his own work.
6. Besides Poole's Index, the Readers' Guide to Periodical Literature, periodicals and serials containing excellent
monthly or quarterly lists of bibliography on certain subjects

will be studied carefully. We feel confident that such a course in bibliography and reference works will enable the student to conduct an original investigation with ease and pleasure and thus we may hope that the student of today will be the scholar of tomorrow.

Training in the Use of Books

William Warner Bishop

Bishop is regarded as one of the leading academic librarians of the twentieth century, having distinguished himself in administration, international cooperation, and public and technical services. Before serving as Librarian at the University of Michigan (1915-1941), he had been Superintendent of the Reading Room at the Library of Congress (1907-1915) and Cataloger and Reference Librarian at Princeton University (1902-1907).

In this address, presented at the College of William and Mary, Bishop described exponential growth in the production of books and recommended training in the use of books to help students and professors deal intelligently with the deluge of new materials published each year. This training he defined as "the acquiring of a scholar's attitude toward the printed page," learning how to discriminate (for research purposes) among books and authors.

As a model for development in the teaching of book and library use, Bishop recommended the faculty at the University of Michigan who, following the lead of German universities, introduced courses by lecturing on the bibliographical sources of the topics to be covered during the semester. He described these lectures as the "most highly prized and faithfully attended" of the course. The author reprinted this speech in his collection, The Backs of Books and Other Essays in Librarianship (Baltimore: Williams and Wilkins, 1926), pp. 99-124. Bishop's articles on closely related topics include "The Amount of Help to Be Given to Readers," Bulletin of the American Library Association 2 (September 1908): 327-334 and "The Library in the American College," in American Library

Association, College and Reference Library Yearbook 1
(1929): 1-12.

Reprinted by permission of the publisher from Sewanee Review 20 (July 1912): 265-81.

•   •   •

It is my good fortune to have in my office in the Library of
Congress a collection of books which recalls to me daily one
of the great men of our country, a man whose memory is
especially dear to Virginians, that most distinguished alumnus
of the College of William and Mary, Thomas Jefferson.
Mr. Jefferson spent much time and money in gathering a library. His efforts extended over many years. In a letter
written in 1814 he described them as follows:

> .... You know my collection, its condition and ex-
> tent. I have been fifty years making it, and have
> spared no pains, opportunity or expense, to make
> it what it is. While residing in Paris, I devoted
> every afternoon I was disengaged, for a summer or
> two in examining all the principal bookstores, turning
> over every book in my hand, and putting by every
> thing which related to America, and indeed whatever
> was rare and valuable in every science. Besides
> this, I had standing orders during the whole time
> I was in Europe, on its principal book-marts, par-
> ticularly Amsterdam, Frankfort, Madrid, and London,
> for such works relating to America as could not be
> found in Paris. So that, in that department particu-
> larly, such a collection was made as probably can
> never again be effected, because it is hardly probable
> that the same opportunities, the same time, industry,
> perseverance and expense, with the same knowledge
> of the bibliography of the subject would again happen
> to be in concurrence. During the same period, and
> after my return to America, I was led to procure also
> whatever related to the duties of those in the high
> concerns of the nation....

This collection gathered with so much pains by the

former President was purchased by the Government in 1815,
and became the nucleus of the present Library of Congress.
The greater part of that library had been destroyed in the
previous August, when the Capitol was burned by the
British troops. For many years Mr. Jefferson's books
formed the most useful and valuable portion of the collection,
and even to-day certain of them are indispensable to inves-
tigators. The collection numbered about 7,000 volumes. The
disastrous fire of 1851, which destroyed a large part of the
library, proved especially destructive to Mr. Jefferson's
books; less than 2,500 survived, and the wear and tear of
ninety-five years has reduced this number to 2,000. These,
carefully preserved as the "Jefferson Collection," remain a
witness to the industry, learning, and zeal of the author of
the Declaration of Independence.

But fortunately we are not left to infer from this--less
than one third--the character of the remainder of the collection formed by Mr. Jefferson. Almost as soon as the books
were put in place, a catalogue of them was issued by the
Library. This catalogue was arranged in forty-four chapters,
following the classification which Mr. Jefferson had himself
devised, and which remained in effect, with some minor
changes, to the end of the century. The library revealed
by the catalogue of 1815 was undoubtedly one of the best
in America at that day. It was strongest in law and in history, especially that of America, but it contained many
valuable works and sets in philosophy, classical literature,
theology, and belles-lettres. The books were of high character, and were mostly in good editions and sound bindings.
When we reflect that it was bought largely in the midst of
engrossing public duties, in time of war, and in great part
under the disadvantage of remoteness from the book-
markets of the old world, the marvel is that it was so good.

In 1815 there were but few libraries of any size, public or private, in the United States. This collection of only
7,000 volumes ranked high in numbers. Harvard college could
boast some 16,000 in 1790; the New York Society Library,
about 14,000; the Library Company and Logonian Library of
Philadelphia, some 18,000; and the Library Society of
Charleston, S.C., about 7,500. There may have been half
a dozen other libraries of over 7,000 volumes scattered along
the Atlantic seaboard. Private libraries numbering more than

a few thousand books were rare, and Mr. Jefferson's collection was a very notable one for that day.

I say "for that day," since the increase in the number
of libraries and in their size since 1815 has been little short
of marvellous. There are to-day in the United States over
2,300 libraries having more than 8,000 volumes each. Their
total numbers reach well over eighty-five millions of volumes,
and eleven million pamphlets, while in the year 1908 nearly
twenty millions of persons are recorded as having actually
read and studied in their reading-rooms. Over seventy-five
million books were issued for home use from only 1,384 of
these 2,300. There are now over 10,000 persons employed in
library work (including those charged with the care of buildings). Six libraries have more than 500,000 volumes; nine,
more than 300,000 but less than half a million; and sixty-two,
less than 300,000 but more than 100,000. Thus there are
to-day in our land seventy-seven libraries, each one of which
is more than fourteen times as large as was the Library of
Congress when it started afresh with President Jefferson's
collection in 1815. And that Library has grown from this
original 7,000 to almost two million books and pamphlets, add-
ing of late years over 100,000 volumes annually. Moreover,
the number of small collections, school, office, village, college, professional libraries, collections which are not included
in this somewhat wearisome array of figures, has increased,
if not proportionately, at least very greatly. There must be
available for use to a greater or less degree in this country
at least sixty-five millions of books--a figure which still
falls far short of one to each inhabitant.

Moreover, the production of books and of magazines
has increased in about the same proportions. Newspapers
are probably no more numerous in proportion to the population than they were in the second decade of the nineteenth
century, for most of the publishing activity of that day was
shown in journalism. We have no reliable figures for the
publication of books and pamphlets in that period of our history. The great scholarly bibliographies have dealt largely
with the colonial period, and the bulky trade bibliographies
begin much later. In the midst of the War of 1812 and the
impoverished condition which preceded and followed it, the
publication of books was probably small. Moreover, it is,
of course, a commonplace of history that the United States
was almost wholly an agricultural country in 1815; and in

communities devoted largely to farming, book publishing does
not ordinarily flourish as it does in an industrial society. A
few hundred books, perhaps a thousand or more pamphlets,
probably made up the annual output of this country in 1815.
In Europe the number was, of course, very much greater,
although the period of the Napoleonic Wars was not favorable
to extensive publishing.

Contrast this meagre production with what has been
aptly termed "our literary deluge." In 1910 there were published in the United States 13,470 books, by 2,217 publishing
firms. This number does not include "directories and similar
publications, official publications (with a very few exceptions),
or minor pamphlets." Thus all but a few dozen of the thousands of publications of the national, state, and municipal
governments are not counted in these figures, nor are the
hosts of catalogues of schools and colleges and many valuable
publications of societies, such as year-books, annuals, bulletins, and journals, all of them materials of some worth, which
are certain to find a resting place on library shelves. No account is taken in arriving at this number, 13,470, by the
Publishers' Weekly, of the extensive magazine output of the
country, nor of the huge number of newspapers of all sorts.
Therefore the formidable array of nearly fourteen thousand
books produced in the United States in one year is far from
being the whole number which is to be reckoned with.

Great Britain produced, in 1910, 10,804 works; Germany, about 31,000; France, 12,615, and Italy 6,788. The
Scandinavian countries, Austria, Spain, Portugal, Holland,
Belgium, Switzerland, Greece, and Turkey must have published among them at least twice as many as Italy, one would
suppose, while Australia, South Africa, and India will easily
bring the total up to 85,000 works in European languages--
not including the literary product of the great Slavic nations.
This makes no account of the very considerable annual output
of books in the Orient and in South America. We shall not
be far wrong if we say that at the very least 100,000 books
are printed each year, any one of which may perhaps be
called for by a reader in one of our great libraries.

This is a deluge indeed. What a contrast to the conditions of Mr. Jefferson's day. Then the well-read man of
letters or affairs, undisturbed by telegrams, cables, newspaper extras, telephone calls, ticket bulletins, automobile

honks, next month's magazines, or "red-hot" fiction, could
sit down to a leisurely perusal of the books his agent had
sent him from Philadelphia or London, could re-read the
classics, could keep abreast of the best thought of the day
with reasonable success, and could master the contents of a
library of 7,000 volumes with the comfortable assurance that
he had read the majority of the best works of the world of
letters.

That day has passed. The scholar of to-day is ever
fearful lest he shall have missed the latest treatise on his
little specialty, which yet, despite its limitations, has a
literature of its own. The average man of intelligence is
well-nigh helpless before the mass of books in even a minor
library. The craze for the "latest" novel, the most "up-to-
date" reference book, is the characteristic note of the
present demand for books. How, in the face of this flood,
shall the young man of our day find his bearings; how shall
he ride the flood a master; by virtue of what training shall
he make it serve him, carry him to his goal, whelmed by
numbers, misled by cheap newness, misguided by advertising,
and lost in a wilderness of printed matter when he essays to
work in a modern library or to attempt the mastery of any
important question? This is my theme: training in the use
of books, the acquiring of a scholar's attitude toward the
printed page. Its timeliness is proven by every library bulletin, every publisher's announcement, by the experience of
every teacher, and, I fear I must add, by the painful witness of much incompetent and careless journalism, and the
enormous profits of the publishers of cheaply made subscrip-
tion books.

How that training may be obtained, and where it shall
begin, I shall endeavor to set forth briefly, in the hope that
such a theme cannot fail to be of interest to all connected
with education.

We may begin with the child in school. Now certain
elementary facts about books one naturally supposes everybody observes and knows. And yet experience shows that
most school children--and many of their elders, for that
matter--are seldom acquainted with the basic fact that a book
has an author. To them a book is a book; their arithmetic
is their arithmetic book; not Robinson's, or Smith's, or
Wentworth's, or anybody else's arithmetic. Nobody ever

points out to them the fact that their text-book was written by anyone, and they usually know it by the color or by the name of the teacher in whose class they used it. This curious ignorance on the part of school children was first brought to my notice years ago, when examining orally a large number of candidates for entrance to a college and to its preparatory department. Out of nearly a hundred young people ranging from twelve to twenty, not one was able to tell us the names of the writers of all the text-books he had used during the previous term, and few, very few, knew the names of any of the authors. The answers were so extremely vague in most cases as to lead me--in my inexperience--to doubt seriously whether there had been any actual study of the various subjects. "We had the same grammar everybody uses;" "The English history was a little green book," was the kind of reply my questioning elicited. And yet these same young folk did well in their classes, and gave evidence of having really worked at the matter of these books concerning whose makers they had so little knowledge. Perhaps the matter is the all-important thing, but the poor author who gave it form--I speak for all makers of text-book--deserves the reward of at least a bowing acquaintance. And the indifference to the author in the school days is too frequently carried over into later life. It is an indifference fostered by the anonymous journalism of the day, whose remote results are seen in part in the greedy devouring in our great circulating libraries of any trash that is called a novel. Perhaps the irresponsibility of school children as respects their author and his work was never better shown than by an incident which has always stood in my mind as the finest example of ineffective teaching I have met with. A young girl of my acquaintance, on being asked in what grade she was in school, said she was in the third year of the high school. "Then you have been reading Cicero's Orations Against Catiline?" "Well," was the meditative answer, "we have been reading somebody's orations about Catiline; I guess they were Cicero's, but whether they were for or against Catiline, I don't remember."

If the author deserves to be known to his readers, the title of his book likewise claims a certain attention. Doubtless it is a less important detail than the other, but nevertheless not wholly negligible. Here again the child in school generally receives small aid and comfort from his teacher. The beginning of a proper training in the use of

books comes when children are taught that books are written
by people, have a definite name, and frequently appear in
different forms. We hear much in pedagogic circles of
training in observation. That observation may well begin
with such elementary details as these.

Any librarian will testify that titles are more frequently remembered than authors, but that they are seldom remembered correctly. The girl who demands the red book
her sister had last month is sometimes less puzzling than
the woman who calls insistently for the book entitled: For
Better or For Worse, finally going off contented with Miss
Johnston's To Have and to Hold, remarking complacently
that she knew it was something out of the marriage service.

It is not too much to expect that school children may
have it pointed out by someone that a book generally has a
table of contents and an index. I wonder how many teachers
ever do this? How frequently do we find children helplessly
turning the pages, looking in vain for some half-forgotten
passage! Makers of text-books generally provide indexes
and tables, and presumably teachers use them, but too seldom are children systematically taught the necessity and use
of these keys to the contents of a book.

If we can secure some such early training in observing
and understanding the primal factors in the make-up of a
book, we may surely demand also of teachers some sort of
instruction in elementary discrimination between books.
Books are not like bricks, or bales of cotton, or bolts of
cloth--a fundamental fact which is not always clear to business men in estimating the cost of handling and buying
them. Each book is a separate entity--a mass of paper, to
be sure, on which there are certain impressions on ink, but
much more than that, the physical expression of someone's
thought. Now if the child has learned that some man or
woman wrote his text-book, he has grasped the prime element in discriminating between books. Given one man's
work, he may be aware that another man has done the same
sort of thing. Hence the necessity of knowing how well
each has done it, in order to make a choice. But while the
selection of books is perhaps too serious a matter to enter
into this primary training in the use of books, the knowledge
of what field or parts of a field different books cover, is
not. Moreover, this knowledge--derived, of course, from a

study of the table of contents; for one seems naturally to come back always to the elements--is of extreme practical importance. The sooner a boy learns that not all American histories come down to the year 1912, and that there are numerous histories devoted to small periods of time, the better for him. That the author has a plan and purpose in writing, and that two books apparently on the same topic may be written from absolutely different points of view and for different ends, he will discover, if only he is made to read prefaces and introductions. If a child once fairly enters into the idea that an author writes for a particular class--as for children; or for a particular purpose, as in a purely outline or elementary history; or from a motive of his own, as a defence of his own conduct or the exposition of a theory,--he has begun to discriminate between books. When he has once begun, he will not be likely to cease. And he will, by virtue of this training, be in the way to acquire an intelligent attitude toward books, a knowledge that they are made by people who differ in gifts and in purpose, in ability and in design. Moreover, he will not be led into the very common error of assuming that a well-known book is necessarily the book he wants. It is a fact to which all librarians will bear witness that the average man who wants to know something in English history asks for Macaulay's History, in entire ignorance of the fact that it is devoted largely to the reign of James II. So Gibbon is asked for by persons who wish to know something about the Gracchi, and Carlyle's French Revolution for the later career of Napoleon. Such elementary training as that which I have urged would do away with this kind of error.

The use of elementary books of reference is more common in schools than is this training in observation. No school room beyond the sixth grade is complete without a dictionary and an atlas. But very few teachers realize what a wealth of information is contained in a modern dictionary, or train their pupils to find it. I may safely say also that they fail to train them so well and thoroughly in the order of the alphabet that it becomes second-nature to them--a key to arrangement of all sorts of books and catalogues, which they will need to use all their lives. I know I am on for-bidden ground here, and that it is unfashionable in these days to teach the alphabet. But I am thankful that I "learned my letters" when a child. I do not insist on that process as a preliminary to learning to read--but very soon

after a child has learned to read, he should be drilled in
the alphabet as a set of symbols. When he has learned this,
he is ready to use a dictionary or an encyclopaedia. Now
the wonders of a modern unabridged dictionary are not revealed to the casual observer. But they are a constant
source of delight to children--I speak from experience--and
of information to the teacher. A little training here will
reveal to a bright child possibilities of which he will be eager
to take advantage later. And how few children are trained
to use by way of quick consultation their atlases or the maps
in their geographies. Here is a fertile field for ingenuity
and resources on the part of teachers. I find very few
grown people who use atlases with speed and certainty.
Usually an uncertain finger wanders over the map in search
of the name of the desired place. The letters and figures in
the margin, the indexes, the table of contents, they ignore.
And yet how simple are these devices. They are so easily
used that children when once introduced to their meaning
make a game of locating a town, a river, a county.

This elementary sort of training can reasonably be expected of all pupils who complete the primary course. The
ordinary text-book, the dictionary, the atlas, are all the
vehicles, all the apparatus required for conveying it. There
is no need of an elaborate library or much formal training,
and yet the results of the teacher's occasional direction and
careful supervision will show later all the difference between a
blind following a set of printed formulas, and a discriminating
and intelligent attitude toward a book.

One serious difficulty should be recognized at this
point. With young pupils only confusion is likely to result
from too great a divergence from a text-book on the part of
the teacher. That blind reverence for the printed page
which it is our purpose to destroy will cause children to lose
confidence in a teacher who puts herself in opposition to the
book too often. All teachers of young children know this,
and govern themselves accordingly. The literalness of the
child mind we all recognize. I well remember a boy who came
to me in great distress because he had found that Caesar
didn't know Latin grammar. He had found in his text a vio-
lation of one of the plainest rules in Allen & Greenough. I
think he never had any confidence in me after my explanation
that there were exceptions to all rules, and that Caesar knew
more about Latin than the distinguished professors who made

the grammar, or the boy who was studying it, and moreover
had written a Latin grammar himself.

Not all children who reach our secondary schools find
in them good school libraries. We have been slow to realize
the need of a school library in the curriculum of the high
school, and the importance of its function in the scheme of
secondary education. And even where books have been provided generously, there has been but little appreciation of
the possibilities of training which are latent in even a small
collection. Too often the care of the high school library has
been an added burden placed on an already heavily-taxed
teacher, or has been left to the ignorant enthusiasm of some
bright pupil. Within the past twenty years many of our larger cities have been appointing librarians for the high
school libraries. Moreover, in a few places these librarians
have become what they should all be, teachers of the art of
using books. Slowly, under the influence of some of our
state library commissions, and of some enlightened high
school principals, teachers and school authorities are beginning to see that the school library affords throughout life a
basis for learning how to use books in collections. Not alone
is this knowledge absolutely needed as an aid to modern instruction in literature, history, and science, but it is even
more valuable as furnishing the means whereby pupils may
become adepts in the use of libraries, an art which has been
won by most of us through hard knocks, but which can be
taught very simply and effectively. Let us not forget the
necessity for that art in modern life, the flood of books with
which the pupil will have to struggle later. In the secondary
school he can and should learn the elements of dealing with
books in libraries, and when he comes to college he should
not be helpless, but happy in the opportunity to make quick
and efficient use of a library of fifty, one hundred, or even
five hundred thousand volumes.

He should learn by formal instruction of the high
school librarian--instruction which, to my knowledge, is now
given with great success in a dozen schools--that books have
to be arranged or classified on some sort of a system.
Usually they are grouped on the principle of likeness--those
treating of the same theme being placed together. If he once
grasps that idea and its corollary--that as one book can go
only in one place, it must be placed with those books which
it most resembles--he will quickly understand classification
notations, and will not be baffled by figures, letters, or

decimal points. He should also learn the use of a simple
catalogue on cards, and should master the principle of alphabetical arrangement. If a boy knows how to use the
card catalogue of a high school library, there is no reason
why he cannot use easily any other catalogue, even so huge
a thing as the card catalogue of the Library of Congress
with its two thousand trays and its hundreds of thousands
of entries.

In the secondary school also the pupils can easily
learn the use of the indexes to magazines. Few tools are
more helpful than Poole's Index and the Reader's Guide to
Periodical Literature. There is no reason why they should
not be known to all high school students, even although the
greater part of the volumes indexed are not in the school or
town library.

When he is ready for college, therefore, a young man
may reasonably be supposed to have an elementary equipment in the use of books, if only his teachers have deliberately tried to give it to him. No extensive apparatus, no
costly library, no great amount of time are needed. Careful
and tactful teaching of the habit of using books as tools;
an intelligent direction of the pupil's attitude toward the
books he has at hand; the fullest possible use of the school
library under competent guidance--these are all that a
training in the use of books demands as a beginning. It
is easy to estimate the advantage which a student thus
equipped has over one who has known books merely as
printed matter containing certain information which he has
more or less reluctantly acquired, and whose ability to use
books in collections is absolutely a negative quantity.

It is a stock complaint against our modern colleges
that they do not acquaint students with the great literatures
of the world. Education for culture is said not to exist, or
at least not to succeed. Whatever measure of truth may be
found in this contention, it may be worth while to point out
that the old-fashioned college course of four years, rigid
and arid as it was, failed even more completely than that of
to-day to introduce students either to the great literatures
of Greece and Rome--small samples of which were minutely
and painfully dissected daily--or to those of the modern languages. In few cases in the earlier two-thirds of the nineteenth century was the routine of text-book recitation or

formal lecture abandoned in favor of a wide comparison of
authorities or an independent study of the literature of a
period.   If I do not read amiss educational history and the
reminiscences of our fathers, the old-fashioned college
course was certainly not that "good old time" to which educational reformers would hark back.   Certainly no young
man in any American college had an opportunity to study in
the forties, or even in the sixties, such topics as the Ro-
mantic Movement in German literature, the French Chansons
de Geste, or the Greek dialectic poets, topics which appear
in catalogues as sample elective courses in colleges of no
great size or extraordinary resources.

We should be far wrong, however, did we infer that
the old-fashioned college with its small faculty, its rigid
curriculum, its hard and fast class lines, failed to foster a
love for literature and reading.   There was more leisure
for reading, both on the part of students and faculty.
There was almost without exception an abundance of life
in the literary and debating societies--organizations which
are not everywhere vigorous to-day.   Athletics did not absorb so much of the energy of the student-body, and it is
probably true that there was more reading on individual
initiative than there is to-day, when formal instruction is
found in so much wider a range of subjects, even in the
smallest colleges.

In fact, the modern college and university have bred
a peculiar attitude toward books on the part of students.
Certain books are required to be read for entrance in
English--books which are the birthright of all who speak the
English tongue.   And many a lad reads and cons notes on
Quentin Durward, or Ivanhoe, or the Princess, in about the
spirit in which boys read the immortal commentaries of
Julius Caesar.   "Collateral reading" has been run so hard
that books to be used in a certain course have become merely an adjunct--Professor So-and-so's books-- and are even
less than a text-book in the eyes of the student.   Worse
than that, the seminar and departmental libraries have had
too frequently a deleterious influence on the advanced student.   No other books interest him--if they are not in the
seminar library, they are not worth while.   Instead of
broadening his range of knowledge, this very convenient
grouping of certain books as tools, tends to restrict it.
Lest I may seem to exaggerate, I will illustrate by an

anecdote which came under my observation. A certain very
distinguished professor in one of our largest universities by
some unusual chance wandered so far from his seminar that
he came on the general card catalogue of the university library. "How convenient and admirable a thing this catalogue is," said he, after half an hour's study of it; "I must
have it copied for the economics seminar."

   There results too frequently, from this and other influences, an attitude of indifference toward the college library on the part of students. I have watched students
who came every day for weeks to read certain required
books, and have never seen them read anything else--doubt-
less it was true that they had not the time. I have seen the
graduate student stick to the seminar until it grew to represent the world of letters to him. I have regretfully noted
the presence in laboratories of students of the sciences for
hours every day--hours so long that they never had a
glimpse of any cultural reading. And--I fear I must say
it--horribile dictu!--I have known boys who passed an entire four years in a college with 350,000 books in its library, and who in those four years never entered its doors.

   Now a large part of this indifference is the result of
at least two factors: the lack of the sort of training in the
secondary schools which I have been emphasizing, and the
almost criminal indifference on the part of college and university authorities, including their librarians, I fear--toward
the development of cultural reading and the sense of mastery of books. Plunge an untrained boy into a library of
thirty, fifty, or hundred thousand books--how is he to
pick and choose, how shall he get his start? He needs formal instruction in the rudiments, nay, even in the refine-
ments, of bibliography. In the German universities the
professor usually lectures at the beginning of each course
on the bibliography of the subject he is about to discuss
before the class during the semester. Those lectures are
generally the most highly prized and faithfully attended of
the course. The custom has had some notable imitators in
America, and I have always been profoundly grateful that
most of my professors at Michigan followed this practice as
a matter of course. Within the past few years Princeton
has been going much further in the work of her "preceptors." Here and there a college librarian has with more or
less success given lectures on the use of the library and

on bibliography. If we will consider the literary deluge of
the day, the ever growing number of books in our college
libraries, we shall perceive the positive necessity for methods
differing alike from the indifference and the ways of the past.

      To go into details of those methods would be unprofit-
able here. They have never been worked out with more than
fair success, but I think I may say that college librarians
and college professors alike are earnestly studying them;
are experimenting, and testing ways and means. The college library must deliberately spend thought and money in
advertising its wares, and must interpose as few obstacles
as possible between its books and its readers.

      What should result from such a bibliographic training?
How should a young man, equipped as we would have him,
face the library and the out-pourings of the press? He
should, it seems to me, show first a certain readiness and
ease among books; he should treat them all as at least dis-
tant acquaintances who may become friends any day. He
does not know them, perhaps, but he knows where they live
and why they live there, and what they purport to do for a
living; and he is not any more surprised than he is with
people to learn that some are existing largely on their past
reputation; others are leading a double life, and a few are
not too reliable or no better than they should be. Secondly,
he should know well and familiarly those directories and
those elite lists, social registers if you please, of the world
of letters--which tell him both where anybody may be found,
or where the best books of any sort dwell. He should--to
drop our metaphor--use easily bibliographic tools of all sorts
from the simple check list to the erudite works of Fabricius
and Poggendorf. And he should know the literature of his
own subject more than fairly well. Only thus will he become
possessed of the historic sense and of the man's attitude
toward the printed page. He will realize that books are but
imperfect media of arriving at knowledge after all, and that
he must put himself into them if he is to profit by them. He
will need little assistance from librarians, but will not hesi-
tate to ask questions when he needs help.

      Of greater value than any facility in the use of cata-
logues, bibliographies, and indexes, will be the ability to
judge of the comparative merits of books both new and old.
If he has learned to read the great reviews, to appreciate

to some extent the personal equations of authors, publishers, and reviewers,--not omitting a suspicion of the power of advertising, even in scientific subjects--if he has acquired some criteria for forming judgments of his own, he has gained from the college library, from the college professor, from his fellow students, (especially in debate), from his earlier training, an attitude toward books which defies definition, but which may perhaps be best termed <u>discriminating</u>. Such a man cannot be "dated" in later life by the opinions and views of his day in college. He is equipped to cope both with books, and, to a lesser degree, with men.

But highly as I rate the power to work easily and familiarly with books in collections, I am not unaware that there lurk certain serious dangers in this very familiarity and facility. It is the peculiar vice of librarians--even more characteristic than their propensity to talk shop--that as they know intimately the backs of so many books, they are likely to persuade themselves that they know their contents as well. The temptation is subtle and powerful, and its operations are not confined to the custodian of books. Let no one deceive himself into thinking that because he knows the royal road to learning, its guide posts, its directories, its ins and outs, the various vehicles that carry men on it, he is necessary travelling thereon himself. There is no virtue and no praise in this knowledge, if it is not applied to help either oneself or another to actual progress.

No one is really trained in the use of books who has not made himself master of a few books. His facility in the use of many books should and must leave him to leisure which is needful to absorb certain great works, to read himself into them, to make them part of his very being. What these books should be is not a matter for dogmatism. One man will feed his soul on Shakespeare, and another on Newton's <u>Principia</u>. But certain works should become a part of the very nature of every man of our race, whatever his profession, who dares call himself educated. The English Bible is still the greatest work in the English tongue. The youth who reaches maturity without a thorough knowledge of its wonderful prose and poetry, and its message of personal religion and of duty toward God and man, has missed the greatest intellectual and moral training the language affords. I care not how he interprets it. Let him <u>know</u> the

Bible from cover to cover, and consider his own relation to
it what he will.

There are other English books, too, which no man can
afford not to know, and know intimately. Shakespeare and
Milton among the poets; Bacon and Addison and Emerson
among essayists; Green, Macaulay, and Parkman among the
historians, are but a few of the names which suggest themselves at once. And who dares affirm himself wholly ignorant of Homer and Vergil, of Dante, and of Goethe and
Schiller, of Cervantes and of Montaigne? The man who has
not as a boy devoted himself to the reading and re-reading
of at least a few of the world's great books is but poorly
prepared to cope with the literary deluge of our day or with
the plausible sophistries of the time. He has necessarily a
low standard of literary judgment. He has sold his birthright of noble books for a mess of pottage whose chief in-
gredients are Sunday newspapers and illustrated weeklies.

With this caution, this admonition to think on the high
things of the world of letters, I reach my conclusion. He
that is faithful to the mastering of a few great books will
use easily the tools provided for handling the lesser books.
Secure in the possession of some works which the ages have
tested, he will welcome the good in the mass of new books,
will make the indifferent, or even the bad, serve his need
without lowering himself to its level, will show his training
in the use of books not alone in the ease with which he
masters bookish problems or acquires information, but much
more in the character of his thinking and in the standard of
his judgments.

Instruction in the Use of a College Library

Lucy M. Salmon

A graduate of Bryn Mawr College and the University of
Michigan, Salmon taught history at Vassar College from 1887
until her death in 1927. The Dictionary of American Biography observed that the cardinal principle of her teaching
was that the student should be the "chief agent in his own
instruction."

Speaking at the ALA conference in Kaaterskill, New
York in 1913, she posed a perennial question: Is library
use instruction given better as an independent course, or
in connection with regular course work? She strongly supported the latter and preferred professors to librarians as
instructors in library use. She cited the advantages professors have in working with small groups of students and
in showing students only as much of the library system as
their course work necessitated. Supported with detailed
descriptions of her library use assignments, these comments
constitute a cogent, closely argued position.

Identifying differences between academic reference librarians and college professors, she defined the responsibilities of reference librarians as supporters of non-curricular
activities such as debates, college publications, and other
work necessary to student (rather than faculty) initiative.
She concluded that librarians could also provide an environment
conducive to user instruction by maintaining open shelf arrangements and aiding in collection development, but that instructional duties should remain with professors.

Reprinted by permission of the American Library Association
from the ALA Bulletin 7 (July 1913): 301-09.

•   •   •

Students who enter college are in an altogether hopeless
state, if we are to believe the lamentations poured out in
educational reviews and in library journals. In familiar
phrase, "they have left undone those things which they
ought to have done, and they have done those things
which they ought not to have done, and there is no health
in them." But it is not given either a college librarian or
a college instructor to remain long hopeless, either for
himself or for others,--the very nature of his calling demands that somebody do something. Discouragement over
ingorant and untrained freshmen dissolves into the bewild-
ering questions of who is to do what, and when, and
where, and how. And so the college year begins.

It is undoubtedly true that a very large majority of
college freshmen are not familiar with a large library such
as they meet in college, that they have never used a card
catalog, and that they would not even recognize it if they
saw one.

But is it reasonable to expect such knowledge? The
majority come from small places where such opportunities
are not found, the work of the secondary schools does not
demand extensive use of a library, and the mental immatu-
rity of pupils of the secondary school age does not augur
well either for an understanding of the intricacies of the
card catalog, or for any special interest in the cataloging
of books, or in general library history and administration.
If the entering student had a knowledge of these things,
one reason for going to college would be lacking,--he goes
to college to learn what he cannot reasonably be expected
to know before that time.

Cheerfully accepting then this condition of ignorance
of all library procedure on the part of the rank and file of
college freshmen everywhere, and unanimously agreeing
that the college student must in some way learn how to use
a library, diversity of opinion is found in regard to these
two questions:--Is this instruction given better as an independent course to the entering students, or is it better to
give it in connection with regular college work? Should the
instruction be given by members of the library staff, or by
college instructors?

The very fact that this question has been broached is
helpful, since it is significant of the great changes that are
coming both in library administration and in educational
theory and practice. It suggests the increasing specialization in library work, the growing co-operation between the
library force and those engaged in the more technical side
of education, newer and, we believe, higher ideals of the
object and therefore of the process of education, and the
reflection of these changes in the development in the student
body of independence, self-reliance, and the desire to do
creative work.

Assuming therefore that we are all interested in securing for the college student fullness of knowledge at the
earliest hour possible, I venture personally to differ somewhat from the report of the majority of the committee of
the New England college librarians and to say that from the
angle of the college instructor, it seems clear to me that
the knowledge is better acquired in connection with regular
college courses and that it can best be given by college instructors. It is with most of us a favorite occupation to
see how many birds we can bring down with one stone, and
this desire is in a sense gratified if we can incorporate
knowledge of how to use a library with the subject matter
included in a particular course,--it seems a saving of time
for student, instructor and librarian. Everything is clear
gain that can be picked up by the way.

But quite apart from this general desire to telescope
several subjects, there are specific advantages gained by the
student when the instruction is given by the instructor of
a regular college class. The knowledge acquired falls naturally into its place in connection with definite, concrete work.
Abstract theory has little place in the mental equipment of
the freshman, he seeks out relationships, adds new knowledge to what he already has, and quite reasonably is impa-
tient, even intolerant in spirit when new ideas and facts
are presented to him that he cannot immediately assimilate.
To use a homely illustration, an article of food, like butter,
that is essential for our physical diet serves its purpose
much better when distributed through other articles of food
than if taken independently and by itself. All new ideas in
regard to library organization, cataloging, bibliography,
searching for material, the handling of books, if gained
through the usual channels of college work, are quickly and

easily assimilated by the college student. If, however,
these same ideas are presented to him unrelated to other
work they are in danger of remaining unassimilated and of
becoming a hindrance rather than a help.

On the other hand, the advantages in having the
instruction given by a regular college instructor are that
he deals with small sections of students, not with "numbers
which are appallingly large;" that he knows the individual
student; that he is able to relate the bibliographical work
with the individual student on the one hand, and on the
other hand with the special subject with which the student
is working.

Personally, I can but feel that the assumption made
by the committee of the New England college librarians,
by the librarian of the Newark public library, by the dean
of the collegiate department of the University of Illinois,
and by others in the library field that college instructors
are not interested in this matter and would oppose instruction in it is not really warranted by the condition that
exists.

May I venture to describe somewhat in detail what
is done in one college in showing students how to use books,
how to become acquainted with the opportunities of a large
library, and how to avail themselves of these opportunities
in a direct personal way. In giving this account of what
is done in Vassar College, may I emphasize the statement
that the work done is by no means peculiar to one college,--
other institutions all over the country are doing much that
in principle is precisely the same, although the details may
vary.

The first aid in knowledge of the library building,
of its equipment, and of how to use its collections is given
the Vassar College student literally during her first hours
on the college campus. She is met by a member of the
senior or the junior class and taken about the campus, and
it is the duty of these student guides to give every entering
student a copy of the Students' Handbook. In this she is
urged to "become acquainted with the library as soon as
possible." "The reference librarian," the Handbook tells
her, "expects every new student to come to the reference
desk to be shown about the arrangement of the library and

the use of the catalog and to receive a copy of the library
Handbook."

The guides point out the library and they are instructed to urge the new students to seek out the reference
librarian at once and to make the library trip immediately.
The new student goes to the residence hall where she is to
live and she finds on the bulletin board in this hall an invitation to take the library trip. The records kept by the
reference librarian show that a very large percentage of
the entering students almost immediately avail themselves
of this invitation extended by guides and reiterated by
Handbook and by bulletin boards.

When the new student first enters the library she is
given a plan of the building showing the arrangement of
the different sections and handbook explaining in full the
library privileges. Armed with this, she is met by the
reference librarian and then joining a group of three others
she is taken through the library where she makes connections
between the plan in her hand, the books on the shelves, "the
inanimate reference librarian--the card catalog--" and the
animate reference librarian in whom she finds a guide, counselor and friend.

This library trip can be, and is intended to be only
general in character. The student gains from it first of
all the consciousness of having found in the reference librarian a friend to whom she can always go for help and advice; second, her interest is aroused to become better
acquainted with the card catalog and with the general facilities for work afforded by the library; and third she
gains a determination to follow the injunction of the Students'
Handbook, "do your part to make the library an ideal place
in which to work."

It is at this stage, after this general instruction given
by the reference librarian, that the majority of the entering
students meet the officers of the department of history.
We give them collectively during the first week, usually
the second day, an illustrated lecture on the library. This
includes slides showing the catalog cards of a few of the
books they will use most in their history work, the cards
of the most important reference works, periodicals, and atlases, slides showing the difference between a "see"

card and a "see also" card, slides that explain incomplete
series, continuation cards, and every variation that concerns
their immediate work. Every slide concerns a work on
history that is to be used almost immediately, and the form
used in cataloging, the notation and the annotation, the
hieroglyphics of the printed card, and the bibliographical
features of the card are fully explained from the screen.

The students then meet their individual instructors,
each one having previously provided herself with a pamphlet called Suggestions for the Year's Study, History I.
This pamphlet, besides giving detailed instructions for the
preparation of the work, includes a plan of the library;
suggestions in regard to its history, as also the description and the meaning of its exterior and interior; a facsimile
and explanation of the catalog card of the text book used
in the course; hints concerning the general card catalog;
an analysis of the general form and different parts of a
book; special directions for preparing the bibliographical
slips or cards that must accompany every topic presented,
together with an illustration of a model card; a full classification, with illustrations under each, of all the works of
references the class will presumably use, including general
works of reference, dictionaries, encyclopaedias, periodicals,
yearbooks, atlases, autobiographical material, including the
various forms of Who's Who? together with biographical,
ecclesiastical and various miscellaneous dictionaries and encyclopaedias; an elaborate chart devised to show the
authoritativeness as history of the textbook used in the
course, accompanied by a full explanation of it; suggestions
in regard to the purchase of histories for a personal library;
and finally, a recommendation to make use of another pamphlet called Suggestive Lists for Reading in History. The
main points in the pamphlet Suggestions for the Year's Study
are talked over between instructor and students, and constant reference is made to it throughout the year.

The next step in the history work is to assign each
student one or more questions written on a slip and drawn
by lot. These questions are intended to test her assimila-
tion of the bibliographical help already given, and her
ability to apply to a concrete case what she has gained. As
soon and as often as possible the students in the different
sections of this class in history go to the library with the
instructor for such additional and special help as they may
need.

From time to time the students in History I prepare
special topics on limited questions. A bibliography must
always preface these topics and if it is in any way at fault,
either as regards form or material, it must be presented
a second time or as many times as is necessary to correct
the defects.

This course in History I is required of every student
in college. Those students who elect other courses based
on this become acquainted with still other features of the
library and acquire added facility in bibliographical work.
Every student, for example, who elects the course in
American history has a pamphlet called Suggestions for the
Year's Study, History A, AA. This pamphlet includes a
chart that shows the location in the library of all the sections of American history, each accompanied by the Dewey
notation for each section, and also the notation for the
sections in political science, law and government, American
literature, English literature, and English history. It also
considers at length the place in the course of the textbook,
secondary works, collections of sources, almanacs, works on
government, guides to literature, state histories, biographies,
travels, and illustrative material. For the latter the students
are again referred to Suggestive Lists for Reading in History.

Another section of the pamphlet considers specific
classes of books which the student uses. It calls attention
to the various kinds of bibliographies, as complete, selected,
classified, and annotated; to library catalogs arranged on the
dictionary, author, subject, and title plan, as also to trade
catalogs; to documents classified by form and by contents;
to official publications, and the publications of historical
societies; to every form of personal record; to descriptions
by travelers; and to general and special histories. It also
takes up periodicals; manuscripts; special facsimiles, like
the B. F. Stevens; geographical material; monumental
records; inscriptions, and pictorial material.

Elaborate directions are given for preparing exhaustive
bibliographies of the material in the college library on special
subjects and suggestions for expanding these in the future
as other opportunities for further library work are presented. In addition, tin trays of cards are provided in the
American history sections. These are bibliographical cards

that supplement but do not duplicate the catalog cards of
the general library catalog.

During the year about twenty special topics are prepared by this class, each prefaced by a bibliography of
the subject. At the end of the year, one special bibliographical topic is presented. This represents what each student
can do in the time given to three classroom hours.

At the end of the first semester of this course the
examination given is not a test of what the students have
remembered but rather a test of what they are able to do
under definite conditions. The class is sent to the library,
each member of it usually receives by lot an individual question, and she then shows what facility she has gained in
the use of books by answering the question with full range
of the library.

Other pamphlets of Suggestions have occasionally been
prepared for the most advanced courses. At the end of
the senior year the students in my own courses are frequently given an examination that calls for the freest use of the
library in the planning of history outlines for club work, in
arranging for a public library selected lists of histories
suitable for "all sorts and conditions of men," and similar
tests that show how far they are able to apply present
bibliographical knowledge to probable future experiences.

All this instruction and opportunity for practice in
bibliography is not left to "the chance instruction of enthusiastic instructors" or to "the insistence of department heads"
to quote Mr. Kendric C. Babcock.[1] It is definitely planned,
it is systematically carried out, there is definite progression
from year to year in the kind of bibliographical work required, and it is directly related to the specific and individual work of every student. From time to time conferences
are held by the members of the library staff and the instructors in history and these conferences enable each department
to supplement and complement the work of the other and thus
avoid repetition and duplication.

This division of labor enables the reference librarian
to play the part of hostess, to make the students feel at
home, to secure their good will and co-operation, to develop
a sense of personal responsibility towards the library and its

treasures. Her work as regards the library is largely general and descriptive; as regards the students it is that of
a friend and counselor; as regards the other officers of the
college it is that of an ally and co-operator.

It is necessary to emphasize at this point the wide
divergence between the work of the reference librarian in
the college or the university and that of the reference librarian in the public library however large or small it may
be.

In the public library the demand made upon the reference librarian is for definite information for immediate use;
the library patron wishes, not training in acquiring information by and for himself, but the information itself; no substitution of deferred dividends will satisfy his insistent
demand for immediate cash payment; he cares not at all for
method but he cares very particularly for instant results.
Moreover, no one intervenes between the reference librarian
and the library patron,--he alone is responsible for giving
the information desired. And again, the reference librarian
has to deal with an irregular, constantly fluctuating clientele. The man who wants to know who first thought the
world was round and whether he was a vegetarian or per-
chance a cannibal may never visit the library again, but
the effort must be made to satisfy his curiosity. The reference librarian of the public library must always be more
or less of a purveyor of miscellaneous information to an irregular fluctuating public.

But the functions of the college reference librarian are
altogether different. It is often his duty not to give, but
temporarily to withhold information; not to answer but to
ask questions; to answer one question by asking another;
to help a student answer his own question for himself, work
out his own problems, and find a way out of his difficulties; to show him how to find for himself the material desired;
to give training rather than specific information; to be himself a teacher and to co-operate with other instructors in
training the students who seek his help. All this is possible
for him for he deals with a regular constituency and he can
build up each year on the foundations of the previous year.
But while progression comes for the students, there is always
the solid permanency of subject with which the reference librarian deals. With the regularity of the passing calendar

there come the questions of the feudal system and the fron-
tier, of the renaissance and of how to follow a bill through
congress. The personnel of the student body changes, but
there is always an unchanging residium of subject matter.
On the side of the regular college work there is therefore
practically no demand whatever made on the college reference
librarian for the miscellaneous information demanded of the
public reference librarian,--he is not the one who writes
for the daily papers the description in verse of the daily
life of the reference librarian.[2] Just what his work is in
the college, from the students' point of view is indicated by
a recent experience.

A class of seventy in American history was recently
asked to what extent the members of it had availed themselves of the services of the reference librarian in that
particular course and the replies seem to show that their
inquiries had chiefly related to the use of government publications, early periodical literature, material not suggested
by the titles of books, out-of-the-way material, source material, and current newspaper material not available through
indexes. The many tributes to the help received from the
Vassar College reference librarian are perhaps best summed
up, so it seems to the teacher, in the statement of one student "she shows you how to go about finding a book better
the next time."

If then it must be evident that the work of the college
reference librarian differs widely from that of the public
reference librarian, it remains to consider specifically what
division of the field should be made between the college
reference librarian and the college instructor. Here a clear
line of demarcation seems evident. The college instructor
must know the student personally and intellectually, as he
must know the conditions from which he has come and the
conditions to which he presumably is to go. He must help
the student relate all the various parts of his college work
and help him relate his college work to the general conditions in which he is placed. Hence he cannot separate
for the student the bibliography of a subject from the subject itself. Nor can he turn over to the librarian the instruction in bibliographical work. The reference librarian
is the only member of the library staff who in the capacity
of a teacher comes into direct personal relationship with the
student, but his work, as has been seen, is entirely different.

In this division of the field that leaves to the college instructor the actual instruction of students in the use of books, a large unoccupied territory is claimed by the reference librarian as peculiarly his own. This concerns the "extra-collegiate activities" and includes help on material needed in inter-class debates, dramatics, pageants, college publications, Bible classes, mission classes, commencement essays, and all the miscellaneous activities in which the student, not the instructor, takes the initiative. This work corresponds somewhat closely to that of the general reference librarian in a public library and it demands about one-half of the time of the librarian.

Instruction in the use of the library is facilitated by unrestricted access to the shelves and here the students are able to put their knowledge to the test and to work out their own independent methods.

What are the advantages and the disadvantages of unrestricted access to the library shelves? The question was recently asked a class of seventy students and their replies show an almost unanimous opinion that the advantages are overwhelmingly in favor of the open shelves.

Among the educational advantages enumerated are that this fosters independence and self-reliance, through encouraging personal investigation; that it enables students to see books in relation to other books, to make comparisons, and therefore to select those that are the best to use; that it shows the library resources and, to a certain extent, the breadth of the investigation that has been done in specific lines. "The open shelf is an instructor, a great indispensable helper, an education in itself," writes one student, while another states, "It gives an opportunity to form a closer acquaintance with books already known by name, and for casual acquaintance with books one has not time to draw out and read at length."

On the more personal side the students have found the advantages to be the pleasure found in handling books; the appeal made by titles and bindings; the inspiration that comes from the feeling of kinship with books; the opportunity given for wide acquaintance with books and authors; more extensive reading; the saving of time; the satisfaction of being able to find what is wanted, freedom from the limitations of specific references. "We become interested in subjects and in books we should not otherwise have known at all," writes one, while another asked a friend who replied, "Well, I don't know exactly what it means, but I guess it means that I for one use books I never otherwise would have used."

On the side of the library as a whole, many have found advantages in the opportunity it gives of doing general and special bibliographical work and in the knowledge afforded of the general plan of arrangement, classification, and cataloging. "If we had to stay in a reading room, how much idea of library organization should we have?" is the clinching question of one enthusiastic student.

The moral advantages are found to be the feeling of responsibility towards books and the training given in not abusing the privilege.

But it is in the failure of some persons to avail themselves of these opportunities for moral training that students find the disadvantages of the open shelf. There are the periodic complaints that books are lost, misplaced, hidden, and monopolized; that the privilege is abused; and that the social conscience is lacking. "The open shelf is the ideal system but it is designed for an ideal society," feelingly writes one, while another, more philosophical, finds that the open shelf has its annoyances, but no disadvantages, and that these are probably to be charged up to human nature, not to the system.

Only an occasional one sees any other disadvantages. One student finds herself bewildered and lost in irrelevant material, while another brought up in the atmosphere of Harvard, thinks that the closed stack encourages greater precision and carefulness, "for if you have to put in a slip and wait for a book you are more careful about your choice than you are when you can easily drop one found to be unsatisfactory and lay your hands immediately upon another one." "It may be," adds a third, "that we do not get all we might from a book when it is so easy to get others. I find myself often putting aside a book when I do not immediately find what I want."

With an occasional plaint about the increased noise and that the open shelf really takes more time since it is easier

to ask for an authority on a specified subject than it is to
look it up for one's self, the case for and against the open
shelf, from the side of the student, seems closed, with the
verdict overwhelmingly in favor of unrestricted access to
the library shelves.

I cannot forbear suggesting two directions in which
it seems to me the library work could be extended to the
advantage of both library and academic force.

The first is the desirability of having connected with
every college library an instructor in the department of
history who gives instruction in one or more courses in
history and who is at the same time definitely responsible
for the development of the bibliographical side of the history
work.

The work of the history librarian on the library side
would be to serve as a consulting expert on all questions
that arise in cataloging books that are on the border lines
between history and other subjects. Such perplexing questions are constantly arising and valuable aid might be given
in such cases by an expert in history.

Another part of the work of the history librarian from
the side of the library would be to keep the librarian and
the history department constantly informed of opportunities
to purchase at advantage works on history that are available
only through the second-hand dealers. It now usually de-
volves on some member of the library staff to study the
catalogs of second-hand books and report "finds" to some
officer of the history department. Could facilities be provided for making it possible to have the initiative come from
the history side it would seem a distinct gain.

The work of the history librarian would also include
the responsibility for the classification, arrangement and
care of the mass of apparently miscellaneous material that
accumulates in every library but does not slip naturally
into a predestined place. All is grist that comes to the history mill, yet it is difficult to know how it can best be
cared for. Miss Hasse in her well-remembered article "On the
Classification of Numismatics"[3] has shown that the utmost diversity has prevailed in regard to the classification of coins
and the literary material dealing with them. This is but one

illustration of the uncertainty, confusion, and diversity that
prevails in classifying much of the material that seems miscellaneous in character, and that yet should be classified
as historical material.

The work of the history librarian on the side of the
students would be concerned during the first semester particularly with the freshmen and the sophomores. The bibliographical and reference work now done could be greatly
enlarged and extended. It would be possible to explain
still more fully the possibilities of assistance from the card
catalog; to help students locate the more special histories
that might seem to be luxuries rather than the necessities
of their work; to make them acquainted with histories as
histories, rather than with histories as furnishing specific
material; to develop their critical appreciation of books and
their judgment in regard to the varying degrees of authoritativeness of well known old and recent histories. Encouragement would be given the students to begin historical
libraries for themselves, advice could be given in making
reasonable selections of books, and help in starting a catalog. Interest in suitable book-plates for historical collections might be roused as well as interest in suitable bindings,
and thus through these luxurious accessories the student
be led on to friendship with the books themselves and with
their authors.

During the second semester the work of the history
librarian would be largely with the seniors and would be
more constructive in its nature. The seniors are looking
forward to taking an active part in the life of their home
communities and they will be interested in the public schools,
in the public library, in social work, in church work, in
history and literary clubs, in historical pageants, fêtes and
excursions, in historical museums, in the celebration of historic days, and in innumerable other civic activities, many
of which are intimately connected with the subject of history.
The history librarian would be able to give invaluable aid
to the seniors in preparing lists of histories suitable for
public libraries in communities where suggestions may prove
welcome; in suggesting histories adapted to all these demands
made by personal, co-operative, and civic activities. This
constructive work of the history librarian would be capable
of infinite extension and variation and its good results would
be far-reaching and of growing momentum.

May I suggest one further possible direction in which
the activities of the library staff would lend interest to the
general work of the college. Every institution needs luxuries
and the members of the library staff have it in their power to
offer courses of lectures open to all members of the college
and also to citizens of the community who are interested in
educational questions. Such courses would include lectures
on the history of libraries; on the great libraries of Europe
and America; on the great libraries of the world; on great
editors like Benjamin F. Stevens; on rare books; on books
famous for the number of copies sold, of editions, of translations, of migrations through auction rooms; on the famous
manuscripts of the world. The possibilities of such courses
are limitless.

There are also the courses of lectures that we are all
eager to hear on the plain necessities that are of even
greater interest than are those that deal with the luxuries.
The college wants to hear about the administration of a library and its general problems; about the special questions
of cataloging, interlibrary loans, the special collections of
the library as well as its general resources. From the standpoint of special departments, lectures might be given by representatives of these departments on the treasures of the
library as they concern their special fields.

Joint department meetings of the members of the library
staff and the officers of the departments of English and of
history for the discussion of questions of mutual interest
have at Vassar College proved stimulating and contributed
much to a mutual understanding of each other's ideals and
to a sympathetic appreciation of the difficulties attending
their realization.

"Why cannot all this work with and about books be explained by the librarians,--" college authorities sometimes
ask. "That is their business; it is the business of the
teacher to teach."

The answer is simple. The good teacher must individualize the student, the good librarian must individualize the
book; and both teacher and librarian must co-operate in
helping the college student get the utmost possible from his
college course in order that in his turn he may help the
community in which he lives in its efforts to realize its ideals.

The endless chain extends to the farthermost confines of heaven!

NOTES

1. Library Journal, March, 1913, p. 135.
2. Library Journal, Oct., 1912. Public Libraries, June, 1913.
3. Library Journal, September, 1904.

Part III

PHILANTHROPY AND INNOVATION FOR UNDERGRADUATES

1918-1940

PHILANTHROPY AND INNOVATION FOR UNDERGRADUATES, 1918-1940

The years between the first and second world wars were discouraging ones for higher education. Grants from private foundations, totalling in the hundreds of millions, had not met earlier, though perhaps unrealistic, expectations. External funds could be expected to support educational innovation and permanent endowments, but could not become integral to an institution's annual budgetary process. In addition, students seemed more obsessed than usual with non-educational matters. Laurence Veysey writes that the general mood of the academic community bespoke a lack of confidence and a fear of economic scarcity. Educators in the 1920s and 1930s confronted a social pattern that was hostile in spirit to the entire curriculum.[1]

Yet, amazingly, out of this period of professional and administrative discontent, arose some of the most compelling curricular innovations of the twentieth century. Disciples of John Dewey urged instructional emphasis on family and social development and civic responsibility. Robert Hutchins and Alexander Meiklejohn attempted new philosophical constructs for the liberal arts. Honors courses were established across the nation and Veysey concluded that by the end of the 1930s "there seemed far more likelihood of widespread curricular rethinking than at any time during the preceding thirty years."[2]

Simultaneously, academic libraries entered a phase that was equally fruitful, especially for the small colleges that benefited from private philanthropy. In 1929 the Carnegie Corporation initiated its program of book collection support, distributing grants of $5,000 to $25,000 to eighty-one institutions, thereby stimulating numerous presidents and trustees to consider a more central role for the library in collegiate education.

User instruction advanced conceptually and program-matically. In 1935 Louis Shores published his first full statement of the "library-college" idea which defined the teaching function of academic libraries and redirected for several decades the continuing dialogue on the library's pur-poses. B. Lamar Johnson, as a college dean and library director, implemented course-related library use instruction throughout the curriculum at Stephens College. Harvie Branscomb conducted research based on library use and urged a stronger librarian-professor partnership.

As a preview of things to come, the 1930s ushered in the first substantial research, based on valid design and measurement techniques, that treated the topics of student knowledge and use of library resources. Articles by library science professor Peyton Hurt and psychologists C. M. Louttit and James Patrick are among the earliest examples.[3] With these developments as a background, the stage was set for dramatic changes in higher education in the postwar period.

NOTES

1. Laurence Veysey, "Stability and Experiment in the American Undergraduate Curriculum," in Content and Con-text: Essays on College Education, Carl Kaysen, ed. (New York: McGraw-Hill, 1973) pp. 1-63.
2. Ibid., p. 10.
3. Peyton Hurt, "The Need of College and University Instruction in Use of the Library," Library Quarterly 4 (July 1934): 436-448; and C. M. Louttit and James R. Patrick, "Study of Students Knowledge in the Use of the Library," Journal of Applied Psychology 16 (October 1932): 475-484.

Bibliographical Instructions for Students

Charles B. Shaw

A former professor of English, Shaw was Librarian at North Carolina College for Women from 1920 to 1927 and at Swarthmore College from 1927 until 1962. In 1931 ALA published his compilation, List of Books for College Libraries, which the Carnegie Corporation used in making book acquisition grants to college libraries. The "Shaw list," as it became popularly known, was the basis for subsequent editions of Books for College Libraries, widely used for collection development in undergraduate institutions. Its historical value is discussed in Neil A. Radford, The Carnegie Corporation and the Development of American College Libraries, 1928-1941 (Chicago: American Library Association, 1984), pp. 103-126.

In this speech presented at Drexel Institute in February 1928, Shaw succinctly stated three propositions designed to alleviate the "haphazard, unscientific" teaching that he claimed had characterized bibliographical instruction. He proposed to eliminate library lectures (described as "love's labor lost") and to replace them with a required course taught by professors of bibliography. He proposed that colleges establish a department of bibliography which would be as accepted and as inevitable as a department of history or English. Finally, he urged that we "evolve and train" a group of bibliographical instructors, "a new species," which would combine the librarian's knowledge of books with the instructor's training and ability to teach. Thus, in the perennial debate of the library lecture versus the credit course, Shaw strongly supported the latter. This speech was regarded by Frances L. Hopkins as a clear call for bibliographic instruction of a high intellectual order in "A

Century of Bibliographic Instruction: The Historical Claim
to Professional and Academic Legitimacy," College and Research Libraries 43 (May 1982): 192-198.

Reprinted from Library Journal 53 (April 1, 1928): 300-301.
Published by R. R. Bowker Co. (a Xerox company).
Copyright © 1928.

•   •   •

The earnest and emphatic request of the chairman of this
meeting was that this should not be a long and formal
paper.

I shall only, then, cite a few articles, and offer for
such discussion as time allows, a few perhaps unorthodox
and extreme propositions.

The articles are three in number. They, with the
numerous citations which are given with them, will lead
you to most of the recent literature in the field. They are:

> Ada J. English.   How shall we instruct the college
> freshman in the use of the library? School and So-
> ciety. 24:779-785. 1926.
> Raymond L. Walkley. A program for practical in-
> struction in college libraries. School and Society.
> 25:371-373. 1927.
> H. B. Van Hoesen. Graduate and undergraduate
> instruction in the bibliography and use of the library.
> School and Society. 21:311-314. 1925.

In the A.L.A. Survey, 2:192-200, there are brief statements
of the bibliographical instruction given in twenty or more
colleges and universities.

The debatably intended propositions are also three in
number.

I.   Somewhat on the principle that a little knowledge
is a dangerous thing, it is suggested that we drop attempts
to teach freshmen the use of the library if it is impossible

to do it thoroly. To do the job thoroly implies, not an optional lecture and demonstration or two, but: (1) a required
course; (2) weekly meetings (about sixteen) during the first
semester; (3) a teaching staff with enough time and adequate
teaching ability; (4) sufficiently small sections to insure the
proper attention to and work from each student; (5) a generous supply of duplicate reference books. Any attempt to
introduce library usage to freshmen which does not measure
up to these standards, it is suggested, is love's labor lost;
a waste of the instructor's time and the mere gilding of ignorance with a superficial smattering of bibliographical technique.

II. A department of bibliography should be as much
the accepted and inevitable thing in any college as a department of English or a department of history. This department
should offer a variety of courses; courses with prerequisites
and progressive relationships, ranging from elementary
courses in the use of library tools and aids, through those
in the evaluation of the contents of current books and the
material aspect of books (paper, printing, binding, etc.)
on to diplomatics, palaeography, or what you choose.

III. Teaching is a profession requiring special abilities and training. Librarianship is likewise a profession requiring special abilities and training. The special abilities
and training of the two by no means coincide. Therefore
to ask a library administrator, a cataloger, a reference librarian or an assistant at the circulation desk to teach freshmen
the use of the library or to teach a course in subject bibliography is to give them an inappropriate burden which is
detrimental to the interests of the library and unfair to the
student. Such haphazard, unscientific teaching as librarians
now undertake must be scrapped; and we must evolve and
train instead a group of bibliographical instructors, a new
species which will combine in one individual the librarian's
knowledge of books and bibliographical procedure with the
instructor's ability in teaching method and in the skilled imparting of information.

Stephens College Library Experiment

B. Lamar Johnson

Johnson was Librarian and Dean of Instruction at Stephens
College from 1931 to 1952. In this capacity he integrated
library use into the course content of the undergraduate curriculum and he produced two excellent discussions of his
ideas and experiences in Vitalizing a College Library (Chicago: American Library Association, 1939) and The Librarian
and the Teacher in General Education: A Report of the Li-
brary-Instructional Activities at Stephens College (Chicago:
American Library Association, 1948); the latter title was co-
authored with Eloise Linstrom. Before going to Stephens,
he had been a high school English teacher and principal.
In 1952 he was appointed Professor of Higher Education at
the University of California at Los Angeles.

In this selection, a speech presented at the ALA Mid-
winter Conference in 1932, he described his newly initiated
program at Stephens which employed three objectives:
1) to teach students how to use reference sources effectively,
2) to teach them good study habits, and 3) to make the library function as the center of the instructional program.
Johnson had one important advantage that few librarians
enjoy--he was dean of instruction as well as librarian. Practically, his role as administrator gave him the authority to
introduce changes in teaching methods and course content
and he admitted that without this dual role, his attempts to
reorganize the college "in such a way as to further" the "library program" would have been virtually impossible. Thus,
as a model for library development Stephens could provide
leadership intellectually but probably not politically.

Reprinted by permission of the American Library Association
from the ALA Bulletin 27 (May 1933): 205-211.

•   •   •

At Stephens College we are this year beginning a five-year
library program; accordingly what I shall have to say must
deal largely with our plans. I should, of course, much
prefer to discuss what we have done. A presentation of
our plans is, however, distinctly advantageous to me, in
that it makes it possible for me to receive your counsel
early in the development of our program. You may be
assured that I shall appreciate such suggestions as you
may be willing to offer.

The library program upon which we are entering at
Stephens College this year is strictly experimental. We
have set up the objectives which we desire to attain and
have made plans which we believe will lead toward the
achievement of those objectives. As the experiment begins,
however, there is no assurance that the procedures tenta-
tively planned are those which will best achieve our aims.
Where experience proves that the methods we are using do
not contribute to the accomplishment of our aims, we are
fully prepared to disregard such methods or modify them.

In his recently published book, The Experimental College, Alexander Meiklejohn presents a number of challenging
ideas. I have been particularly interested in his concept
of the aims of college education and the relation of this
concept to the use of books. He says:

> The college does not build up maturity by
> the same methods as those employed in a mill or
> an office. Its chosen instrument is the book.
> The intention of the college is that in the case
> of those favored young people who are allowed
> to study after the high school period, minds
> shall be fed, and trained, and strengthened, and
> directed by the use of books. The whole pro-
> cedure points forward to a mode of life in which
> persons, by the aid of books, are enabled to live
> in ways which are not open to their nonreading

fellows, are trained to practice special forms of
intelligence in which the use of books plays an
essential part.

Our library program at Stephens College is aiming to
achieve the end thus characterized by Dr. Meiklejohn. We
have, however, stated the aim in terms of the three following objectives: first, to teach students how to use books
effectively; second, to lead students to love books and to
engage in reading for recreation; and, third, to make the
library function as the center of the instructional program
of the college. In short, we are attempting to make the
library the heart of the college to the end that, as Meiklejohn
says, the students may become intelligent readers.

The entire administration of the college has been re-
organized in such a way as to further our library program.
The librarian is dean of instruction and is the ranking
member of the faculty. He is responsible for changes in
the curriculum and for the improvement of teaching methods.
Since at Stephens College faculty meetings are planned to
be professional rather than administrative, the librarian
presides at and is responsible for such meetings; he visits
the classes of all teachers; and he confers with members
of the staff regarding instructional problems. This organization makes it possible for him to be familiar with the
instruction given in the classroom, to adapt the work of
the library to such instruction, and to offer teachers a type
of assistance which would otherwise be difficult, if not impossible.

Trying to Avoid a Pitfall

A danger which you may suggest and one against which we
are consciously guarding is that the librarian may become
so involved in his extra-library duties that he will neglect
his professional responsibilities. From the time of the conception of the library program, President Wood has stressed
the importance of avoiding this pitfall; at all times he has
warned the dean of instruction against assuming administrative responsibilities of any type; such responsibilities are
placed entirely in the hands of the dean of administration.
The dean of instruction is concerned with improving the instruction given the students; as such he must know what is

taught in the classroom; as librarian he knows what is
available in the library; it is his duty to make teachers
conscious of what the library has that will be of value for
class use.

Throughout the program emphasis is being placed
upon teacher-library cooperation. We realize that a major
responsibility for the success of our experiment lies in the
hands of faculty members. Only through instruction given
by faculty members can students be taught to make effective use of books; only with the active assistance of an interested faculty can an effective program be carried on for
guiding recreational reading; only through the cooperation
of teachers can the library become the center of the instructional program of the college. In other words, we regard
our library program as an all-school project which demands
the attention of every faculty member.

Each of the three objectives of the experiment is
large enough to challenge the best thinking of the entire
college. Simultaneously to direct our attention to the three
aims would likely result in the partial achievement of three
ends but in the actual attainment of none. In order that
each objective may be given the thorough and careful attention which its importance demands, we propose to give
particular emphasis to one aim during each of the first three
years of our five-year experiment. This plan should result
in cumulative development of the entire experiment upon
a sound and carefully worked out basis.

This Year's Objective

We are this year stressing that objective of our library
program which relates to teaching the students how to
make effective use of books. Before discussing methods of
approaching this problem, I should like to present a few
thoughts regarding what is meant by the effective use of
books. We will readily agree that the student who wishes
to use books effectively must be acquainted with certain
mechanical features of books, such as the index, the table
of contents, the preface, footnotes, and bibliographies.
The student must likewise know how to use basic library
tools, the card catalog, the Readers' Guide, encyclopedias,
dictionaries, and a number of equally important reference

books. Writers on the subject of the use of books often
go this far and no farther. The result is that many schools
and colleges are claiming to have taught their students how
to make effective use of books when they have instructed
these students with regard to the mechanical make-up of
books and when they have taught them how to use basic
library reference tools. I should not for one minute minimize the importance of instruction of this type. It is vital
and must be included in any program which purposes to
teach students how to use books. We feel, however, that,
if we stop here, our work will have been only partially accomplished. We shall have failed to achieve a major portion
of our objectives. Instruction in the use of books, as we
conceive it, includes two additional fields, namely: instruction in how to study and instruction in silent reading.

Thousands below Normal in Reading

It is a matter of common knowledge that most students entering college do not know how to study; they do not know
how to approach an assignment in such a way as to get
the most out of it. Students themselves recognize the need
of training in how to study. Last year, in an investigation
carried on at Stephens College, three-fourths of the students
indicated that they would like instruction of this type.
Each year colleges and universities enroll thousands of students whose reading ability is below the normal for seventh-
and eight-grade pupils in junior high school. Certainly
such students cannot be expected to use books effectively
until steps have been taken to improve their reading ability.

At Stephens College we are emphasizing the fact that
instruction in the use of books is an integral part of regular
class work; such instruction is not presented as an end in
itself but rather as a means of assisting the student to solve
problems connected with regular class work at the time she
is facing these problems. Instead of telling the student
that she will study the Readers' Guide, the card catalog, or
encyclopedias as such, the teacher makes a regular assignment, perhaps the preparation of a bibliography, and discusses with the students the value of the library tools which
I have mentioned in gathering materials.

Given Basic Tools at Once

In order that we may be certain that all students are given
instruction in the use of books early in their work, teachers
of introductory English and social studies courses give their
students experience with basic library tools and with the
mechanical features of books during the first ten weeks of
the school year. I wish once more to emphasize, however,
that such experience is not given as an end in itself, but
rather as an aid to the preparation of regular assignments
in these courses.

All of the faculty members are advised that students
must be given repeated experience with the basic materials
to which they are introduced in their English and social
studies courses. If students are to learn how to use the
Readers' Guide, the card catalog, encyclopedias, and the
indexes to books, they must be given assignments which
will demand the continued use of these reference aids.

A second type of instruction is instruction in how
to study. Teaching students how to study and how to read
presents varied problems in different courses. The problem
of studying mathematics, for example, is quite different from
that of preparing an assignment for a literature course.
The problem must, therefore, be approached by the individual teacher who works with his students in developing
study habits best suited to their needs in a given course.

The query immediately arises, "How are the teachers
trained to give instruction of the types which I have mentioned, and what is done to follow up this instruction?"
Each fall for two weeks previous to the opening of school
we have at Stephens College a faculty conference. This
conference consists of a series of faculty meetings, of group
meetings, and of individual conferences. The aim is to
assist faculty members to prepare for the year's work.
This fall the theme of the faculty conference was "The
Stephens College Library Program," with particular emphasis on instructing students in the use of books. During
the conference I had the opportunity of presenting to the
entire faculty, as well as to groups and individuals, suggestions for instructing students in the use of books. Following these conferences, each teacher prepared and presented to me a written report of his plans for giving such

instruction. I studied these plans and followed them up
by means of classroom visitation and individual conferences
with teachers. During November, I conferred with each
faculty member regarding the success of his plans and what
he could do to improve them. Next a meeting of the entire
faculty was devoted to a discussion of the problem, the
purpose being to inform faculty members of what their colleagues were doing to instruct their students in how to use
books. At this faculty meeting, I requested several teachers
to describe what they were doing in their classes, and I
made a general summary of the type of instruction which
is being given.

Guide for Instruction Planned

At the close of the semester, the teachers will give me a
report describing and evaluating what they have done to
instruct their students in the use of books. These reports
will be followed by individual conferences, during which I
shall attempt to have clarified the descriptions of activities
and to have amplified the evaluations of these activities.
On the basis of these reports, we shall prepare a summary
list which describes what Stephens College teachers do to
instruct students in the effective use of books. This summary, which will be mimeographed and distributed to
teachers, will be used as a guide for continued instruction
of this type.

In any program of this sort, no matter how effectively
it may be organized and carried out, there are some students
who need special attention. Accordingly during the second
semester, a group of such students selected on the basis of
their first semester's work will be organized to meet for
special instruction in how to study and in silent reading. In
future years such groups will be organized early in the school
year, the students being selected on the basis of tests given
when they enter.

I have spoken at some length regarding instruction in
the use of books, not because I regard this as the most important objective in our library program, but because we
are this year concentrating the attention of the entire college
upon this aim. Our faculty is thinking and working in terms
of this aim. In each of the following two years we shall

concentrate our attention upon one of the remaining two objectives of our program.

Students Asked for Suggestions

Although we are placing an all-college emphasis upon teaching the student how to use books, we are not entirely
neglecting our other objectives. In the field of recreational
reading we are planning to keep books of interest before the
students at all times. We are using book jackets and posters
to advertise books, both in the library and in other parts
of the campus. We seek to chat with students about books
which may interest them. As an important part of our program for recreational reading, we are this year placing in
each dormitory a library of books for pleasure reading.
Early in November, at an all-school assembly, we told the
students that books for their pleasure reading were to be
placed in the dormitories. Emphasis was given to the fact
that these libraries were for the enjoyment of the students,
and every student was invited to suggest books for them.
During the two-week period following this assembly, we set
aside a table in the library for students who wished to locate titles of books dealing with subjects in which they were
interested. On this table we placed various book lists, including the Reading with a Purpose series, the A.L.A. Catalog, Dickinson's One Thousand Best Books, and the same
author's Best Books of Our Time. Students were also invited
to consult with members of the library staff and with faculty
members regarding books dealing with the subjects of their
interest. At an assembly following this period, we gave
each student a sheet of paper upon which she was asked to
suggest books of two types for dormitory libraries: first,
books which she had enjoyed and would like to recommend to
others; and, second, books which she would like to have in
her dormitory in order that she might read them. Student
suggestions were collected by proctors in each dormitory the
evening of the day following the assembly. We have been
well pleased with the response of the students and believe
that their suggestions will help us considerably. In the
first place, from among the fifteen hundred titles suggested
by them, we have been able to select a considerable number
of books appropriate for our dormitory libraries; and, in the
second place, we believe that asking the students for their

suggestions and using these suggestions make the student
body feel that the libraries actually belong to them.

We have not yet opened our dormitory libraries, but
we shall do so during the second semester of the school
year. In three dormitories, books will be placed in the
parlors of the hall; in the remaining three residence halls,
rooms for the libraries have been set aside on the second
floor. We wish to experiment with each location before
finally establishing a policy with regard to the placing of
the libraries. From time to time during the school year,
books in the dormitory libraries will be changed so that
students in a given dormitory may have the opportunity of
becoming acquainted with varied collections of books.

The third objective of our library program is to make
the library function as the center of the instructional program of the college. The very organization of the college
is planned in such a way as to facilitate the achievement of
this objective, for the librarian's position as dean of instruction enables him to know what is going on in the classroom
and to assist the teacher in using the resources of the library. The opportunity to visit classes is of particular value
in this connection. At all times, of course, we aim to keep
teachers informed regarding what we have in the library.
We inform them of new books added to the library; we send
notices to individual teachers regarding books and magazine
articles in which they may be interested; and we compile
for teachers lists of books which relate to their course.

We are also interested in beginning a reorganization
of the library to the end that library books may be placed
where they can be readily accessible to faculty and students
at times when they are most needed. At present we are
making our first efforts in this direction by establishing
classroom libraries. Teachers have been invited to inform
us of books which they should like to have placed in their
classrooms for periods as short as one day or as long as
the school year. A few teachers have already begun the
use of these libraries. Permit me to assure you that we
are not beginning the use of classroom libraries ignorant of
the difficulties we shall encounter. We are, as I have stated
before, working on an experimental program, and we regard
experimentation with classroom libraries as an important element in our program. A second step which we have taken

in order to permit teachers and students to have ready access to books during the class period is to invite teachers
to bring their classes to the library for work during the
class hour. One teacher has a class meet in the library
twice a week, and other teachers bring classes to the library
at irregular intervals. Do not gather from what I say that
we are converting our library into a classroom. Such is not
at all the case. We have set aside space adjoining our stacks
where a class may meet or where a teacher may confer with
his students.

Divisional Libraries Proposed

A third step which we propose taking is the establishment
of divisional libraries in close proximity to the divisional offices. At Stephens College, courses are grouped into four
divisions: humanities, science, social studies, and skills
and techniques. Accordingly, when I speak of a divisional
library, I refer to a collection of books set aside for the use
of one of these four divisions. By placing books close to the
classrooms and to the offices of professors, we hope to encourage the use of books at times when their use will mean
most. In accordance with the experimental nature of our
program, we shall begin the use of the divisional library with
extreme caution. We shall first experiment with the Social
Studies Divisional Library. In our work with this library,
we shall study its use and try out various methods of administration. If we find that the divisional library proves
successful, if it encourages the use of books, and if we are
able to solve administrative problems which we know will be
connected with it, we shall set up similar libraries for each
of the four divisions.

Throughout our work at Stephens College, we are
keeping in mind the following questions and are striving to
answer them:

1. What steps, if any, can be taken to lead college
students to love books and to engage in reading for pleasure?
2. What type of library administration is best suited
to encourage the extensive use of books by teachers and
students in their class work?
3. Should the work of the library be so vitally related

to the instructional program of the college that the librarian may also advantageously be dean of instruction?

In conclusion, I wish to restate three characteristics of our library program:

First: The librarian, by virtue of his position as dean of instruction, has vital contact with the instructional program of the college.

Second: As much as is possible, the book collection is to be decentralized, to the end that books may be placed where both the teachers and the students can have ready access to them.

Third: The Stephens College library program is strictly experimental. We have set up tentative plans to achieve our objectives. We are, however, committed to no plan which experimentation indicates fails to contribute to the achievement of our aims.

The Library Arts College, A Possibility in 1954?

Louis Shores

Shores directed the library school at Florida State University from 1947 to 1967. He had also directed the library school at George Peabody College for Teachers (1933-1942) and had been Head Librarian at Fisk University (1928-1933). A prolific editor and author, he helped establish the Library-College Journal, later renamed Learning Today, and the Journal of Library History, Philosophy, and Comparative Librarianship, often referred to as JLH. From 1946 to 1959 he was editor of Collier's Encyclopedia.

"The Library Arts College" should be regarded as one of the classics of academic librarianship. At once both visionary and impractical, it is perhaps the briefest, clearest explication of the Library-College concept which, for undergraduates, would involve moving the teaching-learning situation from the classroom to the library and emphasizing problem-solving techniques within a liberal arts curriculum.

As a significant educational idea, the Library-College has become the subject of numerous retrospective critiques. One of the most cogent and insightful of these is contained in Patricia Breivik's Open Admissions and the Academic Library (Chicago: American Library Association, 1977), pp. 23-25. Breivik sees the "library-college" as offering "the only clear-cut philosophical statement of service with accompanying objectives of how academic libraries can support the educational trends of this century," notable among which she mentions independent study and research and student-centered interdisciplinary learning. Readers interested in pursuing the topic at length should examine Louis Shores, Robert Jordan, and John Harvey, The Library-College:

Contributions for American Higher Education at the Jamestown College Workshop, 1965 (Philadelphia: Drexel Press, 1966) and Gloria H. P. Terwilliger, "The Library-College: A Movement for Experimental and Innovative Learning Concepts: Applications and Implications for Higher Education" (Ed.D. dissertation, University of Maryland, 1975).

Reprinted from School and Society 41 (26 January 1935): pp. 110-114.

•   •   •

The sponsor of any untried plan, no matter how worth while, faces at the outset two discouraging types of criticism. There are first of all those reactionary critics who defend the status quo by hurling charges of charlatanism or radicalism at any proponent of change, without pretending to examine the proposal itself.   And then, there are those, of course, who will listen kindly and tolerantly to the presentation of a reform, and at the conclusion dismiss it as Utopian and fanciful.

To the first group of critics the sponsor of the present plan can merely say solemnly and with all the sincerity at his command that he honestly believes the changes he proposes are vital to the education of our young men and women, and therefore important to society.   It is somewhat easier to tell the second group of critics that the library arts college idea is not new, that it has been predicted for over a half century, and that trends in current college reform point inevitably to the consummation of the plan, possibly before the assigned 1954 date.

Every librarian has used the Carlyle quotation, "The true university is a collection of books."   That pioneer historian of pedagogy, Gabriel Compayré, commenting on Abelard's ability as a lecturer, prophesied the downfall of classroom methods over a half century ago, when he wrote in his epochal work:

> Human speech, the living word of the teacher, had then an authority, an importance, which it

has lost in part <u>since books, everywhere dis-</u>
<u>tributed, have, to a certain extent, superseded</u>
<u>oral instruction</u>. At a time when printing did not
exist, when manuscript copies were rare, a
teacher who combined knowledge with the gift of
speech was a phenomenon of incomparable
interest....

How much more strongly Monsieur Compayré would
have stated this thought had he lived to witness the replacement of the single-textbook method by our modern reserve
book system can only be surmised.

If time permitted, a series of statements by educators and librarians culled from writings and speeches of the
last half century and arranged chronologically could be
presented here to support the contention that the education
of the future will inevitably be a library education, that is,
an education which will be centered in the library. A few
such quotations may suffice. For example, in the National
Education Association proceedings of 1889, the U.S. Commissioner of Education, W. T. Harris, is quoted as declaring,
"The school is set at the task of teaching the pupil how to
use the library in the best manner--that, I take it, <u>is the</u>
<u>central object toward which our American schools have been</u>
<u>unconsciously tending</u>."

The present president-elect of the American Library
Association, writing in the <u>Library Journal</u> for November,
1910, quoted President Harper, of the University of Chicago,
as follows:

> That factor of our college and university work,
> the library, fifty years ago almost unknown, today
> already the center of the institutional intellectual
> activity, half a century hence, with its sister, the
> laboratory, ... <u>will by absorbing all else have</u>
> <u>become the institution itself</u>.

Nor have these remarks come from educationists alone.
In 1916, Librarian Richardson made a startling substitution
for Mark Hopkins on his end of the log when he declared,

> It is conceivable that a university should be a
> university, and a student get a university education

> if the university consisted only of a library and a
> student, without a lecturer, tutor, or preceptor,
> or research professor, or librarian--absolutely only
> a student and a library on a desert island.

We pass by the hosts of criticisms directed against the
American college during the two decades following Librarian
Richardson's observation, omitting such readable if not ab-
solutely accurate books as Upton Sinclair's "Goose-Step" and
Abraham Flexner's "Universities," for the words of a college
professor and a college student.

The professor is Carter Davidson, writing on the
"University of the Future" in the North American Review for
March, 1931:

> The faculty and the better students find the
> lecture and classroom recitation repetitious, boring,
> and a waste of time; the inferior students feel that
> lectures are hard to understand, and that the
> classroom recitations are too rapid, failing to make
> clear the more difficult problems.

The student is Kenneth Roberts' University of Michigan
composite (referred to by the chairman), who when asked if
he could suggest a remedy for the lack of scholarship in the
"lit" school shot back:

> I certainly can! I came here to study and if
> somebody'd tell me what to study, I could do more
> by myself, in my own room and in a library, than
> I could by tramping around to a lot of lectures....
> I don't get much of anything out of classes....

If these few quotations appear to deal harshly with the
conventional college and the sacred faculty we college librarians so humbly serve, look at what current reform has done
to American higher education. The 31st yearbook of the
National Society for the Study of Education lists 128 reforms
which differ only in the degree of instructional responsibility
placed on the library. Whether the innovation is styled
honors reading, as at Swarthmore, or autonomous courses,
as at Antioch, whether the teacher appointed to instruct is
called tutor, as at Harvard, or preceptor, as at Princeton,
or even professor of books, as at Rollins, whether courses

are abolished, as at Chicago or Olivet, and comprehensive examinations instituted, the educational department fundamentally affected is the college library. Current college reformers have at last begun to realize that the material unit of cultural education is the book, and that actually, as well as oratorically, the library is the liberal arts' laboratory. Only the conception of the library as the college and the college as the library remains prerequisite to the birth of the library arts college.

Just how do these trends affect us as college librarians? In the first place, I should like to make a distinction between educational librarianship on the one hand and research librarianship on the other. This is fundamental because I believe the two (education and research) are as incompatible in the library as they are in education on the secondary school and college levels.

The notion is rapidly gaining ground in college circles that a good researcher is not necessarily a good teacher. Indeed, there are those courageous enough to declare positively that the instructor engaged in research is invariably a poor teacher. No small part of the blame for the inferiority of undergraduate instruction can be traced to the fact that every American college is anxious to become a university engaged in research. The college president is forever exhorting his faculty to produce, because he knows he can interest foundations in studies much more easily than he can in that intangible something called "good teaching." As a result, the college neglects its real job--the training of young men and women. If the truth were told, a high positive correlation would be found to exist between the amount of time and energy expended by the college faculty on research and the amount of time and energy devoted by the students to extracurricular activities. Mutually bored by the learning process as carried on in the classroom, the teacher seeks for fame and advancement through research, and the pupil, left to his own resources, endeavors to while away the four years' times as pleasurably as possible in the fraternity houses and stadia.

It is not the purpose of this paper to disparage the recent movement to create research librarianships. So long as American universities continue to produce tons of studies, useful and otherwise, each year, there will be need for

research libraries and their staffs, whose duties will include
the acquisition and organization of printed material ad
infinitum, and the provision of even larger quarters for
their accommodation.

Far different is the function of the educational library,
such as the average undergraduate college should have.
Its collection should be highly selective and definitely
limited in size and scope. Whereas the research library's
book selection problem may be solely one of acquisition,
the educational library will be equally concerned with
elimination. As protection against the nuisance of research
ambitions, the college collection should have a maximum,
say 35,000 volumes, imposed upon it, beyond which its
collection may never expand. Each year the college may
undertake to purchase 500 new titles, on condition it weed
out 500 old works from its collection for discard or for
presentation to some ambitious research university endeavor-
ing each year to report a bigger and better library. In
this way only the number will remain static; the educational
library's contents will always include the basic books, plus
an ever-changing collection of ephemeral material. The
result will be a highly serviceable educational library with
abundant material to furnish a true culture to young people
who want it. Another result of this selectivity will be to
eliminate the necessity for providing expansion in college
library buildings. Contrary to the Carnegie standard, I
see no reason for planning future expansion in a college
library building, if those responsible for book selection do
a full job.

With the collection definitely limited in size and the
actual titles standardized by some such basic list as that
prepared under Mr. Shaw's direction, the acquisition and
organizational duties in the college library will be reduced
considerably and rendered largely routine. For example,
it is entirely likely that college titles will be purchasable
completely classified and catalogued, or that perhaps the
H. W. Wilson company will issue book catalogs cumulatively
in which each college will be able to indicate its own holdings. In any event, it is very unlikely that the services
of a highly trained cataloger and classifier will ever be
needed in an educational library.

The question then arises what, if any, will be the

librarian's duties? Primarily, the professional librarian will
be a teacher. The positions of librarian and professor will
merge. Every college instructor will be library trained;
every college librarian will be either a professional teacher
in some such field or a semi-professional housekeeper performing the necessary routines accessory to library education.

With this preliminary interpretation of higher educational trends, it is now possible to look at the library arts
college of 1954. A somewhat more detailed description of
the plan has been placed in Professor Austin's hands, and
no doubt his comments will elaborate the bare outline given
here. The plan resulted from the writer's undergraduate
experiences, which, like those of many other college students, convinced him he could learn much more in the library
reading than he could by attending most classes. Since
then, the plan has gradually developed an ambition to undertake undergraduate instruction to a small group of college
men with a selected book collection of not over 1,000 titles,
three library-trained instructors, and a small amount of
equipment.

At the outset it should be realized that the library
arts college is merely the logical culmination of such current
trends in American higher education as are exemplified by
honors courses, comprehensive examinations and other reforms of the last decade. Unencumbered by outworn ap-
pendages, the library arts college benefits from advantages
minimized by the transitory experiments of to-day. It
differs from the conventional college in at least five essentials.

In the first place, the library arts college reverses
the conventional college's practise of compulsory, regular
class attendance supplemented by voluntary and irregular
library reading. The library arts college student is definitely scheduled for supervised reading periods and permitted
to ask for a class meeting whenever he feels his readings
have failed to answer questions in his own mind. The supervisor of the reading period is a library-trained subject-matter
teacher. When the student reports to the history reading
room for his history reading period, he finds there a history
teacher thoroughly trained in library methods, who, among

other things, combines the duties of the history instructor
and the reference librarian.

In the second place, all instructional quarters, like
classrooms, reading rooms and laboratories, are concentrated
in the campus' one educational building--the library. A
plan for such a building drawn to scale is available among
my notes for any one who cares to examine it. In general,
the drawing calls for four units, one for each of the three
subject divisions--humanities, natural sciences, social
sciences--and a fourth for administrative and general reading
quarters.

In the third place, the instructional scheme employs
a principle of the Lancasterian schools which influenced
American educational development in the early years of the
nineteenth century, and which disappeared only because of
improper conditions. Briefly, the principle calls for upper-
class students to tutor lower-class students. This practise
is mutually beneficial since it insures individual instruction
for each lower classman and excellent training for each upper
classman. Beginning teachers frequently attest they
learned more about their major subject the first year they
taught it than they learned in all their undergraduate study.
Obviously, when a student has to know his lesson well
enough to make it clear to an underclassman, that student
not only masters his material, but what is more important,
he is able to express himself clearly on the subject. This
type of tutoring reinforced by faculty supervision, supplemented by occasional inspirational lectures, and checked
by the requirement of frequent papers, tests and a final
comprehensive examination, will do much to restore scholarship to its rightful place on the college campus.

As for the faculty members themselves, they will be
library-trained, subject-matter experts, but not specialists
in the restricted sense which describes our present research
professors who teach only incidentally. The chemistry man,
for example, will not be so thoroughly consumed by his
interest in colloids that he will be unable to supervise a
general reading course in science. It is very likely that
he will be able to express an intelligent opinion on James
Joyce or the Herbartian influence in American education.
But above all, he will be vitally interested in the young
people he teaches, study their development as zealously as

the average researcher does his experiment, and be as proud of the young man or woman he graduates into society as the average scientist is about a notable discovery.

Finally, the curriculum, instead of including a great number of frequently unrelated courses, will represent a carefully planned reading program intended to acquaint the student with man's accomplishments of the past and problems of the present. There is no more direct method of achieving this end than through the reading of the right books. To the library-trained teacher of the future is assigned the task of selecting intelligently the right book for the right student at the right time. That American Library Association motto might well be adopted as the major aim of our library arts college education.

Bridging the Gap

Harvie Branscomb

Branscomb directed the library at Duke University from
1934 to 1941. He also held other administrative positions
at Duke where he was Professor of Early Christian Literature from 1925 to 1946. He was Chancellor of Vanderbilt
University from 1946 to 1963 after which he became a
Consultant to the International Bank of Reconstruction and
Development and Chairman of the U.S. National Commission
to Unesco.

He published Teaching with Books as a result of
visiting more than sixty institutions and compiling data on
library use and student grades. Working under the
auspices of the Association of American Colleges and with a
grant from the Carnegie Corporation, he took a twelve-month
leave from his regular duties in order to complete the investigation. He designed his project to study the college library
from the standpoint of "educational effectiveness" rather than
administrative efficiency, in order to consider the extent to
which the library was integrated into the institution as a
whole.

"Bridging the Gap" is his attempt to define the proper
and ideal relationship between the librarian and the professor. He contended that the librarian should be regarded as
an assistant to the instructor; more specifically, the
reference librarian should work outside the library building
to establish effective communication with faculty members
and even attend classes so as "to assure the fullest cooperation of the library staff with the work of instruction."

Likewise, the instructor should enter the library as an

assistant to the librarian. Undergraduate learning in the form of independent study necessarily occurred in the library outside the classroom, albeit with faculty direction but also with strong dependence on librarian assistance. Such developments encouraged instructors "to take the literature of their subjects [not merely the subjects themselves] much more seriously" than in the past.

Branscomb's book, addressed to college and university administrators, was widely reviewed and well received in both education and library science journals. He published excerpts of his findings in four separate papers, all entitled "Teaching With Books," in Bulletin of the Association of American Colleges 25 (March 1939): 134-141; Peabody Reflector 15 (January 1942): 25-27; Library Journal 64 (15 May 1939): 391-394 and The Development of University Centers in the South, edited by A. F. Kuhlman (Nashville: Joint University Libraries, 1942), pp. 93-103.

Reprinted by permission of the Association of American Colleges from Teaching With Books: A Study of College Libraries, pp. 196-209. Chicago: American Library Association and Association of American Colleges, 1940.

•   •   •

The thesis running through this volume has been that the primary task of the college library is to provide certain facilities for and to aid in carrying out the instructional program of the faculty. Other functions such as the provision of reading materials along non-curricula lines and even of books for faculty research, though desirable and important are secondary to this main task. Yet for reasons which have been discussed, the program of the library and that of the faculty have not been a unit. There has been lacking a sense of common purpose and, consequently, attention to the problem of the most effective coordination of effort.

Librarians are aware of this lack of integration, though the aspects of it which loom largest are, naturally enough, the difference in status and rank between members of the faculty on the one hand and the library staff on the other. They would like to see the "gap," as it is often called, bridged, and would go to almost any lengths toward that end. The matter, however, is not one merely of good-will. It involves certain administrative steps directed toward uniting the efforts of instructors and librarians so that the educational program will function as a single unit. It involves also modifications, in emphasis at least, in the program of many libraries, and a greater concern for student reading and interest in library matters on the part of many faculties.

Some of the emphases and arrangements which will contribute to this integration of effort have already been mentioned, and there are others of which one can speak with fair confidence. The problem ranges out, however, into an area in which only the most tentative steps have been taken and in which there is no authoritative word to be given. In what follows it will be impossible to stay completely within the realm of the tried and proven, but experienced administrators do not need to be warned that all such suggestions of an administrative character, like theological doctrines, have to be applied by the sinner to his own condition.

The first step is one about which there can be little question. If the library is to function intelligently as part of the educational program, the librarian must be placed in a position in which he will be informed as to what is going on. In practical terms this means in most institutions changing the status of the librarian. In a great many colleges and universities they are not even members of the faculty, whose educational objectives they are expected to carry out.

This point has already been discussed and it is not necessary to repeat the arguments which were given for bringing the college librarian more closely into the area of educational discussion. Nor is it necessary to say again that the mere title "professor" has no sacramental efficacy. The problem is one of achieving for the librarian, qua libra-rian, an organizational position corresponding to the centrality of his responsibilities. The values resulting from such arrangements will be not only a fuller cooperation with instructors in the library aspects of this work, but also a

more intelligent understanding of the relation of the library
to the larger issues and efforts of the institution. Of the
latter a striking illustration can be given. When the Joint
Committee on Intellectual Cooperation was set up by the
University of North Carolina and Duke University, the
responsible library officials of both institutions were made
members. Through this contact with the policy forming
committee, they were enabled to plan the cooperative library
program which is functioning so successfully in both institutions.

The second approach to the problem of integrating
library management and educational ends must come from the
library side, though it will flow in part from the above
steps. It consists in reworking the program of the library
from the point of view that the primary concern of the library, as well as of the rest of the college, is the effectiveness of the courses of study. Too frequently even when
this point of view has been accepted, it has been a passive
acquiescence, rather than a positive program.

The writer recalls a conversation with a very competent and successful college librarian who had just completed
a move into a new library building. The president of that
college was keenly aware of the importance of the library
and had increased its budget considerably. After an inspec-
tion of the attractive and well arranged building, we paused
for a cup of tea in the social room. The librarian then
stated her problem: "I have gotten a new building. I have
two additional members of the staff, the book funds have
been increased. Of course we could use additional funds
and would like to have them, but no serious problem exists
here. Now what do I do next?" The problem was clearly
formulated and honestly faced. The familiar library program
has been one of securing more and more facilities, a program which no one could deny to be essential for effective
work. But if its objectives do not look beyond this, or
if these further ends are conceived to be in the hands of
other branches of the college, the facilities secured will
always remain to a certain extent potentialities rather than
active instruments of education. So far as the library itself is concerned a program conceived in terms of facilities
rather than more fundamental ends is all too likely to become
enthralled to its own processes and resources.

A detailed description of the program which should
supplement that of acquisition and preparation, the present
writer would not attempt to supply. Certain directions
which it would take, however, can be seen. It certainly
involves knowing more about the work being carried on in
the several departments than is commonly the case. This
can be secured by study of the catalog and of syllabi of
courses, and by going over points of uncertainty in the
latter in conferences with individual faculty members. Attendance at departmental meetings, particularly when the
work of large courses is to be discussed, would be quite
profitable, although this could only be done by invitation,
a point which the library committee might arrange.

"What do I do next?" One can only suggest that
the courses be taken up one at a time, and their objectives
and library needs examined. Out of such a study would
come several specific steps. Among the first would certainly
be a more intelligent judgment on the subject of the number
of duplicates required for various titles, a point on which
the librarian can speak with more wisdom than can the
faculty member. Closely related would be a modification of
circulation rules which would adjust these more exactly to
the reading demands of the course. A distinction between
three-hour books, three-day books and seven-day books is
carried out without difficulty by a number of libraries. An
effective contribution along a quite different line can also be
anticipated. It would consist in bringing to the attention
of the class--and incidentally of the instructor--materials in
the library related to the course of study. There are
several ways in which this can be done. One would be by
preparing a supplementary bibliography classified under
several headings. Such a list--revised of course by the
instructor--mimeographed and placed in student hands, would
supplement and tend to broaden the instruction from which
some classes at least suffer. A second approach would be to
prepare small exhibits of material in the library dealing
with special topics treated in the course. Library staffs
are skillful at such displays--much more so than most faculty
members--and there seems no reason why this skill should
not be brought to the aid of important courses. A third
method would be to place supplementary material, such as
biographies of important figures touched in the course, on
the shelf alongside the volumes containing the required
readings.[1]

A third result of a fuller acquaintance with the
courses and their objectives would be more adequate assistance in connection with themes and special assignments.
In the first place, every step toward a freer and more
active cooperation between the library staff and the teaching groups makes it easier for the former to report to the
latter difficulties encountered by students in their effort
to carry out these assignments. Mr. Peyton Hurt has described the fruitful results of an analysis of a number of
undergraduate courses in the University of California.
In a number of cases the wording of term paper assignments
was changed at the suggestion of the librarian, with the
result that student access to library materials was made
easier and with gains both to the library and the students. [2]
An even more striking illustration can be drawn from the
Library of the Woman's College of the University of North
Carolina. One of the assignments customarily made to
freshmen in this institution was a "survey theme" involving
the use of material from a number of sources. Difficulties
frequently arose because the subjects assigned called for
material which the library did not possess. The upshot
of a series of discussions was that finally the list of topics
on which these themes could be written was made up by the
library staff and turned over to the departmental faculty
concerned.

There is one objection to all of this. It is that
exhibits, book lists, conferences with instructors and like
activities are all very time consuming. Who is going to do
all of this? Here a proposal which may seem radical will
be made. All but the smallest colleges have reference librarians whose duties are often described in very impressive
general terms--"to interpret the reader to the library and
the library to the reader," etc.--but whose actual work consists to a considerable extent in answering routine questions. [3]
The pattern for this sort of work seems to come from the
public library, where readers of all sorts need help in the
use of even the more familiar reference tools, and suggestions
as to books to read on a variety of subjects. On a college
campus the direction of reading in general is in the hands
of the faculty. A well-qualified librarian who is free to deal
with student questions is an obvious asset, but the definition of his or her duties has not yet been worked out in
college terms. The suggestion is made that the college reference librarian--and may we not find a better title?--should

not be located in a room in the library, but a good part of
the time should be outside the library building in communication with faculty members, and in some cases attending
classes so as to assure the fullest cooperation of the library
staff with the work of instruction. Of such a conception of
the reference librarian's position the distinguished work of
Miss Ludington at Mills College can be cited in illustration.
In smaller libraries this work will of course devolve upon
the librarian; in the larger institutions, on the several subject specialists related to particular departments whose
presence on the staff has been recommended. To the objection of lack of time one further general answer can be
made: such efforts as have been described, undertaken only
in a desire to aid the faculty in its work, will be one of the
most direct ways toward getting the united support of the
faculty for a library staff adequate for the work of the college.

In the above discussion a sort of library service has
been sketched in which the librarian becomes the assistant
to the instructor.   There remains to be mentioned certain
developments in which the instructor is moved into the library and becomes virtually an assistant to the librarian.
This development is related to those changes in the form of
college teaching which leave the student more or less free
from regular class instruction, dependent upon his own labor in the library, though with faculty direction.   When
this takes place the problem arises of giving the student
adequate guidance and assistance, some of which is provided
by regularly preceptorial or tutorial meetings, but some of
which is needed at unexpected times while the student is
reading in the library.   To a certain extent an informed
reference librarian can supply this, but a number of institutions have grasped the problem with more vigor.

Teachers College of Columbia University some years
ago experimented with the plan of placing in the philosophy
of education reading room during the morning hours an assistant from the department to aid students in "questions
arising from class or group discussions, or in the preparation
of term papers and examinations." The experiment proved
very effective. [4] They now have available in the library the
full time services of two faculty members to provide assistance
in any aspect of the educational literature. The "college"
program of the University of Chicago calls for all freshmen

or sophomores to take certain basic survey courses requiring heavy use of the library, and advisors for certain of these courses are located in the college library for most of each day. At Brown University Mr. Van Hoesen suggested that the English Department release an instructor from one course so that he might help select books for general reading and also would be present in the library at certain hours to aid students in choosing their reading materials. After a year's trial the plan was extended into "an experiment" with six library counselors from different departments, each putting in two hours a week at stated times. At Wesleyan University a member of the Classics Department has an office in the library where he is available several afternoons a week to aid students on problems involving foreign languages. The plans for the new library, or "humanistic laboratory," of Princeton University call for preceptors or other student advisors to be located in the library building, not in front offices or reading rooms, but on the several stack levels adjacent to the book collections with which they are most concerned. This plan thus calls for a physical association of the three elements in education, the student, the faculty advisor and the book collection.

This same effort to find a means of integrating more closely library work and teaching efforts appears in the location in some institutions of numerous classes in the library building. In itself this is not new, the new element being the fact that whereas such locations formerly were reserved for seminars or advanced courses, in some institutions they are now being assigned to courses at the sophomore and even freshman level. All such developments point to an effort on the part of college administrators to get instructors and students to take the literature of their subjects of study much more seriously. Which of these arrangements are the more desirable, it is not necessary to say, since the particular plan which would be adopted will depend to a large extent on local policies and developments.

Thus far nothing has been said on the subject of courses on how to use the library, which constitute perhaps the most familiar answer from the library side to the problem of integrating library and classroom work. The argument made for such courses is both specific and general. In the first place, it is maintained that no student can do the best college work unless he can use the varied facilities offered

by a modern library. Students coming from secondary
schools are overwhelmed by the various rooms of the college
library, and baffled by the very multitude of books and the
size and complexity of the catalog. Of the various bibliographic aids to knowledge they are in complete ignorance.
Unless they are given specific instruction on these subjects,
they will go through college unable to use the facilities which
the college has acquired at great expense for their use. In
the second place, it is argued that such a course provides
one with a technique for getting at knowledge, without
which one will be at a disadvantage throughout life. The
world of print nowadays is so voluminous that one must work
in libraries, not with single volumes. Such courses, therefore, justify themselves as a necessary equipment of the
educated citizen. A great number of libraries provide
courses along this line. They vary from required courses at
the freshman level to elective courses on advanced academic
levels. A most powerful support for such courses has
been the data published recently by Mr. Hurt and others
showing that even graduate students were sadly deficient
in a knowledge of library tools and techniques.[5] One
writer goes so far as to recommend three required courses
for college students.[6]

That many students are confused by the developments
of modern libraries goes without saying. Two questions
raised by the fact are more difficult to answer. One is
whether or not library practice, evolved in connection with
much smaller book collections, has not become too elaborate
and complex. The card catalog is the point in question
here. When catalogs begin to run into millions of cards, the
question cannot be avoided whether or not we are trying
to supply too much information by this means. To this
point we shall return in the next chapter.

The second question is that of the best way by which
this needed information can be supplied. The question
divides into two parts; introductory information and the more
advanced work in the bibliography of special subjects.
Nothing could be more useless or deadly to the intellect than
to memorize the names of bibliographies or other guides for
which the student feels no need and has no interest. It is
certainly sound pedagogy to postpone the latter work until
a need for the material is beginning to appear. To illustrate,
an effort to teach freshmen the intricacies of government

documents--a field incidentally in which only a small per
cent of librarians are competent--is surely premature. On
the assumption, then, that the freshmen are to be given
only general or introductory information, how and by whom
should this be given?

There is of course no one and only method, since
information can often be imparted equally well by more than
one means. The two most common methods--aside from an
introductory tour of the library building by freshmen
usually too dazed to take much in--are through some required
course of the general curriculum such as English literature
which gives access to all freshmen, or through classes or
conferences conducted by the library staff. In favor of
the latter are the arguments (a) that the instructors of
subject courses are rather frequently reluctant to give up
time to instruction in the use of the library, (b) that instruction by the library staff establishes contacts with students
which makes them feel free subsequently to ask questions,
and (c) that sometimes the faculty members do not themselves
know very much about how to use the library. The objections to such courses given by the library staff are that
(a) the library staff is extremely busy already, (b) that
many students do not need this introductory training, and
(c) that librarians, like most experts, want to teach students
too much. The last point can be expanded into the general
objection that all efforts of special interests to introduce into
the curriculum courses dealing with methods rather than
cultural content is to be opposed vigorously by those who
would preserve the liberal arts tradition.

While repeating the statement that no way of doing
this work of instruction is better in all cases than others,
two suggestions may be made. These are complementary to
each other, and should be considered together rather than
separately. The first, based on the truisms that unnecessary instruction is deadly for the student and expensive
for the institution, and that students vary greatly in their
need for the sort of instruction under discussion, is that a
test or examination be given all freshmen sometime during the
academic year and that those revealing gross deficiencies be
assigned to the librarian for special instruction of an introductory character. A test which may serve this purpose has
recently been prepared and standardized by Miss Lulu Ruth
Reed. The test has been given to students in a number of

colleges and a normal score established.[7] By the use of
this or some other test, those needing instruction can be
determined. The library staff can then arrange small
groups for instructional purposes. A certificate from the
librarian that the student is qualified to go ahead might well
be required. Some such plan as this is being worked out
at Lawrence College where the Reed test was given to all
undergraduates. It was found that while the score of the
four academic classes rose with their rank, the mark of the
lowest senior was below that of the lowest freshman.

The second suggestion complements the above. It is
that the librarian should endeavor by various means to bring
to the attention of the faculty the problem of student inability to use the library. So much of what is basically essential can be secured indirectly and in connection with other
work, that even a little attention to the problem by faculty
members can assure a reasonable knowledge on the students'
part on all essential points.

This leads to the other aspect of this problem--the
more advanced instruction in bibliography. Excellent courses
of this sort are being given by a number of librarians, but
it would seem that the general solution of the problem can be
achieved only by the experts in various fields and in connection with advanced courses. That this matter is now
neglected and that graduate students report themselves un-
familiar with approaches to library materials which they
should know and use, is simply another piece of evidence
that faculties, for all their concern for libraries for their
own use, have neglected much of their teaching opportunity
as regards them. That the facts justify efforts on the part
of libraries to rig up courses to teach bibliography in all
fields would seem very doubtful. The problem will not be
solved by the assumption by the library of this part of
what is properly the work of each advanced department, but
by bringing to the attention of department heads the deficiency of many graduate students in this respect. If frequent and cooperative contacts are established between the
library staff and the faculty, as has been suggested, information relayed by the former as to difficulties students encounter in writing term papers and other exercises will also
call attention to the point. There can be no possible objection, of course, to the use of the library staff by instructors
for discussions with their classes of special library problems

or materials. The point which should be guarded against
is the library taking over all responsibility for bibliographic
instruction.

One way by which it is proposed that the gap between
the library staff and the faculty be bridged has been discussed in a previous chapter. It is that librarians should
teach courses in the regular departmental fields. By so
doing they become not merely librarians but instructors as
well. No objection to this can be raised, provided the librarian has the qualifications and the time, but it would not
seem to be the basic solution of the problem. This would
seem to rest on opening channels of communication, understanding and cooperation between the reading aspects of
instruction and the classroom aspects rather than by com-
bining in the person of the librarian two disparate functions.
As one means toward this end the teaching of a course by
the librarian might be desirable, but it is not the only way
by which the end can be achieved nor in all cases the best
way. The librarian, by giving formal instruction, would
become closely related to one department of the college, but
he would achieve thereby no similar relationship to the other
departments. A second dubious approach to the general
problem was revealed as such by a very wise university
president to whom it was submitted. The suggestion was
made that since we have in many departments of instruction
assistants to read papers or to aid in research, why not a
"library assistant" who would see that reserve lists were
kept in order and that book orders were timed properly and
other library matters attended to. "If you do that," he remarked, "the faculty members themselves might never come
near the library."

In the last analysis a problem of this sort can be
solved only on the campus itself. Administrators who have
clearly in mind the goal to be reached will find their own
way of making progress toward it.

NOTES

1. The librarian who undertakes to call the attention
of the class to the full resources of the library on the subject studied will meet from some instructors the objection
that they do not want the class to read these additional books

but only the ones specified in the outlines. The difficulty
is not what to do with this objection, but what to do with
such instructors. In most cases, however, no instructor
will object to such efforts unless he misunderstands what is
being attempted. There should be no grounds for such mis-
understanding. All such steps as have been suggested
should follow a discussion with the instructor and should
enlist his assistance.

2. The University Library and Undergraduate Instruction (Berkeley: University of California Press, 1937),
p. 19ff.

3. The Reference Department of the Duke University
Library kept a record of the questions asked from September
4th to April 25th of the academic year 1937-38, classifying
these in two groups. Of 6,852 questions so classified--it
is recognized that the record was never quite complete--68
per cent were grouped as routine questions and 32 per cent
as reference questions. Similar figures for the Woman's
College Library of the same institution, a smaller library
with a less extensive reference collection, and therefore
with fewer questions as to the location of books, etc., showed
40 per cent reference questions. This of course does not
minimize the value of the reference work done, but does suggest that a highly trained librarian will not have his or her
full time and attention taken up by such questions. In the
General Library referred to above these reference questions
averaged about 10 per day.

4. See Ruth Allen Casewell, "A Venture in Vitalizing
Reference Reading," School and Society XXX (1929), 433-
36.

5. Peyton Hurt's article, "The Need of College and
University Instruction in the Use of the Library," Library
Quarterly IV (1934), 436-48, summarized the results of an
examination on the use of the library given to 354 graduate
students at the University of California and at Stanford
University. He cites the following figures: 49 per cent
said they often felt the need of advice in using the card
catalog; 68 per cent that they needed instruction in the use
of the library; and 78 per cent that such instruction would
have been useful in undergraduate work.

6. Elbridge Colby, "The Teaching Librarian," Library
Journal XLIX (1924), 767-73.

7. The test may be secured from the Chicago Plano-
graph Corporation, 517 South Jefferson St., Chicago, at a
cost of 4c each. At first glance one is impressed with the

number of questions that no one but an expert reference librarian or cataloger could answer. Miss Reed explains that these questions are included to assure a sufficient range for the test. It is not expected that undergraduates will score 100.

Part IV

SEARCH FOR IDENTITY IN A TIME OF GROWTH

1941-1968

The 1941-1968 period of library use instruction began much
as the 1918-1940 period ended--with an attempt by an influential librarian to educate a nonlibrarian audience. The
year after the publication of Harvie Branscomb's Teaching
With Books,[1] Louis Round Wilson, probably the most influential librarian of his day, made a presentation to the Institute for Administrative Officers of Higher Education on
"The Use of the Library in Instruction."[2] Wilson confidently
stated:

> I believe the efficiency of the library as an
> educational instrument can likewise be further
> increased, provided the problem is steadily and
> intelligently attacked by college administrators,
> faculties, librarians, and research students.[3]

Nevertheless, despite such an optimistic beginning,
Barbara Phipps found from her survey near the end of the
period that librarians involved in user instruction were
frustrated, disappointed, and demoralized because of "lack
of staff, lack of time, lack of money for experimentation,
lack of cooperation and interest from the faculty and the
administration."[4] The changes in library use instruction
occurring during the intervening years can best be understood in the context of developments in higher education
during the same period.

Before World War II only a small segment of the population attended college. After the war, however, the
meritocratic philosophy and the GI Bill of 1944 opened up
the colleges and universities to the flood of returning vete-
rans. Later, in the next decade, the launching of Sputnik
I by the Soviet Union provided the impetus for a second
major shift in American philosophy toward higher education.

Higher education became part of national defense and egali-
tarian ideals came to support access to higher education for
everyone.

With the increased enrollments came increased funding.
Nevertheless, academic libraries struggled to keep pace
with the general growth in higher education during this
period. In 1939-1940, less than twenty million dollars went
to academic libraries and only three million volumes were
added to their collections. This expenditure, however,
represented 3.7 percent of general and educational expenditures in higher education. This percentage dropped to 3.3
by 1950, and it did not regain the 3.7 figure until near the
end of the "golden years" of the 1960s.[5]

Of importance to library use instruction is that much
of the increase in funds for academic libraries during this
period went to "bricks and books." By 1967-1968, academic
libraries added over twenty-two million volumes annually to
their collections.[6] The libraries needed room both for growing
collections and for increased numbers of students and, supported by federal funds, they went on a post-World War II
building spree that did not end until the 1970s. Meanwhile,
the student-to-librarian ratio continued to increase. From
1959 to 1968, for example, the number of students for each
academic librarian increased from 378 to 446, or twenty-three
percent.[7]

Library use instruction during this period can be
characterized as activity without progress. Numerous programs existed at the freshman orientation and basic instruction levels, but the increasing number of students overwhelmed many of even the well-established programs. As
early as 1949, Erikson reported from his survey that the
most serious deterrent to successful library instruction programs was insufficient library personnel.[8] Librarians of
the day were faced with larger freshman classes each year
and with little time to experiment and reflect thus, according
to Kenneth Brough, the provision of effective library instruction remained an "unsolved problem."[9]

Large numbers of students were not the only hindrance
to library instruction during this period. Programs struggled
because they lacked a viable conceptual framework and many
librarians showed little understanding of either previous or

concurrent efforts. Some librarians simply failed to support
user instruction as an educational function of the academic
library. Tom Kirk has provided a cogent analysis of the
weaknesses of library use instruction during the 1940s and
1950s. He concluded:

1. Those involved failed to distinguish orientation from
   instruction and therefore provided only the former;
2. The instruction or orientation was not given in a
   context of the student's need to know how to use
   the library;
3. The instruction when it went beyond orientation
   tended to take its scope and content from the
   reference training which librarians had received;
4. Librarians were not sensitive to educational
   changes that were occurring. [10]

As a result, many programs struggled and finally foundered
in the 1940s and 1950s.

Librarians turned to other solutions during the 1960s.
Givens has reviewed efforts to use technology during this
time, [11] and the Library-College movement attracted widespread attention as some librarians sought to change the entire structure of higher education. Nevertheless, by the
middle and late 1960s, many librarians involved in user instruction had become frustrated and demoralized, as Phipps
had found in her survey.

NOTES

1. Harvie Branscomb, Teaching With Books: A Study
of College Libraries (Chicago: American Library Association
and Association of American Colleges, 1940).
2. Louis Round Wilson, "The Use of the Library in
Instruction," in Proceedings, Institute for Administrative
Officers of Higher Education (Chicago: University of Chicago
Press, 1941), pp. 115-127.
3. Ibid., pp. 124-125.
4. Barbara H. Phipps, "Library Instruction for the
Undergraduate," College and Research Libraries 29 (September 1968): 411-412.
5. W. Vance Grant and C. George Lind, Digest of

Educational Statistics, 1973 (Washington, D.C.: United States Government Printing Office, 1974), p. 111.

    6. The Bowker Annual 1970, edited by Carole Collins and Frank Schick (New York: R. R. Bowker, 1970), p. 15.

    7. Ibid., p. 14.

    8. E. Walfred Erickson, "Library Instruction in the Freshman Orientation Program," College and Research Libraries 10 (October 1949): 445.

    9. Kenneth J. Brough, Scholar's Workshop: Evolving Conceptions of Library Service (Urbana: University of Illinois Press, 1953), p. 159.

    10. Thomas Kirk, "Past, Present, and Future of Library Instruction," Southeastern Librarian 27 (Spring 1977): 16-17.

    11. Johnnie Givens, "The Use of Resources in the Learning Experience," in Advances in Librarianship, vol. 4, edited by Melvin J. Voigt (New York: Academic Press, 1974), pp. 160-164.

A Suggested Program of College Instruction in the Use
of the Library

Patricia R. Knapp

Despite the lack of significant advances during the 1940s
and 1950s in the practice of library use instruction,
Patricia Knapp made a series of theoretical contributions
during this period. Her proposals outlined in this selection have served as the foundation for numerous later programs and, by the 1970s, she had become probably the
most frequently cited author in the literature of user
instruction.

From 1937 to 1943, Knapp held various positions with
the Chicago Teachers College Library, and during the later
years of World War II, she served as a librarian with the
armed forces. While librarian at George Williams College
from 1945 to 1955, she completed her Ph.D. at the University of Chicago. Her dissertation, published as College
Teaching and the College Library (Chicago: American
Library Association, 1959), dealt with the use of the library
at Knox College. As Harvie Branscomb had concluded some
fifteen years earlier, Knapp found that the college library
played only a marginal role in the education of most undergraduate students.

Strongly influenced by her research, Knapp focused
on the importance of teaching faculty in student use of the
library. In an article summarizing the major conclusions of
her dissertation, she wrote:

> Neither subject field, nor teaching method, nor
> kind of assignment nor quality of students in a
> class is of crucial importance in determining

151

whether or not a given course will be dependent on
the library. The only decisive factor seemed to
be--and this is a subjective judgment--the instructor's attitude. Where the instructor expected and
planned for student use of the library, it occurred.
Where he did not, it did not occur ("College
Teaching and the Library," Illinois Libraries 40
[December 1958]: 829).

Unlike many librarians of the period, Knapp in this
selection demonstrates both an awareness of the history of
library use instruction and the current trends in higher
education. Key educational concepts, such as problem-
solving, continuity, practice, and planned learning experiences, are important elements in the program she proposes.
Above all else, Knapp emphasizes the role of the teaching
faculty in library use instruction.

Reprinted by permission from Library Quarterly 26 (July
1956) 224-231. Copyright © 1956 by The University of
Chicago Press.

•   •   •

The fundamental aim is to induce students
to use books for many sorts of purposes. The
first is for work, for study. When the freshman enters college, he comes for the first
time into contact with a library designed primarily for that purpose. The character of
his work requires him, as never before, seriously to search for the right books, and to
use them wisely. Immediately there is a
temptation to instruct him in the use of the
library directly. That is often done in lectures during Freshman Week, or in a short
orientation course. While it is the obvious
thing to do, it is really putting the cart before the horse; a student does not learn by
being told how to use the library, but by
using it. Moreover the responsibility for the
use of books should not be centered in the

librarian, but in the faculty. All the work
of instruction must be so organized that the
student will need library books. Once that
need is clear to him, he is in a mood to
learn how to supply it. His first efforts
will be awkward and clumsy, as all first efforts are, but if he is convinced that he is
going to use the library frequently in the
work of science, in literature and the humanities, as well as in the social studies, he will
want to know how to use it effectively. Moreover his use of the library is not merely a
phase of some fraction of his course of study;
it becomes an inevitable part of his whole
college experience.[1]

This statement may well serve as the text for this paper.
Though it appeared almost twenty years ago, planned instruction in the use of the library at the college level is
still quite generally limited to one or two orientation lectures and perhaps a "library paper" in Freshman English.
The shortcomings of this kind of program have long been
apparent and are still perfectly obvious.[2] Competence in
library use, like competence in reading, is clearly not a
skill to be acquired once and for all at any one given
level in any one given course. It is, rather, a complex of
knowledge, skills, and attitudes which must be developed
over a period of time through repeated and varied experiences
in the use of library resources.

The usual college-level instruction in library use is
simply incapable of developing such competence. At the same
time, current developments in higher education indicate an increasingly urgent need for good instruction in library use.
These developments may be summarized as follows:

First, educators recognize that accelerated social change
requires that education, particularly general education, be
concerned not with solutions for today's problems but with
methods of solving tomorrow's. Since the library is an important storehouse of social resources for the solution of problems, the need for training in the use of the library is under-
lined by the current emphasis on problem-solving in education.

Second, as Lacy points out in a recent article on the

role of the college library, the function of scholarship
itself has changed: "The acquisition of new knowledge by
empirical methods has replaced the preservation and trans-
mission of a heritage as the central function of scholarship.
Western learning has become a dynamic force of change.[3]
Here, again, the emphasis is on methods rather than on
static solutions. And here, again, the library, viewed as
the storehouse of the resources for scholarship, has a
central role. Furthermore, lest it be assumed that the
changing function of scholarship affects only the minority
of our college students, Lacy may be cited further:

> [One] effect of this penetration of nonacademic
> life by scholarship is that higher learning is no
> longer the ornament of a small elite. The very
> operation of our society requires that higher
> learning be shared by tens of millions who
> need its skills and technique to participate ef-
> fectively in the economy or to act intelligently
> as citizens.[4]

And, finally, the overwhelming increase in the quantity and diversity of library materials sets an increasingly
high premium upon skill in their use.

Because of these developments, we must agree with
Stanley Gwynn that

> the skill required to use a library--that enables
> the student to select, from that portion of so-
> ciety's memory which is represented by his college
> or university library collection, those materials
> pertinent to his problems--seems to be one of
> the skills which the college exists to provide.
> Indeed, I will boldly assert that in these times
> and in our present state of learning, with the
> records of knowledge multiplying at an almost un-
> controllable rate (bibliographically speaking), the
> knowledge and skills we have been talking about
> actually constitute one of the liberal arts.[5]

Why, then, do we still rely on the orientation lecture and
the Freshman library paper to provide this necessary skill?
Several reasons may be suggested. In spite of the changes
in scholarship that Lacy notes, most college instructors are

content-oriented rather than method-oriented. In spite of
the emphasis upon problem-solving, they tend to teach what
they know rather than ways of finding out. For all the
lip service they give the library as the "heart of the college," many instructors do not recognize its full potentiality.
Those instructors who have themselves acquired competence
in library use have acquired it through advanced work in
one special field. Not appreciating the fact that higher
learning is no longer the ornament of a small elite, they may
assume that only those students who go on to advanced
work will need library skills. Or perhaps they assume
that most college students acquire these skills as a natural
by-product of their work in content courses.

College librarians know better. College librarians know
that many students use only the reserve collection and that
very few go beyond the authors and titles specifically recommended by instructors. On the other hand, librarians
must share the blame for the fact that after fifteen years the
college faculty is still not "teaching with books" in the style
proposed by Branscomb.[6] Too often college librarians have
squandered their most creative efforts on devices to stimulate
extracurricular use of the library. Those who have given
serious attention to the problem have, as a rule, recommended
the inclusion of new courses in an already crowded curriculum.
They have advocated that the library staff should teach these
courses because "(1) it is competent to explain the library,
whereas many faculty members are not themselves sure of
library techniques, and (2) the contacts established probably
make the students more willing to ask questions subsequently."[7] It is hard to imagine two arguments less likely to
convince the faculty that instruction in library use is an
essential element of the curriculum. Librarians, then, are
to blame for using the wrong reasons.

This paper contends, further, that they are not even
arguing for the right things. With Wriston, it maintains
that instruction in the use of the library will be really
effective only if it is presented by the regular teaching
faculty as an integral part of content courses in all subject
fields. Only if it is presented in this way will it appear to
the student to be functionally related to the real business of
higher education. This is the only method which gives
proper recognition to the complexity of the competence the
student should acquire. This is the only method which meets

the criteria for effective organization of learning as noted
below.

Clearly, however, the problem of developing such integrated instruction is not a simple one. It requires careful thought in the determination of objectives. It requires
the planning of learning experiences in accordance with
recognized principles of learning. The co-operative efforts
of most of the faculty must be enlisted in working through
the processes involved, and the whole faculty must be committed to the fundamental value of the project. The librarian's task is most important at this point, for the success
of the whole undertaking hinges upon his success in educating the faculty to an appreciation of competence in
library use as "one of the liberal arts."

Basically, the job is an individual one, to be done
independently in each college. This paper, therefore, will
merely offer suggestions. These suggestions will be concerned with (1) the formulation of objectives for instruction;
(2) relevant principles of learning and curriculum construction; (3) the development of appropriate learning experiences;
and (4) possible procedures for the librarian.

                          OBJECTIVES

In the process of formulating objectives for instruction in
the use of the library, the college should consider the whole
range of knowledge and skills desirable for the student to
achieve. Some are probably achieved through present instruction. For instance, students probably acquire understanding of the contribution of the classic works in the major
subject fields of general education through presently required general education courses. They presumably acquire
elementary skill in the use of the card catalog and Readers'
Guide in their Freshman English course. They unquestionably
acquire the ability to understand, interpret, and evaluate
whatever reading they are required to do.

We are concerned here, however, with suggesting
what seem to be important objectives that are probably not
now achieved. These may be listed as follows:

1. The student should understand the nature and function

of reference materials; that is, the kinds of information available in various kinds of sources in special subject fields.

He is introduced to general reference works in Freshman English, and, if he does advanced work in one field, he may be introduced to the relevant tools. He probably is not made aware of the fact that such sources are an important part of the literature of every subject field.

2. The student should appreciate the value of the library as a source of information.

This objective may be unteachable, and, in any case, is probably a corollary of the first. But, in the light of the findings of the Public Library Inquiry, it is worth stating separately.

3. The student should understand the nature and function of bibliographical apparatus; that is, the way books, periodicals, government documents, etc., are listed, so that (a) the general reader can find his way around in the literature of a field, and (b) the subject specialist can keep up with new developments.
4. The student should understand the function of literature-searching as a necessary step in problem-solving, as simply the use of an important and available resource.

These two objectives echo our introductory comments on the problem-solving skills currently emphasized in general education and on the acquisition of new knowledge currently emphasized in scholarship. It is probable that only graduate students or, at best, honors students at the undergraduate level achieve them.

5. The student should be able to locate and to select various kinds of library materials from the subject approach, such as:
    a) General background reading matter
    b) Critical and evaluative material, reviews, etc.
    c) Opinion, theory--both sides of controversial issues
    d) Factual data, information, how-to-do-it material, etc.
    e) Materials for illustration, aesthetic enjoyment, etc.

Present undergraduate instruction gives the student

very little experience with the subject approach to the library
and almost no opportunity to select his reading. Here, again,
the objective echoes the recognized importance of providing
skills for tomorrow's problems.

The objectives as stated above result from an attempt
to indicate the implications for library instruction of current
trends in higher education. Much more specific formulations
are necessary before the objectives can be used as guides
to the planning of learning experiences. For recommended
procedures in working out such specific formulations, the
reader is referred to Tyler's Basic Principles of Curriculum
and Instruction. [8]

RELEVANT PRINCIPLES OF LEARNING
AND CURRICULUM CONSTRUCTION

Tyler's booklet is useful, too, for its brief and lucid
presentation of currently accepted principles of learning
relevant not only to the formulation of objectives but also
to the planning of learning experiences. For example, he
says:

> For a given objective to be attained, a student
> must have experiences that give him an opportunity
> to practice the kind of behavior implied by the ob-
> jective. That is to say, if one of the objectives is
> to develop skill in problem solving, this cannot be
> attained unless the learning experiences give the
> student ample opportunity to solve problems.
> Correspondingly, if another objective is to develop
> interest in reading a wide variety of books, this
> objective cannot be attained unless the student
> has opportunity to read a wide variety of books in
> a way that gives him satisfaction. [9]

It should be noted that this statement relates to planned
learning experiences, to curriculum-making. The very existence of the college library on the campus obviously provides
"opportunity" of a sort for the student to learn to use it.
But the student who is never stimulated to go beyond the
reserve-book collection is not getting a planned opportunity
really to use the library. The student who is always told
what to read is not given the opportunity to develop skill in

selecting his own reading. The student who is always given author and title is not given the opportunity to acquire the skill of finding information about a given subject.

Tyler states further that there is "evidence that learnings which are consistent with each other, which are in that sense integrated and coherent, reinforce each other; whereas, learnings which are compartmentalized or are inconsistent with each other require greater time and may actually interfere with each other in learning."[10]

It is no wonder that the brief experience with the Freshman library paper is forgotten in the flood of textbooks, reserve books, required readings, and optional reading lists. Furthermore, when the library paper is presented, as it so often is, as a kind of busy-work exercise, unrelated to content courses--which seem to the student to be the meaningful aspect of college--its inefficiency may be explained by another of the principles expounded by Tyler: "A second general principle is that the learning experiences must be such that the student obtains satisfactions from carrying on the kind of behavior implied by the objectives."[11] Finally, Tyler describes

> a theory of learning called generalization which viewed learning as the development of generalized modes of attack upon problems, generalized modes of reaction to generalized types of situations. Judd and Freeman showed that many types of learning could be explained largely in terms of the learner's perceiving general principles that he might use or developing a general attitude towards the situation or method of attack which he could utilize in meeting new situations.[12]

In this instance we want the learner to perceive general principles which are implicit in the nature of the literature and its organization in all subject fields. The general attitude we want him to develop is one of appreciation and interest in making use of this literature. But one cannot generalize from a single experience. The generalization theory of learning, therefore, calls for repeated experiences in which the learner can perceive similarities. From this perception he develops general principles and attitudes.

Tyler's application of the generalization theory of learning is revealed in his criteria for effective organization of learning experiences:

> There are three major criteria to be met in building an effectively organized group of learning experiences. These are: continuity, sequence, and integration. Continuity refers to the vertical reiteration of major curriculum elements.... Sequence as a criterion emphasizes the importance of having each successive experience build upon the preceding one but to go more broadly and deeply into the matters involved.... Integration refers to the horizontal relationship of curriculum experiences. The organization of these experiences should be such that they help the student increasingly to get a unified view and to unify his behavior in relation to the elements dealt with.[13]

Here we find the primary justification for presenting instruction in library use as an integrated part of content courses. The student's experiences with the library should have continuity throughout the four years of his college education. They should be integrated through repetition of unifying principles in more than one course at each horizontal level. And they should provide sequence through increasing breadth and depth of the knowledge, skills, and attitudes required.

In summary, relevant principles of learning and curriculum construction indicate that we must plan learning experiences (1) which offer opportunities to practice using the library; (2) which are consistent with each other and with our desired objectives; (3) which provide satisfaction to the student; (4) which enable the student to perceive general principles and develop general attitudes; and (5) which are organized to maximize generalized learning.

SUGGESTED KINDS OF LEARNING EXPERIENCES

The assignments suggested here are not unusual in the liberal arts college. Typically, however, they are not deliberately planned to provide the student with experiences in the use of the library. They are not deliberately organized

to increase the student's library knowledge and skills. It
is the library aspect which this paper seeks to emphasize.

Since the first-year college courses are introductory,
an appropriate objective is that of developing skill in the
selection of background reading. In Freshman psychology,
for example, the instructor often gives the student an optional reading list to accompany the text. The purpose of
this optional reading is not specified, nor is the student
guided in selecting from the list. Presumably the instructor
hopes that his list will make up for the gaps in the background of some students, stimulate others to pursue special
interests, and enrich the learning of others. These several
purposes should be specified in class discussion. Individual
differences in background, interest, reading skill, and
purpose should be identified as criteria which govern selection of appropriate reading. Parallel discussion in Freshman
English, identifying individual differences in aesthetic appreciation as well, would produce the desired integration
of the learning.

Even more important would be assignments designed
to provide the student with experiences in locating back
ground reading. A later assignment, again in psychology
and in English, might require the student to prepare his
own optional reading list. He would be directed in the use
of the encyclopedia, yearbooks and annuals, the Book Review Digest, and selective bibliographies. He would be expected to understand and defend the criteria used in
selecting from these sources.

Other courses usually required in the first year might
provide experiences in locating other kinds of materials.
In political science, for example, the student could be required to gather references to material on a current political issue. This material would consist not only of general
background reading but also of factual information, statistics, and opposing theories and opinions. He would use,
with guidance, almanacs and other sources of statistical
data, current periodicals and newspapers, the proceedings
of legislative bodies, etc.

Integration of learning could again be provided
through comparable and concurrent assignments in other
Freshman courses. In physics, for instance, the student

could be required to locate background readings on a hobby, such as photography, for which physics has relevance. In physiology he might be required to locate factual information and divided opinion on a current health problem such as smoking.

Assignments in the second year should be planned to give continuity and sequence. The humanities course in music appreciation, for example, might require the student to plan his own record library. He would again use the individual criteria for selecting, but this time he would apply them to another kind of material, and he would be introduced to other selection aids, the record guides and the record-reviewing periodicals.

In urban sociology the student might be asked to survey an urban community through the library. He would use census reports and other government publications, newspapers and periodicals, reports of social and civic agencies, and so on. He would identify social and political problems and the forces engaged in dealing with them.

At the upper-class level subject specialization begins. Assignments for all subjects cannot be suggested here, but a few general comments are pertinent. In the first place, the student at this level should be ready to develop understanding of the nature and function of the bibliographical apparatus in special subject areas and of the importance of literature-searching in problem-solving. If his experiences in the Freshman and Sophomore years were properly planned, he would have acquired skill in the location and selection of background reading, factual information, controversial opinion, and theory. He would understand the characteristics of reference sources.

Because of this background, the term paper commonly assigned in upper-class courses can be more meaningful from the library point of view. In the first place, the instructor can use a subject or topic approach and still be confident that the student will be able to locate sound and relevant materials. In the second place, he can justify the requirement that the term paper be supported by a better bibliography than is usually provided.

Another kind of assignment would be equally appro-

priate to this level of college work and would be even more
valuable as a library experience. This is the bibliographical review. It would require the student to locate, select,
describe, and evaluate the literature available on a fairly
limited topic. He would need to make intensive use of the
bibliographical apparatus and organize his findings into a
coherent presentation.

Finally, it should be noted that colleges are aware of
the danger of overspecialization at the upper-class level
and that they guard against this by requiring students to
take advanced courses in more than one field. This re
quirement should provide the opportunity for emphasis upon
the general characteristics and function of reference and
bibliographical sources. This opportunity should not be
lost through haphazard planning of library experiences.

SUGGESTED IMPLEMENTATION OF THE PROGRAM

At this point the reasoning implicit or stated in the
discussion above may be summarized.

Competence in the use of the library is one of the
liberal arts. It deserves recognition and acceptance as such
in the college curriculum. It is, furthermore, a complex of
knowledge, skills, and attitudes not to be acquired in any
one course but functionally related to the content of many.
It should, therefore, be integrated into the total curriculum. But it cannot be so integrated until the faculty as
a whole is ready to recognize the validity of its claim and
to implement this recognition through regularly established
procedures of curriculum development. Logically, then, the
faculty as a body, or through its appropriate committees,
must implement the objective. It is probably true, on the
other hand, that at present the college librarian is more
conscious of the inadequacy of present instruction than is
any other member of the faculty. Furthermore, he has the
advantage of a broad perspective on the whole curriculum.

For these reasons, the librarian should accept the responsibility of initiating the program, remaining constantly
aware, at the same time, that ultimate implementation must
come through the teaching faculty. In other words, the
librarian must convince the faculty that library instruction

is necessary; he must educate the faculty on the potential role of the library and assist it in planning instruction. And he must do all this with consummate skill and tact. These considerations underlie the suggested steps presented below.

1. The librarian should discuss with sympathetic and library-minded instructors the problem of students' incompetence in the use of the library. He should provide as much objective evidence as is available.

2. If possible, he should persuade some of these instructors to set up experimental assignments which involve library use of the kind desired.

3. He should work with these few instructors individually and as closely as possible in planning learning experiences. He should make the material and personnel resources of the library available as generously as possible.

4. He should use the opportunity afforded in this co-operative work to stress the general values inherent in library competence.

5. With the help of instructors thus oriented to the idea, he should draw up an analysis of the problem and a proposed program for its solution.

6. Again with the support of the "educated" instructors, he should present his statement through the library committee, if there is one, to the curriculum committee.

The steps suggested so far are designed to produce a group of faculty members who have become adherents to the cause of library instruction and who, furthermore, understand what library competence is and what learning experiences are effective in helping the student to acquire it. (It should be understood, incidentally, that this process will be a slow one.) In the succeeding steps, this group may be expected to take over the initiating role of the librarian.

7. The curriculum committee, basing its work on the librarian's presentation, will prepare and present to the faculty a statement which sets forth the basic objectives

of library instruction and a proposed program for its implementation in curricular planning.

8. If the faculty as a whole agrees, it will, perhaps,
set up a special committee to formulate specific objectives
and to indicate specific courses in the curriculum which
might provide for them. (Actual units of instruction must
be individual, but the faculty as a whole or through its
curriculum committee would agree on objectives.)

9. The librarian, or members of the library staff as
assigned, will work closely with individual members of the
faculty in planning and preparing learning experiences wherever they appear in the curriculum.

CONCLUSION

This paper has presented an analysis of the objectives
of instruction in the use of the library, some examples of
possible ways to achieve these objectives, and some suggested
steps to implement an over-all program. These are not to be
considered as final answers but rather as suggestions regarding the kind of thinking which must be involved in
finding answers. Instruction in the use of the library has
been described as one of the "persisting problems [which]
need[s] vigorous new attack."[14] This paper does not lead
the attack, but it may join others in supplying some of the
ammunition.

NOTES

1. Henry M. Wriston, The Nature of a Liberal
College (Appleton, Wis.: Lawrence College Press, 1937),
pp. 64-65.
2. William Vernon Jackson, "The Interpretation of
Public Services," Library Trends III (October, 1954,
188-94. A few universities offer advanced courses, but the
practice does not appear to be widespread.
3. Dan Lacy, "Tradition and Change: The Role of
the College Library Today," Essential Books I (October,
1955), 29.
4. Ibid., p. 30.

5. Stanley E. Gwynn, "The Liberal Arts Function of the University Library," Library Quarterly XXIV (October, 1954), 316.

6. Harvie Branscomb, Teaching with Books (Chicago: Association of American Colleges, 1940).

7. Jackson, op. cit., p. 192.

8. Ralph W. Tyler, Basic Principles of Curriculum and Instruction (Chicago: University of Chicago Press, 1950).

9. Ibid., p. 42.

10. Ibid., p. 27.

11. Ibid., p. 43.

12. Ibid., p. 27.

13. Ibid., p. 55.

14. Jackson, op. cit., p. 188, quoting K. J. Brough, Scholar's Workshop ("Illinois Contributions to Librarianship," No. 5 [Urbana: University of Illinois Press, 1953]), p. 175.

The Methodology and Results of the Monteith Pilot Project

Patricia B. Knapp

Knapp reports in this article on the opportunity to implement many of the ideas she put forth in the previous
selection. In 1959 Wayne State University, with assistance
from the Ford Foundation, established Monteith College as
an experimental undergraduate college within the university.
As director of the Monteith Library Project, Knapp used
anthropological and sociological methods to study the implementation of problem-solving techniques in undergraduate
student use of the academic library. For two years, from
the spring of 1960 to the spring of 1962, Knapp and her
colleagues studied the development and adoption of assignments involving library competence.

The results of the Monteith Library Project were mixed.
Knapp and her colleagues successfully implemented only a
few of her ideas, and they met with resistance from both
students and teaching faculty. Nevertheless, the insights
she provided regarding the roles and values of librarians,
teaching faculty, and students are a major contribution to
library use instruction theory. A generation later, in "A
Century of Bibliographic Instruction: The Historical
Claim to Professional and Academic Legitimacy," College and
Research Libraries 43 (May 1982): 192-198, Frances L.
Hopkins placed in perspective the significance of Knapp's
contribution in concluding that theoretical progress in library
use instruction had been "painfully slow" since Knapp's
work of the early 1960s.

Knapp later wrote a full report of the project under
the title The Monteith College Library Experiment (New York:
Scarecrow Press, 1966) and several additional articles on the

topic including "The Monteith Library Project: An Experiment in Library-College Relationship," College and Research
Libraries 21 (July 1961): 256-263; and "The Meaning of the
Monteith College Library Program for Library Education,"
The Journal of Education for Librarianship 6 (Fall 1965):
117-127. Readers interested in Knapp's proposals for overcoming some of the difficulties encountered during the
Monteith Library Project are referred to her article "Guidelines for Bucking the System: A System for Moving Toward
the Ideal of the Undergraduate Library as a Teaching Instrument," Drexel Library Quarterly 7 (July/October 1971):
217-221.

Knapp later served as professor of library science at
Wayne State University; she was a prolific writer and speaker
on library use instruction until her death in 1972 at the age
of fifty-seven.

Reprinted with permission from Library Trends, vol. 13,
no. 1, July, 1964, pp. 84-102. © 1964 The Board of
Trustees of the University of Illinois.

•   •   •

This paper reports on only one of several aspects of the
Monteith Pilot Project which has interest as an innovation
in library research. Other aspects of the research will be
covered in the final report to the Cooperative Research
Program, which is now nearing completion.[1] The one aspect to be discussed here, and discussed in some detail,
is the analysis of the social structure in which the Project
was carried on.

Research in librarianship draws upon the methods and
techniques developed in other fields and applies them to
library problems. The Monteith research reported here uses
the methods of anthropology and sociology. There is nothing
new, of course, in the use of sociological methods in library
research. The social survey technique, which is borrowed
from sociology, has probably been used more than any other
in the study of library problems. But the methods used in
the sociological analysis of processes in a single institution

have rarely been applied in library investigation. Such
methods were clearly called for in the Monteith Pilot Project.

The long-range goal of the Monteith Library Program
is that of helping undergraduate students attain a high
level of competence in the use of the library. In the pilot
phase of our program we proposed to concern ourselves
not with obtaining evidence on the validity of library competence as an objective of undergraduate education nor with
the potential contribution of such competence to the achievement of other educational objectives. We were interested
in learning what we could about library competence, about
what it involves, about what we mean when we use the term.
At this stage of our work, however, we were content to
limit ourselves to very tentative investigations into these
questions.

We started our work with the conviction that students
attain library competence, however it is defined, only
when they actually use the library and only when their use
of it is significantly related to what they consider the real
business of college, that is, to courses of substantive content. Since it is only through the teaching faculty that
library experiences can be related to regular course work,
we undertook to set up a social structure in which librarians could work with teaching faculty in developing a curriculum in which student use of the library was an integral
element. The primary objective of our research, therefore,
was to focus our attention firmly upon the relations between
faculty and librarians as they changed and developed
through the two years of the Pilot Project.

The analysis of social structure was the responsibility,
exclusively, of our project research analyst Carol Ballingall,
an anthropologist who has had much training and experience
in sociological research. She is a member of the teaching
staff of the social sciences division of Monteith College,
having served in that capacity half-time while the Library
Project was in operation. It is Ballingall's analysis that is
reported here, but the report, itself, is my own. It stems
from reading, from discussions with Ballingall and with
other colleagues at Monteith, and from my own experience.
I have assumed that librarians would be interested in the observations, the reflections, and the comments of a librarian,
a nonspecialist in the social sciences.

First, however, some background information is necessary. Monteith College, which was founded in 1959 with
assistance from the Ford Foundation, is one of the eleven
colleges of Wayne State University in Detroit. It is a small
college, admitting less than 400 freshmen each year. At
present the enrollment is about 700 and the faculty numbers
about 30. The basic courses in the Monteith curriculum are
required of every Monteith student. They take about half
of the student's time through his four years in college; the
other half he spends on his pre-professional, specialized,
or advanced studies. A student planning to enter the
medical school, for example, begins his pre-medical work in
his freshman year and continues it concurrently with his
Monteith courses through the rest of his undergraduate
career. The Monteith curriculum begins in the freshman
year with a year-and-a-half course sequence in the social
sciences and a two-year course sequence in the natural
sciences. A year-and-a-half course sequence in the humanities begins in the middle of the sophomore year. A
colloquium in the senior year draws on all three areas, and
a substantial senior essay is required of every student.

The teaching staff of the college is organized into
three divisions, each of which is responsible for one of
the three basic course sequences. The courses are staff-
planned and staff-taught. Each member of a staff shares
in the divisional responsibility for the two lectures and is
individually responsible for the two discussion sections presented each week in each course. The discussion sections
are limited to twelve students in the freshman year, but
they increase in size through each class level. It is a
stated aim of the college to foster in the student an increasing capacity for independent study. Thus the freshman
receives a great deal of faculty attention, but he is expected
to work more and more on his own as he proceeds through
college. Every student is required to take the final segment of one of the basic courses without attending the discussion sections, though he may attend the lectures, and
students are generally encouraged to take any course independently if they feel competent to do so.

All of these features of Monteith College made it seem
an ideal setting in which to develop an integrated program
of library instruction and course work. Because the faculty
was new, we would not have to overcome old habits.

Because the courses were to be staff-planned and staff-taught, we were not obliged to deal with instructors individually. We were in on the ground floor as the actual planning of new courses began. And we benefited from the commitment to the idea of independent study since surely this implied an important role for the library. (It should be understood, by the way, that Monteith has no library of its own. The students use the general facilities, including the libraries, of the University.)

Planning for the Library Project began as soon as faculty members began to assemble in the summer of 1959. A proposal to the Cooperative Research Branch of the Office of Education was approved in March 1960, and the pilot project began officially in April. The proposal called for a project staff consisting of a director, serving half-time, a research analyst, also half-time, a full-time project librarian and a number of graduate students, who were to work under the supervision of the project librarian to provide bibliographical services to the faculty. All three principal members of the project staff were to participate in the course-planning deliberations of the three divisional teaching staffs of the college. We were to begin in the fall of 1960 by working with the social sciences division. Beginning in the spring and continuing into the fall semester of 1961, we were to work also with the natural sciences and the humanities divisions. Thus the action phase of the project was to extend through three semesters, ending in the spring of 1962. A fourth semester was to be devoted to analysis and reporting.

The General Nature of Social Structure Research

In essence, social structure research involves the examination of a particular situation or institution in the light of certain potentially relevant models which may serve to highlight the many values and activities perceived.[2] The models serve as convenient approximations which allow the researcher to grasp a given situation rapidly and to categorize it properly. Once the researcher has found the appropriate category, he knows what kinds of behavior he can expect to observe. After a remarkably short period of actual contact, he is able to frame questions which will bring pertinent answers

about the characteristics of the particular situation he is
analyzing.

This kind of research derives from both sociology and
anthropology, or, more precisely, from an area of study in
which there is considerable overlapping between the two.
As sociology, the study falls into the category of institutional
sociology and, more specifically, into that branch of institutional sociology which is concerned with the study of formal
organizations.[3] As anthropology, the study falls into the
area of social anthropology of the structural type. The primary discipline of our research analyst is social anthropology.
Her methods, therefore, were inevitably shaped by certain
characteristics of this field.

Anthropology is holistic; it strives to see a social
unit as a whole. The anthropologist most often uses non-
quantitative methods. He looks for "regularities," "configu-
ration," and "pattern" in the whole. Most anthropologists
attempt to approach the social unit without perceptions.
Some make a point of avoiding hypotheses to be tested.[4]
They strive for an "inside view," distorted as little as possible by their own personal and cultural biases. For these
reasons, the anthropologist is inclusive in his gathering of
data. He attempts to encompass everything in his notes on
observation, in his recording of interviews, in his collection
of artifacts and documents. However, his perception and
consequently, his selection of data, is inevitably influenced
by concepts which have theoretical weight, concepts which
have proved meaningful in anthropological studies. His
analysis, moreover, involves a great deal of systematic
working and reworking of the data collected.[5]

The Academic Institution as a Formal Organization

The study of formal organizations has been much influenced
by the classic statement of Max Weber on the nature of
bureaucracy.[6] The features of bureaucracy as Weber
enumerates them include a clear-cut division of labor and a
high degree of specialization, the organization of offices
into a hierarchical structure, behavior governed in accordance with formal rules and procedures, the expectation of
an impersonal relationship between officials and clients, and
a career orientation of staff.

Like practically all modern large-scale organizations, colleges are bureaucratically administered, and a small college imbedded in a huge university faces not only its own bureaucratic administrative structure but also the bureaucratic demands of the giant institution of which it is a part. In the academic institution, however, the tendency toward bureaucracy is always tempered by the ancient tradition of the university as a community of scholars. In Monteith, moreover, this tradition was deliberately emphasized; so that we find all the features characteristic of the bureaucracy considerably modified in this setting. So, for instance, while a division of labor and a degree of specialization is reflected in the organization of the teaching staff into three divisions, there is no departmentalization according to discipline and interdivisional studies are fostered. The de-emphasis on hierarchy is apparent in the fact that the policy-making Administrative Council is made up of the chairmen of the three divisions, each of whom is in close contact with his respective teaching staff. Very little hierarchical structure has developed within the divisional staffs partly because practically all instructors started at the same time and partly because the development of a staff-taught course fostered a sense of colleagueship. Bureaucratic rules and procedures do govern some Monteith activities, but such formalities are likely to have emanated from the bureaucracy of the University rather than from within the College, where flexibility and rule-by-consensus are cherished.

The impersonality of the official-client relationship is less likely to appear in the academic institution than in such bureaucracies as the unemployment service or the social service agency. It is particularly minimized at Monteith because the College has always been committed to the aim of creating a small-college atmosphere. The career orientation of the college instructor generally involves a strong identification with a specialized field. At Monteith the interdisciplinary staff group pulls in the opposite direction. Relatively few Monteith instructors have even attempted to make contacts with their opposite numbers in the College of Liberal Arts. Thus the Monteith situation has strong collegial aspects which might recall earlier patterns of the English common room where every member was a peer, where tolerance of eccentricity did not exclude vigorous debate of ideas, where each person acted when outside the common room

as an independent, autonomous scholar, responsible only to
the judgment of his peers and of history.

But Monteith College exists, nevertheless, as a formal
organization. The formal organization is the context in
which the college teacher must function. Like the doctor,
who needs a hospital, the academic intellectual needs the
university to provide him with students, classrooms, laboratories, a library, an office, and a salary. He must give up
some of the freedom of action of the free-lance artist or
writer, though not so much as the civil servant or the technician. He must find acceptance among his peers who
expect him to be independent and autonomous. He must
regulate his activity to the extent that his students have a
reasonable expectation of seeing him at class time, hearing
his thoughts on roughly the areas he is scheduled to cover,
receiving his criticism and evaluation of their performance.
But how the man teaches, the standards he sets for the
performance of his students, these are matters ordinarily
thought of as entirely his own business. Only extraordinary
infractions of expectations will be noticed by peers, who will,
in any case, tend to defend his, and potentially their own,
individuality and style as a matter of academic freedom.

In short, each of the three models is partly reflected
in the Monteith situation: (1) the model of the bureaucracy;
(2) the model of the collegial organization, and (3) the model
of the free and independent teacher. The Library Project
faced the challenge of coming to terms with this hybrid
creature. Our structural analysis reveals the lessons we
learned through two years of trial and error before we
finally achieved a moderate acceptance.

Analysis of the Monteith Structure

The analysis of our experiences in the Pilot Project
was based on three kinds of data: notes on observation,
transcriptions of interviews, and transcriptions of tape-
recorded reminiscences. The research analyst kept detailed
notes on her observation of every formal and informal
meeting which involved project staff members along with
faculty individuals or groups. Three series of interviews
with the faculty were conducted, one at the beginning, one
in the middle, and one at the end of the Project. In addition,

Ballingall and I each dictated a lengthy reminiscence, about forty typewritten pages, covering the entire period of the Project. We attempted to recall our own changing views with regard to it as well as our estimate of our relationships with each individual faculty member at every stage in the enterprise.

This voluminous body of data, approximately four file-cabinet drawers full, was systematically examined and re-examined by the research analyst as she looked for regularities and deviations in the many patterns of relationship which appeared in the Monteith structure. This analysis resulted in the identification of four characteristics which seem to have been particularly significant for the development of the Library Project. Each of these characteristics is related to concepts implied in the discussion, above, of the academic institution as a formal organization, and of Monteith as a particularly hybrid species.

The Dual Role Concept at Monteith. The concept of role is essential in the analysis of any social system, but it has a particular flavor in the consideration of a structure which is at all bureaucratic. In the bureaucracy, role is associated with office rather than with person. The concept of role implies the idea that people behave the way other people expect them to behave. An individual's behavior reflects not only such general roles as those determined by his age, his sex, his family, his social class, his occupation, etc., but also his membership in this, that, or another group, his "place" in the group, and the duties and responsibilities, the ideas and sentiments, in short, the expectations attached to that place. In this sense, an individual's identity is conferred upon him by the social definition of the behavior appropriate to a particular group, whether that group is defined by an office held in a bureaucracy or by membership in a collegial organization.

The concept of role does not imply conscious play-acting, however; it refers to a largely unreflective acceptance of the socially conferred identity. Furthermore, behavior in accordance with a role not only expresses the ideas and feelings which are consistent with the role, but produces them. The individual identifies with his role.

Many individuals in the Monteith College structure carry

responsibilities in two areas and consequently the dual role
is accepted as a normal pattern.   An individual who has a
dual role acts in any given social situation in accordance
with his perception of the expectations attaching to one or
the other of his two roles.   The fact that the dual role pattern was accepted in the Monteith structure meant that
usually the "others" expected the individual to be able to
separate his two roles in his thinking and behavior.

    The Concept of "Social" Distance.   The Monteith struc-
ture is marked by relatively little social distance between
individuals at various levels in the hierarchy, but by considerable social distance between different groups at the same
level, especially between the three divisional teaching staffs.
The concept of social distance is related to the familiar concept of "status" which is associated with the view of bureaucracy as a system which prescribes and defines relationships
in an organization which is hierarchical and in which functions
are highly specialized.   But social distance also implies distance on the horizontal, the socially, or organizationally defined separation which is a factor in the ability of individuals
and groups at the same status level to communicate with one
another.   Thus it applies equally well to the colleague-group
relationships which characterize the three divisions of the
teaching staff.

    The Divisional Organization and Group Allegiance.   The
organization of the teaching staff into three divisions has had
a crucial significance upon the group organization of the
College, since each staff has developed distinctive ways of
organizing itself, assigning responsibilities, and providing
for internal communication and coordination.   The "group,"
we are concerned with here is a task-oriented group, not a
primary group like family or close friends.   But neither is it
simply an aggregate of individuals who fall into a particular
classification.   The concept implies not only a common task
and a real interaction in dealing with this task; it implies
also a more or less cohesive body which develops its own
style of working, sets its own boundaries and responsibilities, and defines the roles of its members.   Like all groups
in the sociological sense, it is a mechanism for the control
and coordination of behavior.

    Ambivalence Between Roles.   The Monteith instructor
must deal with a degree of ambivalence between his role as

a member of a staff, sharing the responsibility for a whole
course, and his role as an instructor, individually responsible for his own discussion sections. This characteristic
of the Monteith structure is illuminated by the concept of
the "reference group." The "reference group" does not
mean necessarily an actual interacting group of people; it
does mean those groups or individuals to whom one refers
for standards of value and behavior.[7] The concept is related to the concepts of role and status, since the group to
which one refers for standards is likely to be determined
by one's own role and status in a given social situation,
or more accurately, by one's perception of that role and
status. As indicated, each staff became a powerful reference
group for every member in it. But it was not the only
reference group. A chronic problem of the service organization, of which the college is an example, is that of the professional's ambivalence between his own definition of his
client's "best interests," and the client's definition, or, in
other words, the client's wishes.[8]

In the Monteith structure, the instructor is responsible
with his colleagues for total course planning and for planning
and presenting lectures, but he meets individually with each
of his discussion sections and is solely responsible for what
occurs in them. His ambivalence reflects the tensions between
the collegial model of the staff and the model of the free and
independent teacher. It also reflects the instructor's reference group conflicts. In deciding what is in the "best interests" of the students, he can refer to the definition of the
staff, the definition of the students or the definition of his
own internalized standards which have been set by such
"others" as former teachers, former colleagues, the "teaching
profession," or the "scientific community."

Stages in the Development of the Library Project

The Pre-Project Stage. The four characteristics of the
Monteith structure which have been discussed--the dual role
pattern, social distance, the division of the teaching staff
into three divisions, and the instructor's staff-discussion
section ambivalence--were all of crucial importance for the
Library Project at each stage in its development. From the
outset I have had a dual role at Monteith. I was employed
originally as a half-time executive secretary for the College.

My second role was that of emissary, or salesman, if you like, from the Wayne State University Library. Dr. Flint Purdy, Director of the Library, assigned me half-time to the task of developing and gaining acceptance of an integrated library program. As executive secretary my role was clearly subordinate. I was responsible for implementing policies determined by the Administrative Council. Because of the lack of social distance in the vertical structure of Monteith, however, I had no hesitance about campaigning for my ideas to my superiors, and I experienced no difficulty in getting a hearing and support for the proposed program.

As soon as the faculty of the social sciences division arrived on the scene and began to meet in course-planning sessions, the chairman of the division invited me to meet with them. Because of the pressure of other duties, however, it was impossible for me to do so regularly. I soon found that when I was there my presence was accepted with grace and friendliness, but I was not a part of the cohesive interacting group which they quickly became. In short, I was not accepted into full membership.

During the first year of the College, the year in which the Library Project was being planned and the proposal to the Cooperative Research Program formulated, we presented two library assignments. For a number of reasons, students found one of these assignments both difficult and burdensome. They expressed their dissatisfaction forcibly in their discussion sections, thus bringing to the surface the instructor's reference group ambivalence. As a member of the staff the instructor had, along with his colleagues, agreed to the assignment. As an individual, responsible for a discussion section, he faced a number of rebellious students. To some of the instructors the rebellion seemed justified; the assignment was interpreted as meaningless busywork, and the students became the effective reference group. The lack of social distance within the divisional staff, moreover, made it possible for student dissatisfaction and the instructor's acceptance of validity of this dissatisfaction to be quickly and effectively communicated to the divisional chairman.

The First Stage. As the project began officially in the spring of 1960, then, it had already felt the effect of the four structural factors, though, of course, we were not consciously aware of these characteristics at the time.

Gilbert Donahue was appointed project librarian, and was expected to serve the Project full time. But he also had two roles, in that he joined me in participating with the teaching faculty in course planning while at the same time he was assigned the responsibility for supervising the work of the bibliographical assistants. These two roles were complementary in the sense that each was concerned with furthering the aims of the faculty, rather than with shaping them. As supervisor of bibliographical services, he supplied skilled assistance; as participant in course planning, he presented the library as means for achieving objectives determined by the faculty. Similarly my two roles were parallel, if not complementary. Both as executive secretary and as director on the Project, I saw myself as implementing rather than determining faculty goals.

There was the possibility of conflict, however, in the two roles carried by Ballingall, our research analyst. As a member of the teaching staff in the social sciences division, she carried her full share of responsibility for course planning, for lectures, and for leading her own discussion sections. As a research analyst on the Project, on the other hand, she was expected to stand a bit apart to observe and analyze the relationship between the faculty and the Project. Probably her experience as an anthropologist led her to accept without hesitation this dual role. The anthropologist is accustomed to dealing with a situation in which he participates in the daily life of the community he is studying while at the same time he maintains the necessary detachment of the scientist.

The dual role pattern involved even our bibliographical assistants. Initially these students were assigned to work for individual members of the social sciences staff. They were expressly given the responsibility of interpreting the individual needs and demands of the instructor to the library on the one hand, and the necessarily bureaucratic regulations and procedures of the library to the faculty, on the other. They were expected to work closely under the supervision of the project librarian, not only in order that what they produced would profit from his professional knowledge and skills but also in order that they might demonstrate the value of library competence. In this role we expected them to be good-will ambassadors for the Project. In their role

of assisting the faculty, we expected them to adopt the
values and style of the academic researcher.

Here, however, the dual role pattern failed. Almost
every assistant formed a fairly firm one-to-one attachment
with his faculty principal. Most of them avoided the supervision and guidance of the project librarian. They were
reluctant to report to the research analyst on the nature of
the tasks the faculty asked them to perform or on their own
relationships with the faculty. Actually, some instructors
used the assistants merely as messengers, some treated them
like apprentices, and some gave them a sort of junior colleague role. But however they were treated, they saw themselves not as representatives of the Library Project but as
research assistants for the faculty. Perhaps this was the
only model of behavior with which they were familiar.

There was no notable difference in the operation of
the social distance factor on the Project during the first
semester. But there was a new development in the effect
of the factor of the group organization. During the period
before the Project started, the social sciences staff worked
together as a total group. In the fall of 1960, however,
having grown from 10 or 11 to 13 or 14 in number, the staff
decided to break into small committees for preliminary planning of various segments of the course. The three principal
Library Project staff members, therefore, spread themselves
among these committees. Meeting with groups of two or three
or four, we were able to get more library assignments accepted
than either before or after this period. But the assignments
were not very successful. One difficulty had to do with the
fact that three or four people can discuss informally rather
than call a formal meeting. Since our offices were not close
to the faculty offices, Donahue and I were often simply not
around when informal gatherings took place. We were frequently not fully aware of all the considerations involved in
the committee's plans. Consequently, some of the assignments we proposed, though accepted, were not really in tune
with the units to which they were expected to contribute.

Another difficulty which stemmed from the changed organization of the social sciences staff arose from the fact
that the total staff did not feel fully committed to the plans
developed in committees, plans which did not reflect the
thinking of the staff as a whole. As a result, individual

instructors worked quite autonomously in their discussion
sections, emphasizing those aspects of a given unit with
which they felt sympathy, de-emphasizing other aspects.
The aspect most often de-emphasized was the library assignment. The chain of relationships might be summarized
as follows: With the increasing cohesiveness of the committees, the solidarity of the total staff decreased. As the
solidarity of the staff decreased, its power as a reference
group diminished, and students or "generalized others"
gained reference group power proportionately.

The Second Stage. During the second semester of
our operation, which was from February to June 1961, all
four of the structural factors had a negative influence on
the development of the Project. It was at this time that
we extended our operation to include not only the social
sciences division but the natural sciences and the humanities divisions as well. We provided bibliographical assistants
for the instructors, and we began to meet with them in
their course-planning sessions.

And now we began to meet lack of acceptance of our
dual role pattern. As executive secretary, I had by this
time become an ex officio, non-voting member of the Administrative Council of the College, which is made up of the
three instructional divisions. I was never conscious of this
making any difference in my role as director of the Library
Project, but evidence later appeared that some instructors
saw me primarily as a member of the reputedly powerful
Council. My role as a librarian, attempting to serve the
instructional goals of the faculty, or, at worst, trying to gain
acceptance for my own library goals, was quite overshadowed.
Similarly, as we began to work with the faculty in the two
additional divisions, all three Project staff members were
seen not so much as representatives of the Library Project
but rather as social scientists or quasi-social scientists
meddling in the business of natural scientists and humanists.

In a sense, this view was justified. Ballingall is,
indeed, a social scientist and Donahue and I, by training
and inclination, probably merit the label "quasi-social
scientist." Nevertheless, in our Library Project roles we
did not see ourselves as representing the social scientists.
We were, in fact, painfully conscious of the fact that the
librarians among us had never won full membership in the

social sciences staff. We were unprepared to find, therefore, that the Library Project had come to be identified not as a general educational effort, but as a social science enterprise.

Now these comments on our relationship with the humanities and natural sciences divisions should not convey the impression that we or the Library Project were completely rejected. I should make it clear that I am describing neither outward behavior nor individual relationships. The natural sciences staff was gracious and friendly in inviting us to participate in its deliberations. What I have tried to express, rather, is the general, perhaps largely unconscious, attitude of the "ideal-typical" instructor. Certain individuals on each staff were most sympathetic to both our aims and our methods. They really acted as sponsors for the Project. And some instructors were always willing to give us a chance to try out our ideas, whether or not they found these ideas persuasive to begin with. Our experience during these months, nevertheless, indicated a breakdown of acceptance of the dual role pattern. It reflected, furthermore, the considerable horizontal social distance between the three staffs.

The group organization factor created additional difficulties for the Project in the second semester. As we continued to have trouble relating ourselves to the subgroup organization of the social sciences staff, we were now faced with a similar sub-group organization in the other two divisions. The natural sciences staff had from the very beginning tended to organize itself into subgroups based upon disciplinary specialization. The humanities staff, consisting of only four members, had no need of such subdivision. On the other hand, the three rank-and-file members often gathered informally. The chairman of this division was also Director of the College and was frequently occupied with general administrative duties. Formal meetings of the humanities staff, therefore, came more and more to serve the purpose merely of crystallizing the results of informal discussion. The formal meetings of the natural sciences staff served similarly to crystallize the plans developed in the specialist committees. When the Library Project personnel participated in these meetings, therefore, we found that we could contribute little. The library assignments we suggested were likely to be out of tune with prior discussion. We succeeded in getting acceptance of one assignment in the humanities

course and one in the natural sciences course, but neither
of these was successfully carried out.

As we ended the second semester of the Project, our
morale was, understandably, at low ebb. We felt ineffec-
tual and rejected. Naturally enough, we began to turn to
one another for comfort and support. Eventually, as we
became increasingly aware of our own solidarity as a group,
we found ourselves able to take a more constructive approach
to our work.

The Third Stage. During the summer of 1961, we devoted major attention to analyzing and discussing our
experiences thus far and to developing plans for what was
to be the last semester of the Project's operation. By the
end of the summer, we had decided upon three important
changes in our organizational structure. We dropped the
attempt to meet regularly with the three divisional staffs.
Instead we asked one member of the natural sciences staff
and one member of the humanities staff to serve as Library
Project representative for his colleagues. Our research
analyst continued her dual role in relationship to the social
sciences staff. These two teaching staff representatives met
with the three Project staff members to consider the objectives and methods of the library program in general. We
worked with them individually in making detailed plans for
assignments in their respective areas. Our new structure
preserved the dual role pattern--in fact, it extended it--but
it also recognized the importance of full membership in the
interacting faculty group responsible for course planning.
We felt that by giving the dual role responsibility to the
instructor we would make it possible for library assignments
to be in tune with the objectives and pedagogical style of
the faculty and to be presented at the crucial decision-
making moments in the course-planning process.

The second change in our organizational structure was
the discontinuation of the individual assignment of bibliographical assistants to instructors. We decreased the number of
assistants and pooled those remaining into a group who would
work directly under the Project librarian. Requests for
bibliographical service were channeled through him to which-
ever assistant he thought best qualified for the particular
job, though for a long-term or highly specialized project he
might send the assistant to work directly with an instructor.

All of the assistants were given a carefully worked out
training program which included a series of bibliographical
problem tasks. As a result of these changes the bibliographic assistants became a highly cohesive group, a group which
clearly identified itself with the Library Project. By the end
of the term, as their employment by the Project was about
to terminate, some of them felt so competent that they took
tentative and, as it turned out, inconclusive steps toward
setting themselves up as a bibliographical search service.
Five of the fifteen, incidentally, decided to become librarians.
Two of these, I believe, are now in library school. In
general, this new organization of our bibliographical services
departed from the dual role pattern, but it created a loyal,
cohesive group, capable of producing high quality work.

The third major change in our structure was in the
presentation of assignments to students. The assignments,
themselves, were considerably different from those we had
tried previously. Our experience with previous assignments
had taught us a good deal about what kinds of library instruction and experiences are appropriate for college work.
In our new assignments we found ourselves at last with
a product to sell that the faculty would buy. (This change,
of course, was a crucial factor in the acceptance we managed
to achieve in the last semester of the Project. But it is
not a structural change, so it is not pertinent to the present
discussion.) The structural change we now put into effect
was that of having librarians take an active part in the
presentation of assignments.

We had originally assumed that the librarians should
remain as much in the background as possible and had left
the implementation of library assignments to the faculty.
Now, beginning in the fall of 1961, every assignment, once
accepted by the teaching staff, was presented by and discussed under the leadership of one or another of the three
members of the Library Project staff. We made every effort
to see that each instructor demonstrated his support by
participating fully in discussion of the assignment and by
showing that he considered the assignment an essential part
of the student's experience. This change in procedure reinforced the power of the divisional staff as reference
group because our very presence in the discussion section
represented a staff decision. At the same time, the new
procedure gave us an opportunity to contribute to students'

thinking about the assignment and thus to influence the
standards that they, as a reference group, presented.

As the final semester of the operational phase of the
Pilot Project ended in February 1962, we felt that we had
finally arrived at a workable social structure for our purposes. In the future of the Monteith Library Program, we
plan to maintain this organization. A review of this structure may serve to summarize the findings just presented.

The organization calls for the dual role pattern
which is accepted in the Monteith structure, but by shifting
the dual role assignment to a representative of each of the
three staffs, it attempts to ensure that each role is fully
accepted. The instructor who serves as a Library Project
representative will have already been accepted to full membership in his staff-colleague group. We know from our
own experience that he will have no difficulty attaining full
membership in the smaller and intensively interacting Library
Project staff group. We are reasonably certain that in this
group he will acquire a more sophisticated view of what
real knowledge and skill in the use of library resources
involves.

The new arrangement also recognizes the impossibility
of having two or three librarians participate effectively
in the dispersed subgroup organization which exists in each
of the three divisions. Our faculty representative will have
a much better opportunity to do so. He should find it possible to play the role of Library Project sponsor at those
crucial points of interaction when presuppositions are being
expressed, when ideas are taking shape, when plans have
not yet crystallized.

The participation of an instructor from each division,
together with the Library Project staff, in discussions per-
taining to one element common to all three course sequences
may help to bridge the social distance between the three
staffs. It should, in any case, lessen the significance of
this factor in the development of the Library Project, since
no one identified with one staff will be put in the position
of having to concern himself directly with the teaching
plans and procedures of the others. And finally, our new
procedures for presenting assignments to students helps to

overcome the problem of the instructor's reference group
ambivalence.

Implications for Library Research

The significance of the structural analysis of the Monteith
Library Project as a sociological study must be determined
by others. Its significance as a demonstration of the value
of applying sociological-anthropological concepts and methods
to the study of library problems seems to me unquestionable.
The insights associated with this type of approach were
manifestly crucial in helping us at Monteith to understand
and overcome the difficulties we encountered in the Pilot
Project.

Such insights would probably be similarly useful in
helping us understand, and perhaps overcome, some of the
problems we face in other parts of the library world. Think,
for example, of the academic library as an organizational
element in the overall structure of the college or university.
By its very nature, the library has a much more sharply
hierarchical organization than the college, which strives to
carry on the tradition of the "community of peers." In such
a situation, there is a natural tendency for the library to
feel uncomfortable unless it adopts the mode of social control
which prevails in the larger institution. But the pattern of
professional peer group control may be meaningless in the
steeply hierarchical organization of the library. It may, indeed, jeopardize the efficiency of an organization whose
operation depends so heavily upon the coordination of a
great many and diverse activities, upon reasonably uniform
rules and procedures. On the other hand, the library suffers from the tendency of every bureaucracy to value its
rules and procedures for their own sake, losing sight of
the ends for which they were established. A strong identification with the interest of the client, that is, the faculty
and students, as defined by the profession rather than by
the organization, may serve to guard against over-bureau-
cratization. This dilemma for the academic library is
revealed through the use of social science concepts.

The field of library cooperation offers another example
in which such concepts might be illuminating. In the state
of Michigan, we have found that librarians of small,

substandard libraries are often reluctant to support a state plan which calls for regional cooperation. This reluctance can be understood as stemming from the difficulty that such librarians have in identifying with the standards and values determined by the profession. These isolated librarians are likely to receive status and recognition locally from the patrons they serve. Seeing their situation in this light, we might be less likely to embark on educational or promotional programs to overcome their reluctance and more likely to attempt to find ways of providing them with a different kind of group support, perhaps by improving their status in professional circles, perhaps by attempting to enlarge their patrons' understanding of the library resources and services made possible by cooperative library programs.

Here, then, are examples of two library problems upon which a sociological approach could probably shed some light. We hope that our application of sociological concepts and methods in the Monteith study will encourage others to try such an approach to other library problems such as those suggested.

NOTES

1. Cooperative Research Branch, Office of Education, U.S. Department of Health, Education, and Welfare. An Experiment in Coordination between Teaching and Library Staff for Changing Student Use of University Library Resources. Final report. (In preparation.)
2. Lévi-Strauss, Claude. "Social Structure." In Anthropology Today. Chicago, University of Chicago Press, 1953, p. 525.
3. A survey of research in this area is presented in: Blau, Peter M. Formal Organizations: A Comparative Approach. San Francisco, Chandler Publishing Co., 1962.
4. Malinowski, Bronislaw. Argonauts of the Western Pacific. New York, E. P. Dutton Co., Inc., 1961, p. 9.
5. Ibid., pp. 11-25.
6. Weber, Max. From Max Weber: Essays in Sociology. New York, Oxford University Press, 1946, pp. 196-204.
7. Merton, Robert K. Social Theory and Social

Structure. rev. and enl. ed.   Chicago, The Free Press of
Glencoe, 1957, p. 284.
    8.   Blau, op. cit., pp. 42-45.

Additional References

Kluckholm, "Common Humanity and Diverse Cultures,"
In Daniel Lerner, ed., The Human Meaning of the Social
Sciences.   New York, Meridian Books, Inc., 1959, pp. 259-
261.
    Redfield, Robert.   The Little Community.   Chicago,
University of Chicago Press, 1955.
    Redfield, Robert.   Peasant Society and Culture.
Chicago, University of Chicago Press, 1956.

Reference Service: Instruction or Information[1]

Anita R. Schiller

Library use instruction has not been without its critics. Speaking in 1954, the eminent librarian Jesse Shera called for librarians to "forget this silly pretense of playing teacher," in "The Role of the College Librarian--A Reappraisal," in Library-Instruction Integration on the College Level, Report of the 40th Conference of Eastern College Librarians (Chicago: Association of College and Reference Libraries, 1955), p. 13. Such criticism has continued to the present and, recently, Arthur P. Young reviewed the reservations voiced by the critics of the 1970s in his article "And Gladly Teach: Bibliographic Instruction and the Library," in Advances in Librarianship, vol. 10, edited by Michael H. Harris (New York: Academic Press, 1980), p. 67. Young observes that critics of library use instruction focus on three major points of concern:

1. The validity of library use instruction, particularly as a function of reference service;
2. The relationship between library use instruction and library use proficiency; and
3. The educational role of libraries and librarians.

Schiller's work, however, remains the seminal article on the incompatibility of library use instruction and the provision of information as a reference service. A librarian with wide-ranging experience and a number of years as a reference librarian-bibliographer at the University of California, San Diego, Schiller articulated a view of library instruction shared by many of the period and that is still much in evidence. She clearly questions the teaching function as part of the library's information-providing obligation, and the prevalence of this view partially explains the inadequate progress of user instruction during the two decades following World War II.

By the 1980s Schiller, having been influenced by recent economic and technological developments, modified her views considerably, concluding that instruction and information were becoming much less distinguishable from one another than previously. See "Instruction or Information: What's Changed?" The Reference Librarian 1/2 (Fall/Winter 1981): 3-11.

Reprinted by permission of the author and publisher from Library Quarterly 35 (January 1965) 52-60. Copyright © 1965 by The University of Chicago Press.

• • •

Measurement and evaluation of reference service have become matters of increasing concern to libraries, where scarce personnel and limited resources are being challenged by the growing informational and educational requirements of modern society. The development of measurement techniques in other disciplines has supplied an additional impetus, and many efforts to quantify various aspects of the reference function have been reported. Most often the approach has been to isolate and then measure one of several elements of reference service, but seldom has this been preceded by an examination of the basic objectives of reference service. While present methods for measurement of reference questions, clientele, collections, and personnel have sometimes been adequate and useful in individual libraries, no satisfactory tools have been developed for the measurement of reference service among groups of libraries. Furthermore, despite considerable interest in evaluation of reference service (as distinct from measurement), this has proved even more difficult to accomplish in quantitative terms applicable to many libraries. The most recent review of the literature explains, in fact, that "all in all, the evaluation of reference service thus far can best be depicted as a closed circle of futility."[2] It is the purpose of this paper to explore some possible reasons for this and to consider the objectives of reference service. Measurement and evaluation can follow only when the area to be measured has been defined.

To discuss the objectives of reference service implies that reference service is a distinct entity; that despite the

different activities which arise from the needs of particular
communities of users, there is some significant quality common to all reference service, regardless of the particular
type, size, or location of the library in which it is performed.
The very different nature of school, academic, public, and
special libraries makes such an assumption appear arbitrary,
and even highly questionable. Reference service, however,
has evolved in such a way that common properties have
become attached to it regardless of the type of library in
which it takes place. The Standards Committee of the
Reference Services Division of the American Library Association has expressed an interest in measurement and evaluation of reference services in terms applicable to all libraries,
and Louis Shores, former chairman of that committee, has
asked: "What constitutes the reference function in every
library type?"[3] An answer to this question involves an
examination of explicit and implicit goals as well as recognition of existing trends in reference service and of the
influence of tradition upon current practice.

REFERENCE SERVICE--INSTRUCTION AND INFORMATION

Since the end of the nineteenth century in America, personal
service to the patron has been characteristic of reference
service, which has conventionally comprised two factors:
information and instruction. Definitions have frequently
taken cognizance of both components. Thus, the ALA Glossary in 1943 defined reference work as "that phase of
library work which is directly concerned with assistance to
readers in securing information and in using the resources
of the library in study and research."[4] In 1961, the
Standards Committee developed a statement on the content
of reference services rendered to library patrons. Direct
reference service, which "consists of personal assistance
provided to library patrons in pursuit of information," they
catagorized as instruction and information service. The
central feature of instruction "is to provide guidance and
direction in the pursuit of information, rather than providing
the information itself." The central feature of information
service "is to provide an end product in terms of information
sought by the library's patron."[5]

Over the years these two functions have been stressed
with varying emphasis, depending on the period, the kind of

library, its resources, and the outlook of the librarian.
Reference service has generally included both the informational and instructional functions, but these have often been
at cross purposes to one another, because each has been
associated with a conflicting view of the kind and amount of
assistance to be offered. Historically, emphasis on the informational aspect has been coupled with an interest in
providing the greatest possible amount of service. The
reference librarian not only supplies direct information in
response to requests and anticipates demand by acquiring
new materials in areas known to be of interest to patrons,
but also creates demand by calling the patron's attention
to these materials. Such comprehensive information service
exemplifies what Samuel Rothstein has described as the
"maximum theory of reference work."[6]

In contrast, the instructional approach emphasizes the
patron's essential obligation to locate his own information and
restricts the librarian's responsibility to pointing the way.
It is apparent that the maximum and minimum theories represent two antagonistic philosophies of service, but both
views have been adopted simultaneously to serve a common
end. Rather than supplement one another, however, the
two opposing and often inimical views, when incorporated
within reference service, often reduce overall effectiveness
of this service.

In the current period, expanding needs, resources,
and the increasing specialization of knowledge have focused
attention on the informational aspect of reference service,
and recent statements by professional authorities have under-
lined the importance of providing information service. Less
and less weight is given to instruction as an element of
reference service and in some cases it has been eliminated
entirely as a reference function.[7] Stressing the "crucial
concern" many people have for information and the need for
libraries to serve as community information centers, as well
as the limited resources allocated for this purpose in public
libraries, Rothstein has suggested that

> we should give up our reservations about the
> direct provision of information and recognize in-
> formation service as a principal and worthy obli-
> gation of the library, something we should try to
> push forward as far as we can. Let us admit

frankly that our <u>instructional</u> efforts are logically applicable only to <u>students</u>, and that our other customers have no more reason to be guided in the techniques of finding out than they have in being shown how to fix a defective carburetor.[8]

In many special and research libraries, instruction has been specifically excluded from reference service:

> The special librarian finds the information rather than teaching the user how to find it for himself. Only in the case of special collections serving instructional programs is the teaching function recognized.[9]

Demand for reference service flows from currents which originate outside the library in other institutions and in society at large, and the effects of the information revolution on this type of library service cannot be over-emphasized. Where the direct relationship of information service to the requirements of research and to the educational process is clearly perceived, this service has received the interest, and sometimes the support, required to extend and intensify it. Current informational activities generated in some libraries by the requirements of research and technology exemplify in actual practice those professional statements which stress the informational goal of reference service. Despite these developments, however, the instructional aspect has persisted, diminishing the effectiveness of information service to the extent that it serves as a substitute for it, offering less service instead of more, and leaving the library clientele unsure of just what kind of service is being offered.

THE PERSISTENCE OF INSTRUCTION

Katharine Harris has stated that public libraries "have taken on the role of information centers as opposed to teaching centers."[10] Yet, she continues,

> as it becomes more costly in materials and staff, we are forced to give up some of our ideals of complete service to patrons and to return to the "conservative" theory of reference work where we

> help the patrons to help themselves. Department
> heads ... say that we do less and less reference
> work in depth, but much of the work is instruc-
> tional.[11]

A lack of resources, then, rather than institutional purpose
alone, has often required the substitution of instruction
for information and more complete service.

The persistence of instruction as an essential reference
function may also be explained by another factor, and perhaps this is really the heart of the matter. Many librarians
have been reluctant to exclude instruction on the grounds
that the reference librarian has a "teaching obligation to the
society he serves."[12] Thus, Anne Morris Boyd expressed
a still widely held belief when she stated that "the teaching
function of reference work is as important in all libraries as
the information-giving function, if we believe in the library
as an educational institution."[13] The exact nature of the
library's educational role is of such crucial relevance to
reference service that it requires careful scrutiny and will
be discussed at some length below. For the moment, however, an examination of the attitudes held by reference
librarians about their educational obligations is pertinent.
Nowhere have these attitudes been brought into sharper
focus than in their application to students, where traditional
views have had to be re-evaluated in the light of the new
educational demands and the burgeoning student population.

Students have generally been recognized as constituting
the largest single group of users of public library reference
service; yet, despite the library's avowal of an educational
role, students have been singled out as a group least
deserving of assistance, either instructional or informational.
Countless references to the necessity for restricting student
use, in fact, abound in the literature of the past sixty
years. It is only today, oddly enough, when the increase
of already great student use has become overwhelming, that
expansion, rather than limitation, is seen as a way of meeting
the problem. Restriction of student use has created yet
another paradox. On the one hand, students have been regarded as not fully deserving of service. On the other hand,
when students complete their schooling, frequently never
again to return to the public library, their disappearance is

noted with concern: for when the library is ready to serve
them as adults, they do not come to be served.

How can these apparent conflicts be explained?
First, whether correctly or not, where the library has felt
an obligation to serve all groups in a community, students,
as the largest group, have received less service individually, so that the total limited resources might be apportioned
equitably among all groups. Second, however, confusing
the library's actual educational objective with their attitudes
about what they think it should be, librarians have also
felt that students were not entitled to full service.

Lowell Martin has stated that "just below the surface
of the attitudes of some public librarians is the feeling that
the community agency stands for informal education, and
that this is somehow a higher function than reading done
[or information required] for classwork or for degrees,
which they are prepared to tolerate but not to encourage."[14]
Also digging deeper for basic elements, Pierce Butler found,
however, that "librarians, without being fully aware of their
attitude, hold a strong conviction that somehow reading for
information is nobler than reading for emotional experience....
This quaint prejudice among librarians is of more than passing
academic interest. It is profoundly significant for any
serious examination of current reference activities."[15]

INFORMATION AND EDUCATION

The idea that reading for information has greater value than
reading for emotional experience appears to contradict the
view that some readers who come in search of the former are
not to be given as much help as others who come in quest of
the latter. Both ideas, however, stem from the same underlying belief, which has strongly influenced the character of
reference service. This belief, around which a whole system
of values has developed, is simply that in stating the library's
educational role, librarians have regarded the patron's self-
improvement as the library's ultimate achievement.

Passing judgment on the use patrons make of the library
has deep roots in library tradition. Discussing the emergence
of the public library, Shera stated:

The objectives of its founders were very specific
and very real. They wished to promote equality
of educational opportunity, to advance scientific
investigation, to save the youth from the evils of
an ill-spent leisure, and to promote the vocational
advance of the workers. In short, they were ...
interested in normative ends--in the improvement
of men and women and through them of society.[16]

The early emphasis in public libraries on self-improvement,
rather than simply on making the means of education
available, has been largely responsible for the moralistic
overtones of reference work expressed in the instructional
function.

The extension of formal education to a greater percentage of the population, taken with today's heightened
informational needs, demands a new set of priorities more
in keeping with current requirements, but the earlier view
of the library's educational responsibility is generally still
accepted as the standard that determines the kind of service
the patron receives. Thus students who come to the library
through the intermediary inspiration of formal education have
no place there and are not to be accorded assistance unless
they come, not as students, but freely as individuals willing
to improve themselves. It is not as paradoxical as it seems,
although nonetheless surprising, that the library, as an
educational institution, has offered its resources generously
for the purpose of serious study, and yet has restricted
them most when students require information. It is no
wonder that the large numbers of young people who come to
the library expecting assistance, after receiving only brusque
or casual attention, leave it in numbers almost equally as
great as soon as they can possibly do without it.

Educational illusion, then, has been largely responsible
for the persistence of the instructional function. When illusion is stripped away, and the educational role is disen-
tangled from the subjective attitudes that have become
twisted around it, reference service in all libraries will be
seen to have a common goal, and this goal is not achieved
by instruction in the use of materials.[17] The library's essential educational obligation consists in something quite
different from teaching its use.

The common goal of reference work is actively to anticipate informational needs and to respond to requests for
information by providing direct answers to questions and by
identifying and supplying, regardless of their form or location, those sources most suited to the user's requirements.
But making information and materials available cannot be
equated with education; to be informed (or to be taught) is
not necessarily to be educated. The reference department
or library, however, does more than simply provide a quantity of information. As a central information source it can
bring newly available knowledge to the attention of users,
provide scope and depth in its collections, indicate op
posing viewpoints on controversial subjects, supply
specialized and technical sources regardless of their form,
locate and make available additional materials through
knowledge of resources of other libraries and select from
existing materials those of the highest standard of quality,
presented in the form most suited to local needs. These
activities do have an educational objective, but only within
certain limits. The library supplies the most accurate and
complete information--the sources for education. Whether
the user derives an educational benefit is determined entirely by the user himself.

An understanding of the use to which inquirers put
information is often essential to the way in which the library
collection is to be organized and the kind of emphasis it is
to have. Reference librarians, however, rather than
directing their interest in reference use to the improvement
of service alone, providing the most authoritative sources,
and letting the user educate himself or not, have felt an
obligation to concern themselves with the user's improvement
and have regarded library instruction as necessary to this
end. Consequently the focus of their attention has shifted
from the provision of information to judgment on the user's
motives for requesting it. They have minimized their role
as trained professionals genuinely dedicated to anticipate
and provide for informational or educational needs. Despite
the statements of leading professionals and the general
recognition in the field that has been accorded the informational function of reference service, instruction in techniques
has been considered necessary to imagined educational goals.
As a result, the reference process has become inefficient at
its very outset.

Reference librarians frequently have stated that it requires special techniques to ferret out what the patron really wants from what he says he needs to know. In 1908, William Warner Bishop wrote:

> The chief art of a desk assistant or a reference librarian is--as we all know--the knack of divining by long experience what is actually wanted by inquirers. The fact that so few readers will ask directly for what they want, even when they have a clear idea of their needs--which is seldom the case--is perhaps a greater obstacle to successful reference work than poor equipment, poor catalogs, few bibliographies. 18

Perhaps the necessity for such psychological detective work comes, in part, not so much from the patron's inability to express himself, as from his feeling that he is not really entitled to request specific information, and that instead he must indicate his willingness to do his own work and contribute his share to his education. Also, by stressing the need for psychological ability on the part of the librarian, the real rapport required between librarian and inquirer through a common subject interest has frequently been ignored as an important factor in the reference process.

Typical examples of reference situations reported in the literature may serve to bring out this point:

> "I need material on medicine," says the frantic student. Fifteen minutes of questioning finally narrows the scope of medicine to information sufficient for a five-minute speech on the role of the white corpuscle in combating disease. "Have you got anything on American literature?" is reduced by careful interrogating to a critical analysis of Hawthorne's Marble Faun. 19

It is doubtful that these students would have entitled their talks "Medicine," or "American Literature," or that much interrogation would have been required from another classmate interested in his fellow student's assignment, who simply asked, "What is your topic?" Assuming that the student has been assigned a specific topic and requires information, it is likely that, unaware of the librarian's skills, his phrasing of

the request in a generic rather than specific way is an attempt to find some common ground (common subject knowledge)
between himself and the librarian which will lead to assistance.
He knows the librarian will be able to tell him where there
are books in the library about medicine or American literature.
He has not come to expect reference librarians to know anything about white corpuscles or The Marble Faun, nor, in
fact, where or how information on these topics may be found,
and, even if the librarian knows, that he will tell a student.
It is apparent that some common recognition of the subject
must exist between the inquirer and the librarian before an
answer can be supplied. Although it seems apparent that
the public's image of a librarian creates some barriers to the
achievement of this understanding, perhaps the librarians'
image of the public needs re-evaluation too. For instance,
while personal service to the patron has established itself so
deeply in the tradition of reference librarianship, the
reference patron has been regarded either as backward about
making direct inquiries or as incapable of expressing himself.
This attitude toward the patron must puzzle the inquirer as
much as the patron's attitude puzzles the librarian.

    Both this reluctance on the part of patrons to ask
directly for information and the need for the divining skill
on the part of the librarian seem unnecessary to the reference process, for both have possibly arisen from the ambi-
guity of the instructional function and the eclectic nature of
the librarian's subject knowledge. The importance of subject
knowledge in reference work has often gone unnoted because
personal characteristics rather than professional abilities
have appeared so necessary to the reference process. Since
teaching the use of the library has been tacitly accepted and
the provision of information has not been clearly established
in practice as the ultimate goal of reference policy, library
patrons have been left uncertain as to just how much and
what kind of instruction or information is offered, or how
much they may justifiably expect of a librarian. This uncertainty is compounded by the existence of different degrees
of emphasis on the teaching function in different libraries
and, indeed, in different departments of the same library.
Also, since the patron's habits of reference use have often
been conditioned by his previous experience with limited
service, he may anticipate minimum assistance even when he
applies for information in libraries that set out to offer comprehensive service.

EMPHASIS ON FORMAL INSTRUCTION

Concurrently with the singling out of information as the
proper goal of reference service, formal instruction in
the use of the library is now advocated by a number of
librarians, who seek to acknowledge and recognize its place
and to clarify the role of instruction in the reference framework. Lowell Martin has suggested that the Enoch Pratt
Free Library consider a more formal instructional program
so that students may make more effective use of the library,[20] and it has been proposed for college libraries, that
"The time is at hand ... to begin teaching students the
principles of bibliographic procedure as part of the required
curriculum, so they will not remain forever dependent on
the costly and inefficient services of the reference librarian."[21]

To make available, and even to require, instruction
for groups or individuals on a formal basis seems a more
efficient utilization of resources than to repeat the same
process endlessly with individuals in an informal and haphazard way. Such instruction also brings greater efficiency
because it is deliberately offered and the user knows exactly
what to expect and what is expected of him. The reasons
for providing such instruction, however, must be very
clear. If resources are accepted as limited and optimum use
is the goal within these limits, then the formal instruction
in library use may be the best solution. However, instruction is no substitute for resources.

The justification of instruction in the use of library
resources on educational grounds assumes that an awareness
of the library's potentialities will bring forth more effective
use. The result of informed instruction has often been just
the reverse because it has set conditions upon the direct
availability of information. By stressing the inquirer's obligation to locate his own information and by directing the
librarian's attention to showing him how, the library snarls
the line of communication between the inquirer and the librarian.

SUMMARY

This discussion has been concerned with two antithetical
principles underlying the provision of reference service in

libraries--one aiming to show the patron how to go about
finding the sources of information, the other aiming to provide him with the precise information he desires. These
principles are antithetical because in the latter case direct
information is offered freely, and in the former it frequently
is not.

Both approaches, however, are strongly based in the
historical development of American libraries. The instructional approach seems to be based on certain educational
goals which emphasize the patron's self-reliance and place
deliberate limits on the librarian's assistance. The information approach is based on the belief that reference service
best fulfills the library's role in the dissemination of knowledge
when information is made available without restrictions. James
I. Wyer identified these two approaches to reference work as
"Conservative" and "Liberal" and proferred the "Moderate"
theory as a practical compromise.[22] Librarians have continued to accept this compromise as desirable.

Failure to recognize the antagonism between these two
approaches has confused the library's role in various ways.
Patrons are uncertain about what kinds of questions they can
put to a librarian, and they modify their requests to conform
to their expectations of limited service. Librarians in turn
have had to reinterpret questions to discover what is actually
wanted, and mind-reading skill has seemed as important a
qualification for reference work as professional ability. Young
people, especially students, who constitute a major source of
potential users, are neglected and the potentialities of the
library as an information center are diminished.

There are indications that the amplified-service theory
will continue to gain ground in libraries of all types. The
expanding information services in special libraries, the unprecedented attention that has been directed by the federal
government to the information needs of scientists, the development of regional reference systems, and the increasing reference and research facilities being made available to students,
all demonstrate positive responses to the challenge of providing direct information; in some cases, though not all, librarians have supplied the leadership for these developments.
The real future of library reference service lies in the direct
provision of comprehensive and accurate information to satisfy
user demands; instructing the user in the technique of infor-

mation-searching is an important, but secondary, goal and
is not necessarily a reference function.

NOTES

1. The research reported here was supported by a
grant from the Illinois State Library to the Library Research
Center, University of Illinois Graduate School of Library
Science.
2. Samuel L. Rothstein, "The Measurement and Evaluation of Reference Service," Library Trends XII (January,
1964), 461.
3. "The Measure of Reference," Southeastern Librarian XI (Winter, 1961), 300.
4. Elizabeth Hardy Thomas (ed.), ALA Glossary of
Library Terms (Chicago: American Library Association,
1943), p. 113.
5. Shores, op. cit., p. 299.
6. "Reference Service: The New Dimension in Librarianship," College and Research Libraries XXII (January,
1961), 14.
7. In 1956, the ALA's Public Library Service: A
Guide to Evaluation, with Minimum Standards referred to
"information services" rather than "reference service."
"Guidance services" was referred to separately, although
no specific relationship was stated or excluded. In 1964,
the draft of a new Glossary being prepared by the ALA
Statistics Coordinating Project defines reference work as "a
library's activity in seeking to locate and supply specific
information as requested for library users" (March, 1964
[mimeographed]).
8. "Reference Service," loc. cit.
9. Mary Edna Anders, "Reference Service in Special
Libraries," Library Trends XII (January, 1964), 397.
10. "Reference Service in Public Libraries," Library
Trends XII (January, 1964), 382.
11. Ibid., p. 385.
12. Anne Morris Boyd, "Personnel and Training for
Reference Work," The Reference Function of the Library, ed.
Pierce Butler (Chicago: University of Chicago Press, 1943),
p. 254.
13. Ibid.
14. Students and the Pratt Library: Challenge and
Opportunity ("Deiches Fund Studies of Library Service,"

No. 1 [Baltimore: Enoch Pratt Free Library, 1963]), p. 45.
    15. "Survey of the Reference Field," The Reference
Function of the Library, p. 6.
    16. Jesse H. Shera, Foundations of the Public Library:
The Origins of the Public Library Movement in New England,
1629-1855 (Chicago: University of Chicago Press, 1949),
p. 247.
    17. As one example of how education is best served
by providing sources, rather than by training library users
in the skills required to find them, see Leonard Freiser,
"Information Retrieval for Students," Library Journal
LXXXVIII (March 15, 1963), 1121. This article describes
how the Toronto Board of Education "has started a program
of information retrieval for students--literally placing into
the student's hand articles, books and sources from all
media in response to his request for specific information.
Revolutionary in terms of current school practice and thinking, the program is very much in tune with the direction
education is now taking.... This program will gradually be
extended to students in all grades so that they may spend
their time and energy working with information rather than
overcoming library obstacles in trying to find it." This
policy was met with reactions of shock by some librarians
who called it "spoon-feeding," "evasive," and "harmful" (see
Library Journal, LXXXVIII [September 15, 1963], 3251).
    18. "The Amount of Help To Be Given to Readers,"
Library Journal XXXIII (July, 1908), 265-66.
    19. Rose Z. Sellers, "Oh Brave New (Push Button)
World!" Library Journal LXXXIX (January 1, 1964), 6.
    20. Op. cit., pp. 44-45.
    21. Daniel Gore, "Anachronistic Wizard: The College
Reference Librarian," Library Journal LXXXIX (April 15,
1964), 1690.
    22. Reference Work: A Textbook for Students of Li-
brary Work and Librarians (Chicago: American Library
Association, 1930), pp. 6-13.

The College Becomes a Library

Louis Shores

The Library-College movement has been harshly criticized
from several quarters. Nevertheless, it is important to understand its contribution to library use instruction and to
judge it within the context of the 1960s. Looking back, it
is hard to imagine that it captured the imagination of
hundreds of librarians and not a few teaching faculty and
administrators. However, it was not an accident that it
took thirty years for the ideas that Louis Shores put forth
in 1934 to gain widespread attention and support. Growing
enrollments accompanied by the impersonalization of the multiversities, seemingly endless federal funds, and an atmosphere of innovation in higher education provided fertile
ground for the Library-College movement in the 1960s.

In this selection, written at the height of the movement, Shores writes with characteristic enthusiasm and
optimism. He cites numerous examples of institutions that
adopted Library-College ideas, and he writes in glowing, if
somewhat vague, terms about the role of librarians, teaching
faculty, students, and the library in the Library-College.

Within two years of the publication of this selection,
Fay Blake would write the obituary of the movement in "The
Library-College Movement: Dying of Old Age at Thirty: A
Personal View," Wilson Library Bulletin 44 (January 1970):
557-560. With a handful of followers, the movement did sur-
vive the retrenchment of the 1970s. Nevertheless, with the
death of Louis Shores in 1981, only a few vestiges of the
movement remain.

However, many of the ideas and principles of the
Library-College have influenced instructional efforts. Blake

acknowledged the inspiration it provided in her follow-up
article "The Library-College Movement," Drexel Library
Quarterly 7 (July/October 1971): 175-188. In a companion
piece, Joan B. Bechtell described in detail the heritage that
instruction librarians owe the movement in "A Possible Contribution of the Library-College Idea to Modern Education,"
Drexel Library Quarterly 7 (July/October 1971): 189-201.

In the final analysis, however, the Library-College
idea never really took hold. Few, if any, of the examples
cited by Shores were extensive implementations of his ideas,
and seldom did they last beyond a few years. In addition
to the enormous reallocation of financial resources and at-
titudinal changes the movement required, one further reason
for its failure is offered by Patricia Breivik in Open Admissions and the Academic Library (Chicago: American Library
Association, 1977), p. 24. She concludes that the enthusiasm
that served as the strength of the Library-College also
blinded its followers to the obstacles they needed to overcome
and alienated many librarians and teaching faculty.

•   •   •

The College of the immediate future will be a library. All
the trends of the present point to independent study by
the student as the dominant pattern of American higher
education. Group teaching in a classroom is relentlessly
being subordinated to individual learning in a carrel. The
faculty is lecturing information less and guiding bibliographically more. And that part of the faculty called "professional
librarians" is more willing than ever to let clericals and automation take over management and housekeeping chores, so
that at long last librarianship may devote itself to one of its
high roles--education. What is emerging, inevitably, from
the trend to independent study is what we call the library-
college.

Others may offer better variations on this definition.
To me a library-college is a college in which the dominant

learning mode is independent study by the student in the library, bibliographically guided, intellectually aroused, and spiritually stirred by the faculty.

The <u>learning mode</u> of the library-college is universal, and followed by all students regardless of their individual differences.

The <u>library</u> of the library-college is selected to match the individual differences in the student population of the college community. All subjects, levels, and formats are represented in the collection. In this library the term book means the "generic book," which comprises all the media through which educator and student communicate.

The <u>faculty</u> of the library-college is a cross between today's teaching-committed librarian and library-using teacher.

The <u>curriculum</u> of the library-college is the sum total of the students' experience under the influence of the college. Content is interdisciplinary, crossing the sacred boundary lines of predatory disciplines, and exposing to the student interstices often excluded from consideration in the current college courses of study. Specialisms are cushioned by general education in the beginning that integrates not alone with the sciences, the social sciences, and the humanities; but <u>among</u> them; and at the end by a capstone synthesis.

The <u>facility</u> of the library-college is fundamentally a library learning resource center, surrounded by laboratories, gymnasium-athletic fields, auditoria, residences, recreational, health, and meditation and worship areas.

The <u>organization</u> of the library-college is committed to encouraging intimate informality in learning. Its total student body numbers under 500. As enrollments increase, new colleges are opened, and gathered into a cluster, Cambridge University-like.

From this overview some specifications for the library-college are offered both confidently and diffidently.

Evolution of the Library-College Idea

The library-college was inevitable once printing was invented
and books became ever more plentiful. What hastened this
inevitability was the concurrent spread of educational opportunity to every one, first on the elementary, then on the
secondary, and now even on the higher educational level.
Because of the ever-widening range of individual differences,
group teaching in the classroom became steadily less commu-
nicative to more students. With the proliferation of print
and other media, independent learning in the library became
insistently more rewarding.

In 1880, Justin Winsor, eminent historian and the first
president of the American Library Association, who was then
directing Harvard's Library toward newer educational opportunities, wrote, in his eight-page contribution for the U.S.
Bureau of Education's historic document,

> I will not say that the library is the antagonist of
> the textbook; but it is, I claim, its generous rival
> and abettor, helping where it fails and leading
> where it falters. If this is so, it follows that we
> must build our libraries with classrooms annexed,
> and we must learn our way through the wilderness
> of books until we have the instinct of the red
> man when he knows the north by the thickness of
> the tree-boles...

> The proposition then is to make the library the
> grand rendezvous of the college for teacher and
> pupil alike, and to do it in as much as the teaching
> as is convenient and practicable.[1]

Perhaps Justin Winsor's essay was one of the earliest
implementations of the Carlyle philosophy and the herald of
the independent study movement. Just which U.S. college
was the birthplace of the so-called honors program is less
important than the fact that through numerous variations at
Harvard, Princeton, Swarthmore, Colgate, Antioch, Southwestern in Memphis, Stephens, Oberlin, Rollins and a score
or more campuses the learning accent was shifting from classroom to library. The movement began to gain impetus after
World War I. Typically, Swarthmore's Honors Program was
described in 1927:

Topics are assigned by professors a fortnight or
more in advance, with brief indication of the
literature available. Such bibliographical suggestions are never complete and it is always understood that the student must ransack the library
for additional sources.[2]

At Colgate, a few years later, President Cutten defined
the aim of their "preceptorial" variation on the independent
study theme "as that of broadening the intellectual horizon
... developing the student intellectually as a whole man ...
In general we find this aim is best achieved by stimulating
the leading interest of the college man along lines which
might not occur to him. For this purpose we have extensive
reading lists and reading facilities ... The reading, however,
is not compulsory for the group, the whole thing being at
the discretion of the faculty member in question."[3]

Sample descriptions of innovations in learning mode
that featured varieties of independent study can be extracted
from the pre-World War II higher educational literature.
Notable examples would include Lamar Johnson's "Vitalized
Library" at Stephens[4]; President Conant's "Hobby Study"[5]
at Harvard; President Diehl's Tutorial Plan at Southwestern,
Memphis; President Arthur Morgan's Autonomous Courses at
Antioch. Possibly the impact of a September visit in 1928
to an Antioch beginning economics class crystallized a
cumulative urge for independent library study in my own
undergraduate days.

It was the opening day. As I recall it, the professor
gave the students a syllabus; a list of basic sources in
economics; his office hours and room number; and a calendar
of quiz, essay, mid-term, and final examination dates. As I
remember, there were only four lectures scheduled for the
whole semester, on subjects not covered by print, and upon
which the professor was an expert. One of these lectures
was the one I heard on the opening class day: an inspired
overview of the subject of economics, such as might rarely
occur in one of the better general encyclopedias. At the
conclusion of the lecture, the professor distributed a list of
possible subjects for investigation, and the form in which the
investigations were to be reported. Only the first topic was
required of every one and was due in two weeks. Three
other subjects were to be selected by the student from the

list, or independently in conference with the professor. His
final words to the class, "Happy library hunting; the next
time we meet as a class will be at the first of the term's
four scheduled lectures, unless you request a class meeting
before."

Post World War II Developments

Up through V-J Day the independent-study movement was a
phenomenon reserved for the superior student--"the upper
10%" who had inherited the intellectual talents labelled educationally as "gifted." But in the two decades that followed, this nation boldly committed itself to a "first" in the
history of the world: not only to educate, but to higher-
educate every one. There is no time here to endorse this
commitment, philosophically and enthusiastically, except,
telescopically. Fundamentally I believe all of us are gifted
in some directions; less talented in others. This goes for
the so-called "10%" as well as for the other "90%."
Historically, I observe that violent revolutions (political)
have occurred when the 10% and the 90% were educationally
so far removed from each other that they were no longer
able to communicate. The hope here is that universal
higher education will lay a foundation for gradual rather
than explosive political and social change.

Whether these philosophical assumptions can be de-
fended or not the fact remains that universal higher education in the United States is almost here. With the help of
the exciting junior college phenomenon it has become almost
anti-social for the high school graduate to go anywhere
except to college. By 1970, we are told, there will be eight
million students in college, the highest per cent ever of that
age group.

What confronts those of us who gladly or sadly teach
are two phenomena unknown to higher education before, at
least in such proportions. One of these is the growing
threat of impersonality caused by numbers. Mob scenes in
gymnasia on registration days have become a major obstacle
to higher education in our so-called multiversities. The
other hazard is in the classroom, group-teaching of the
widest range of individual differences among students ever
enrolled in our colleges. Unless students can be communicated

with as individuals rather than in numbers, and talent diver-
sifications permitted in the classroom, the present spasmodic
student insurrections will grow into a continuous rebellion.

Fortunately, solutions for both problems are at hand.
The hazard of numbers can be met by reorganization of our
multiversities into cluster-colleges. For the first time in
the history of education it is now possible to meet individual
differences in students with individual differences in media.

Paralleling the college student population growth, which
our pedagogical orators like to call one of the several "explo-
sions," media of all formats have been proliferating in
geometric proportions. The beginning may have occurred in
Mainz, Germany, about 1450, if the invention of printing be
credited to Johannes Gutenberg Gensfleisch. As the making
of books increased, and various new formats entered the educational world, the quantity and range of subjects and levels
proliferated as well. By the beginning of the 19th century,
no library apologized for the presence of non-manuscript
material as did the Duke of Urbino in the 15th century
when he noted:

> In this library all the books are superlatively
> good, and written with pen, and had there been
> one printed volume it would have been ashamed
> in such company. [6]

Rather, libraries began to accession other forms of
print: newspapers, periodicals, pamphlets, broadsides,
minibooks. The introduction of photography brought pictures into the collection. How early other graphics entered
the library is indefinite, but bulletin boards and exhibits
steadily became important library media of communication.
Nor is the inclusion of museum objects a very recent library
phenomenon. Certainly maps and globes have had a centuries-
old place in libraries.

Toward the end of the last century, probably in the
St. Louis school system, Superintendent W. T. Harris, later
to become U.S. Commissioner of Education, added the graphic,
realia, and geographic media to the newly invented phono-
recording and motion picture to herald what was later to
become known as the audio-visual movement. Although some
librarians persisted in referring to these newer formats, and

to radio, TV, teaching machines and computer consoles as
"non-book," much in the manner of the Duke of Urbino on
the subject of print in the 15th century, there was no question that all of these newer media were part of the "generic
book."

The proliferation of media since World War II armed
librarianship to lead the educational world to meet the challenge of universal education. Ever since Binet and Cattell
at the turn of this century, pedagogy had been paying lip
service to something called "individual differences" without
really doing very much about it. Pedagogy could not do
much about it as long as it was tied to the lockstep of classroom group teaching. Nor was pedagogy likely to have much
help from a librarianship that, on the school and college
level, made a fetish of supporting classroom instruction. In
the words of Harvie Branscomb in that monumental volume,
Teaching with Books:

> To sum up, it may be said without hesitation that
> the fundamental need of the college library is to
> develop a distinctive program of its own. Ab-
> sorbed as it has been in the task of increasing
> its supply of books and compelled to serve a con-
> stantly increasing student body, paying small
> salaries and getting usually--although not always--
> no more than it paid for, it has been too imitative
> of other institutions.[7]

Well, the proliferation of media provides librarianship with
the opportunity to develop a distinctive program of its own.

In 1934 at the Chicago Century of Progress A.L.A.
convention I read my paper on the "Library-Arts College."[8]
It was described as "the logical culmination of such current
trends in American higher education as are exemplified by
honors courses, comprehensive examinations and other reforms..." and differing from the conventional college in at
least five essentials: 1) a learning mode that reverses the
library-classroom relationship by having the latter support
the former; 2) an educational plant that consists of a library,
which contains all of the classrooms and laboratories as well
as the reading facilities; 3) an instructional method that bor-
rows the "each one teach one" principle of the Bell-Lancaster
monitorial schools; 4) a faculty that is bibliographically

competent to guide student independent study in the library
and generalist enough to cross sacred disciplines' boundary
lines; 5) a curriculum which follows the library, rather than
vice versa, which school and college librarians proclaim so
self-righteously now.

Here was a distinctive program of its own for the
American college library. Few will remember the shock and
indignation with which this proposal was met some three
decades ago. As Dr. Branscomb might have observed,
librarians more than educators considered the proposal pre-
posterous. I recall that in my youthful feeling of discouragement I compared my Chicago reception with the booing
Stravinsky got in Paris about a quarter of a century before
for introducing a new musical dimension.

All during those dark, Hitler pre-war days I studied
innovation in our U.S. colleges for features that might re-
enforce the library-arts college idea. I took notes constantly,
sketched a campus plan, and sought to enlist financial back-
ing for a prototype college. But these were post-depression
WPA years, and my meager college librarian's salary prohibited even minor expenditures for explorations. Pearl
Harbor relegated the stack of notes to a farm house in
Michigan as I went off to war. But I never forgot the idea.
Even in the far off China-Burma-India theatre (my war-time
substitute for my library CBI) I used to discuss the library-
arts college with an intelligent staff sergeant, whose father
was fairly affluent, and who promised that if he came out
alive he would work with me to establish the college. He
was killed in action.

Nevertheless, upon discharge from the army in the
spring of 1946, a friend and I set out to establish a library-
arts college in South Florida. We almost succeeded in
Sarasota. With the help of a newspaperman and several
prominent citizens we nearly enlisted the Crosley family to
donate their estate, close by the present airport, as a site
and as the first building. But at the last moment, the
Crosleys decided to sell instead, and after following up a
few more futile leads in Venice and Miami, we accepted
President Campbell's invitation to join the Florida State University faculty.

I had just decided that if the library-arts college was

ever to be tried out anywhere I would have to write another
book, when Bob Jordan sent me an announcement of the
Kenyon Talkshop. Since 1962 I have lived library-college
as I never have before, because of Bob Jordan, Lamar
Johnson, Dan Sillers, Patricia Knapp, Lee Sutton, Dan
Bergen, John Harvey and all of the others you will find in
the Library-College volume. In that year, two fellow deans
and I, on our way to join a Southern Association evaluation
team for Texas Tech at Lubbock, began talking experimental
college at Florida State University. Two other deans, the
director of the university library and the chairman of our
department of higher education joined us, and one night a
week, for a full year, we met in one of our homes to design
our prototype college for the eventual cluster-organization
of the university. Of course, the library-college concept
received regular and full attention. At these meetings, we
planned also the Wakulla Springs Colloquium at which ten
invited experimenting institutions from California, Michigan,
Ohio, Iowa, Missouri and Florida described their innovations.[9]

    Innovation is of urgent concern to higher education to-
day. The Magnolia, Massachusetts, conference of May 1966
revealed the commitments of additional colleges. Perhaps no
description there of an experiment in operations seemed
farther along the way toward a library-college than that of
Stafford North of Oklahoma Christian. Elsewhere, unmistak-
able features of the library-college can be found at Antioch,
where the autonomous course approach has now been extended
to the entire freshman class; at Florida Presbyterian, where
classes are replaced completely by independent study in the
library during the winter inter-term; at Parsons, Monteith,
Oakland Community College, where components of the concept
are being successfully demonstrated; and of course, at
Jamestown, the first college to commit itself to the idea.

The Library-College

Permit me now to sketch my designs for six elements of the
library-college. These are only sketches and certainly open
to suggestion: 1) Learning Mode; 2) Library; 3) Faculty;
4) Curriculum; 5) Facility; 6) Organization.

The Learning Mode

Of the learning mode enough has been said to emphasize the
locus shift from group-teaching in the classroom to individual
learning in the library carrel. The philosophy of this mode
was well put for Bennington College when education was conceived as "intellectual adventure rather than indoctrination,"[10]
and the college bulletin announced as a principal aim "to ac-
custom its students to the habit of engaging voluntarily in
learning rather than submitting involuntarily at certain
periods to formal instruction."[11]

     In the library-college the student learns primarily by
reading. This is not unlike the English university where
the student records not that he is attending a class in economics but rather that he is "reading" in economics, or in
philosophy, or Greek, or whatever. Although a major part
of this reading is done in the format known as the hard
cover, the library-college faculty guides and encourages students to read in all formats. Such reading may include
listening to tapes and discs; viewing transparencies, filmstrips, motion pictures; listening and viewing radio, television,
and the entire repertoire of educational media formats; it may,
indeed, enlist sensory-experiencing with all of the five
senses. To quote Saturday Review's Frank G. Jennings:

> But reading, remember, is not restricted to the
> printed page. Actually it never was ... through-
> out his history man has 'read' many things: the
> flight of birds, the guts of sheep, sun spots,
> liver spots, and the life lines on a hand. He has
> read the lore of the jungle, the spoor of the beast
> and the portents in a dish of tea. But whatever
> he has read and however he has read, it has al-
> ways been for 'reason.'[12]

     Yes, reading encompasses the generic book in all of
its formats. In the course of his college life the student's
reading will add up to all of the sensory responses to his
environment, and learning will come through that mystical
extrasensory flash which we are only beginning to investigate in some of the "far out" parapsychological laboratories
like the one at Duke. To encourage this extrasensory perception on the part of the student, reading should include
also meditation, and deep introspection on such impractical

questions as "Who am I?" "Where did I come from?" "Why
am I here?"

But in the library-college the student is also learning
by doing, by demonstrating, by performing, by manipulating,
and by speaking, writing and teaching. One measure of an
educated man or woman is the ability to communicate. In the
library-college the student will write as well as read. He
will write well and frequently reports, papers, essays, and
even imaginative literature, including poetry. He will speak
informally in conferences with faculty and fellow students,
with continuous, conscious and critical effort to improve the
form of his speech and add a creative element to it.

The library-college student will strive to do the many
things required to maintain life. Part of each day will be
devoted to perfecting himself in the tasks of homemaking and
earning a living. This may involve agriculture and horti-
culture on the college farms; carpentering in the shops;
cooking, sewing, home maintenance and repair; auto-driving
and servicing. He will practice the art of self-defense under
expert instruction; learn to swim, and perfect himself in a
sport of his own choice. And there will be both intramural
and intercollegiate athletics. Yes, even football, and the
team will be coached and urged on to win, to strive for the
coveted number one spot in the AP weekly poll, and to aim
to take on the winner of the pro super bowl to prove that
college football is better than the professional brand, even
as certain students of the game, like the late General Neyland
of Tennessee, and Earl Blake of the Army, and most recently
in Sports Illustrated, John Sutherland.[13] Because I believe
football has a unique place in education, and in our national
life. And it has far more color and meaning than is revealed
in Ernest Hemingway's glorification of the bull fight.

The library-college student will perform in any of the
arts he selects. Music, the dance, sculpture, painting,
architecture. The college theater will offer opportunity for
every dramatic talent. Editing and writing experience beyond
that afforded by educational assignments will be available
through college publications, all joint faculty-student ventures,
from campus newspaper through annual, and monthly literary
and humor magazines. If campus or community radio and
television stations exist these will be additional performance
opportunities.

Not the least performing opportunity will be the "each
one teach one" requirement of all students. Toward the end
of the 18th century two English educators, Andrew Bell
(1753-1832) and Joseph Lancaster (1778-1838) each claimed
to have originated the "monitorial" system of instruction
under which advanced students drilled their juniors in funda-
mentals. In recent years this system has been used by the
missionary Dr. Laubach to advance literacy in backward nations. The advantage of this system is mutual to both
monitor and learner. Every one who has ever taught will
affirm that knowledge is reenforced by the teaching of it.
The monitorial system is especially made-to-order for an independent study program.

There are other characteristics of the library-college
learning mode. One dramatic device to stimulate fact
learning is to adapt the GE television "College Bowl" for
intramural competitions. The questions can be selected from
various national examinations which students may need to
take at times and whose outcomes may reflect on the college.
Public debates, addresses, forums, panels are other devices.
Above all else the learning mode aims to be student-initiated,
individual and independent.

The Library

The library-college library is, to paraphrase Carlyle, the
true college, since it is primarily a collection of books.
But the book in the library-college library is the generic
book. It includes a selection of every subject, level and
format pertinent to the educational mission. Subject selection reflects not only the curriculum disciplines we accept
today, but some areas that fall outside and in-between. An
example might be the subjects beyond the borderlines of
science, the occult, flying saucers and Bridie Murphy.
Levels should represent the range of individual differences
in the student population of a particular college community.
This could mean school-encyclopedia level of science for
some; post-graduate for others.

When it comes to format, my classification of the
generic book, as it appears in my book Instructional Materials, is a beginning.[14] There are at least a hundred or
more physical makeups of educational media found in the

schools and colleges of the nation. Representations of all
or most of them belong in the collection if only because one
kind of format will communicate better with the background
of an individual student for a particular learning situation.
It is fashionable intellectually these days to quote Marshall
McLuhan on media. I have served with him on the ASCD
Instructional Materials Commission. Much of what he says
does not communicate with me. But this much I have be-
lieved all of these years of my educational effort to effect a
marriage between audio-visualists and librarians: "the form
of the medium may influence communication." Indeed it is
entirely possible that format may change meaning for different individuals. If this is so, then it is more important
than ever that the library stock be representative of items
in all formats. Nor should so-called audio-visual media ever
be considered non-book material, and therefore reduced in
its educational status.

Furthermore, new dimensions of access to these materials must now be envisaged. The open stack is certainly
made to order for the library-college. But so also is the
recent extension of remote access. If the carrel is to become
truly the student's work bench, the library-college library
must be prepared to go as far as possible from dry through
damp to wet carrel. For our glossary, I understand the wet
carrel to mean the carrel equipped with dial access to audio
and visual material such as tape, disc, radio, to still projec-
tions like transparencies, slides, filmstrips, films, and possibly to closed circuit television, and remote console,
computer-assisted instruction; to facsimile and radioteletype,
etc. "Dampness" to me represents various stages along the
way from dry to wet carrels.

With regard to bibliographic access, we should look
forward to the computerized printout book catalog as an
eventual replacement for the card catalog. Present imper-
fections are only a delay. No phase of library automation
excites me more than the potential of unlimited instant-
printout index-bibliographies to any portion of the collection,
to any topic, and with many more analytics or descriptors
for each item than the standard five analytics on cards. In
embryo, such cataloging can be found at a number of colleges and universities now: Florida Atlantic, Louisiana State
at New Orleans, Missouri. And as for classification we may
yet justify observations by some foreign librarians that

expensive L.C. reclassification was unnecessary when the
computer works better with a simple I.D. number.

Besides the generic book stock, the library-college
library will accommodate people. These will include students,
faculty and staff. For students, the first departure will be
to increase the percentage of student body seated at one
time from a conservative 25%, beyond generous 50%, to 100%.
This has been done at Oklahoma Christian, where the
present library seating capacity is 110%. There will be an
individual carrel for each student, his individual work
bench to which he can come any time of the day and night
the library is open. This does not prevent the student
from studying in his own room, if he prefers, with the radio
on, or during a conversation in progress between his room-
mate and a dropper-in; or in the play room with every other
sentence punctuated by a popping ping pong. But he will
also begin to live as he will after he leaves college and has
a place of work to report to daily. Nor will this prove ar-
chitecturally uneconomical when reckoned against unused
class space-time.

Faculty offices, one for each faculty member, will be
in the library. This should stir some librarian opposition
based on previous experiences. But recall, please, that the
learning mode then was not that of the library-college. And
for each four faculty offices there should be one seminar
room. Faculty offices will be used for study, conference
with colleagues and students.

Most of the special areas provided in libraries will be
represented: public catalog and bibliography-index area;
reference; current periodicals; browsing; rare materials;
exhibit and display. Equipment storage for projectors, re-
corders, playbacks, readers, etc., for use with the related
formats of the generic book, as well as maintenance and
service space areas, will be planned. Laboratory and demonstration space will be provided, although the Purdue experiment with its biological laboratory may point to the ideal
accommodation for a laboratory in a library.[15]

The Faculty

The new-breed faculty that will be required for the library-

college is a cross between those librarians who like to teach
and those classroom instructors who like to use the library
in their teaching. There are enough of both today to provide a nucleus for the faculty of tomorrow's prototype.
Essentially, this faculty member's job will be to guide bibliographically the great adventure in learning by the student.
Inspirationally, the faculty member will arouse through about
a half dozen carefully prepared lectures of such significance
as to be worthy of public billing on the campus. He will
stimulate by stirring seminar discussion; through individual
or small group conferences. Bibliographically, he will attempt to tailor media-selection to the individual differences
of his students, prescribing much as the skilled medical
diagnostician does.

To accomplish this, the faculty member will have to
know media, not incidentally as he was taught them in his
liberal arts or teachers college days, but per se. He will
have to know his sources not alone for subject but for level.
And above all he will have to know the strengths and weaknesses of the various formats for individual learning situations. For example, time-lapse motion pictures can accomplish
communication of certain concepts better than almost any
other medium. Yet there are some abstractions that cannot
be mastered except by wrestling with the printed word. How
better can a youngster gather the nuance of Spanish
idiomatic conversation than through tape exchanges with college students in Latin American countries?

The time is coming when college orientation and teaching in library use will assume a new importance. With that
will come a more creative approach to communicating this important half of knowledge--knowing where to find it. For the
present, in-service education is called for. One device is for
the faculty to undertake continuous indexing of library materials for computerized retrieval much as is now carried on in
scientific libraries. A thesaurus of descriptors, fields, and
groups, based on units and terms in the curriculum, could
be used as a basis. And the librarian could lead the way by
establishing a college-interest profile related to faculty research, to specialist and hobby interests.

Prophetically, Carter Alexander anticipated the role of
the faculty in this new and more exciting relationship to the
student when he wrote:

A plan must be developed ... where the teaching
process can be started and finished by the instructor and the learning process carried on effectively
in the library ... where suggestions can be given
in the library as well as in the office of the pro-
fessor.16

Curriculum

"The curriculum is commonly defined," says the Encyclopedia
of Educational Research, "as all the experiences that a
learner has under the guidance of the school."17 Although
the library-college accents intellectual development in the
library, it by no means neglects "the effects upon learners
of all aspects of the community, the home and the school."
The library-college will periodically invite student diaries
for review and exchange, with the purpose of encouraging
students to revise continuously the total experiences planned.

Of the many statements of a liberal education aim, perhaps none will fit the purpose of the library-college better
than this by Professor Richardson to the President of
Dartmouth College:

> ... the stimulation and development of those gifts
> of intellect with which nature has endowed the
> student, so that he becomes, first, a better com-
> panion to himself through life, and, second, a
> more efficient force in his contacts with his fellow
> men.18

To accomplish this purpose the library-college departs
from the curriculum of many contemporary liberal arts colleges by: 1) intellectually accenting general background
more, and specialism less; 2) physically and spiritually, converting elements of college life formerly looked upon as
"extra" or "co" curriculum to an integral part of the curriculum.

The college curriculum today suffers from the compart-
mentalization enforced by the predatory rights and privileges
of our contemporary academic disciplines. The library-college
will have to recognize these subject areas for some time to
come, but it can more solidly develop the student's general
background on which to build a specialism by including in its

curriculum two "generalia" areas, both in the beginning and
as a capstone. One of these areas is "the half of knowledge,"
that is, "knowing where to find it." It is an area devoted to
the study of media, to sources of information, per se, done
with a dimension and imagination not yet accomplished by our
one-hour courses on the use of the library, or certainly by
our freshman orientation week. One possible approach is the
continuous building of a student-interest profile, covering the
range of interests of the student population, and becoming a
continuous printout catalog. The student would pursue this
course in the library-college learning mode, working independently under the bibliographic guidance of the instructor.

The other area of "Generalia" would simply be called
"Knowledge," for want of a better title at the moment. It
would be an overview or summary of the wisdom of mankind;
of the thought, actions, and achievements that have most
significantly been responsible for man's present state. A beginning might be made through the "Good Books," a collection
like that of Harvard President Eliot's the Harvard Classics, or
Chicago President Hutchins' Great Books, if we could eliminate
the provincialism of the latter and add the classics of the
Eastern World. The student would be encouraged to read
across boundary lines, not only within the sciences, the social sciences and the humanities, as our now "old hat" integrated courses do in most colleges, but across these broad
areas, so that C.P. Snow's doubtful accusation against the
humanists might never be thought again of a college graduate.

On the physical side, the library-college proposes to
include without apology in its curriculum: how to make a
living, how to perform in the world, how to get along with
his fellow men. Without particularizing further here, the
library-college curriculum has a place for such sacrilegious
subjects (in the opinion of the intellectualists) as marriage
and the family, infant care; the dance-ballroom, go go, and
ballet; intercollegiate football; farming; carpentry, etc.

And on the spiritual side, there must be time for meditation. "Where the action is" apparently sells commercially.
But if this nation is to be great it must begin to balance its
national mind with more contemplation, with time to consider
the ultimates. The other day I discovered tucked away in
the New Orleans airport a room for meditation. All of us
know the famous meditation room in the United Nations.

Meditation must be provided for and encouraged in our
library-college, even if it does not involve worship of God.
There is no thinking agnostic or atheist I know who does not
welcome an opportunity to consider introspectively his decision.

Facility

The library-college does not consider that the last word in
library architecture has yet been written. In 1930 I introduced or reintroduced with architect Henry Hibbs the tower
stack for Fisk University in Nashville, of which I was librarian at the time. The next innovation was probably modular
construction. As one who has been frustrated by the fixed
columns of the module, and has questioned the advantages
of "flexibility" and the uneconomical, reinforced floors
throughout, I hope this architectural fashion will at least be
critically reexamined by library-college building planners.

In my opinion, fixed stacks for the varied formats of
our generic book now seem more justified than ever.
Storage for films and hard covers is not practically inter-
changeable, nor will the space for projectors lend itself eco-
nomically or conveniently to conversions. At the moment I
favor a fixed allotment for the bulk of stock accommodation.
As far as possible, media which depend on equipment for
use should be placed in proximity to that equipment; at least
until remote access is feasible.

Reader-accommodation departs from college library
building standards quantitatively by specifying that 100% of
the student body be seated at one time. Qualitatively, the
individual carrel rather than the group reading table becomes
standard. Typical designs for these carrels are available in
such publications as the booklet issued by the Educational
Facilities Laboratory Office.[19]

Staff-accommodation must now provide offices for the
new-breed of faculty; seminar rooms; and auxiliary bibliographic, browsing, reference, special format, and other work
areas. Since the professional librarian will now have merged
with the classroom instructor to become the faculty, there
will still be need to accommodate the management and housekeeping staff, probably according to the "100-foot per" standard.

Organization

For the library-college to function properly, enrollment should
be organized. For the cluster of colleges, the university
should perform certain resource and evaluation functions. Research and other expensive resources which can be shared by
all of the colleges will be housed in the university library.
All-university lectures by nationally and internationally distinguished scholars will be open to all of the colleges. The
university will act as an evaluative agency for the programs
of the various colleges, each of which may have different accents. A federation of library colleges, therefore, becomes a
library-university.

Conclusions

The report of the president of the Carnegie Corporation for
the year ending September 30, 1931, contains these words:

> Whether the liberal arts college can continue to be
> the characteristic element in American life which it
> has been in the past will probably depend more
> than anything else upon the colleges themselves.
> They must demonstrate anew the capacity to produce
> the men and women whose influence in the world
> they will enter after graduation can never be meas-
> ured by mere numbers. This the college succeeded
> in doing in the past, and can do again in the fu-
> ture, but not by repeating the old techniques, for
> the world of tomorrow will be a very different place
> from the world today. As one element in meeting
> these conditions, the library must be actively and
> intelligently used by students.

I submit that the library-college is designed to meet
precisely this challenge of preparing a generation for tomorrow.

NOTES

1. U.S. Bureau of Education, College Libraries as
Aids to Instruction. 1880. p. 8-9. (Circulars of Information, No. 1)

2. Brooks, R. C., Reading for Honors at Swarthmore.
1927, p. 36.
3. Cutten, G. B., "The Preceptorial System at Colgate
University," Association of American Colleges Bulletin, 1935.
V. 21, p. 493-95.
4. Johnson, B. L., Vitalizing the College Library.
5. Harvard.
6. The Vespassiano Memoirs (Lives of Illustrious Men
of the XVth Century); by Vespassiano de Bisticci, Bookseller: Now first translated into English by William George
and Emily Waters. Lincoln Mac Veigh, 19, p. 104.
7. Branscomb, Harvie, Teaching with Books; A Study
of College Libraries. 1940. p. 9-10.
8. Shores, Louis, "The Library Arts College."
School and Society, 1935. V. 61, p. 110-14. (also in
The Library-College, 1966. p. 3-9) as well as in several
anthologies.
9. Experimental Colleges; Their Role in American
Higher Education; ed. by W. Hugh Stickler, 1964. p. 185.
10. Duffus, R. L., Democracy Enters College. 1936.
p. 205.
11. Bennington College, Announcement for the First
Year, 1932-33. 1932. (Publications, V. 1, Series No. 9,
August 1932, No. 1, Part 4)
12. Jennings, F. G., This is Reading. 1965. p. 11.
13. Sutherland, "The College Game is Best." Sports
Illustrated.
14. Shores, Louis, Instructional Materials. 1960.
15. Purdue Lab Experiment.
16. Carter, Alexander. "The Library Professor and
Educational Research," School and Society, 1934. V. 39,
p. 457-69.
17. Kearney, N. C., and Cook, W. W., "Curriculum,"
(In Encyclopedia of Educational Research. 1960. p. 358-63).
18. Richardson, L. B., A Study of the Liberal College; A Report to the President of Dartmouth College. 1924.
p. 17.
19. Educational Facilities Laboratory. Carrels.

Part V

IMPLEMENTATION IN A TIME OF RETRENCHMENT

1969–1980

IMPLEMENTATION IN A TIME OF RETRENCHMENT, 1969-1980

For a variety of reasons yet to be fully understood, library use instruction emerged as a vital force in academic librarianship during the first few years of the period. Paradoxically, as it gained momentum, the financial and enrollment situation of higher education changed dramatically. After a century of relatively steady and certain growth, higher education in the United States became "unsteady and uncertain."[1]

This retrenchment in higher education affected academic libraries in a number of ways which, in turn, affected library use instruction. First, as David Kaser describes in his essay on "the revolution of 1969-1970," the change had a profound effect on the leadership of academic libraries because of the "frustration of unrealized expectations."[2] Despite, for example, the biggest building boom in library history, book collections grew faster than the space to hold them, and the library space problem worsened.[3] Disenchanted with old solutions, many academic librarians looked to other methods to involve the academic library in the educational process.

Secondly, newly-graduated scholars who in better economic times might have pursued careers in the classroom now entered academic librarianship. They brought with them increased sophistication and they introduced to an already awakening profession an additional element of concern for "social responsibilities" that grew out of the 1960s. Perhaps remembering their own days as undergraduate students during the "baby boom" of the 1960s, they took a strong interest in undergraduate students. The leadership of Evan Farber, Miriam Dudley, and others of an "older" generation notwithstanding, librarians in their thirties and younger dominated the grassroots library use instruction movement of the early 1970s.

227

User instruction moved swiftly. By 1969 the Earlham College program had become widely known and the Council on Library Resources initiated the College Library Program. By 1971 the movement had an annual conference at Eastern Michigan University and its own Ad Hoc Committee on Bibliographic Instruction within the Association of College and Research Libraries. From 1969 to 1971, Verna Melum found in two surveys that the intensity of experimentation in library use instruction had greatly increased.[4] By 1974, Farber and Kirk observed that the articles listed in Library Literature on the topic had doubled from an annual average of thirty-five between 1958 and 1971 to seventy in 1974.[5] Other supporters noted the increase in the number of professional positions available for instruction librarians. Finally, by the end of the decade, the newly-formed Bibliographic Instruction Section had become the most active section within the Association of College and Research Libraries.

All has not been well for library use instruction during this period. In our final selection, Nancy Gwinn questions the success achieved by the Council on Library Resources in its efforts to promote library use instruction. In the midst of the decade, the editors of The Journal of Academic Librarianship felt it necessary to caution librarians to review the literature in order to learn of past efforts.[6] Others have criticized it for "lack of conceptual definition, spotty research, uneven financial support, and insufficient endorsement outside the library community."[7] Even staunch advocates Farber and Kirk admit that "... one looks almost in vain for serious recognition of bibliographic instruction by college and university faculty and administrators...."[8] They conclude that user instruction still has a long way to go.

NOTES

    1. Carnegie Foundation for the Advancement of Teaching, More Than Survival (San Francisco: Jossey-Bass, 1975), p. ix.
    2. David Kaser, "The Effect of the Revolution of 1969-1970 on University Library Administration," in Academic Libraries by the Year 2000: Essays Honoring Jerrold Orne, edited by Herbert Poole (New York: R. R. Bowker, 1977), p. 64.

3. Daniel Gore, "The View from the Tower of Babel," Library Journal 100 (15 September 1975): 1600.

4. Verna V. Melum, "1971 Survey of Library Orientation and Instruction Programs," Drexel Library Quarterly 7 (July/October 1971): 227.

5. Evan I. Farber and Thomas G. Kirk, Jr., "Instruction in Library Use," in The ALA Yearbook (Chicago: American Library Association, 1976), p. 59.

6. Richard M. Dougherty and William H. Webb, "Editorial--Library Instruction," The Journal of Academic Librarianship 2 (September 1976): 171.

7. Arthur P. Young, "And Gladly Teach: Bibliographic Instruction and the Library," in Advances in Librarianship, vol. 10, edited by Michael H. Harris (New York: Academic Press, 1980), p. 80.

8. Farber and Kirk, p. 59.

Integrated Library Instruction

James R. Kennedy, Jr.

No college or university has provided a finer example from the late 1960s to the present of the active involvement of the library in the education process than has Earlham College. Although Evan Farber, long-time head librarian at Earlham, insists that the Earlham program is unique and not exportable, the program has served as a model and an inspiration for a number of librarians.

This article by Jim Kennedy, reference librarian at Earlham College for a number of years, followed a talk Farber gave as the Chairman of the Association of College and Research Libraries College Libraries Section at the 1969 American Library Association conference. In correspondence with Larry Hardesty (April 6, 1981), Farber wrote:

> We (Tom [Kirk], Jim [Kennedy] and myself) expected the usual two- or three hundred attendees, and had brought along enough handouts (mostly, sample bibliographies) for that many. This was the first time, as far as we knew, that there was a public presentation on bibliographic instruction and we anticipated some interest, but viewed it mainly as an occasion for proselytizing. To our surprise and delight, the room was overflowing, and there were, we estimated, at least eight hundred in the audience. Moreover, the response was tremendous. The obvious enthusiasm, the questions we got there, and the follow-up letters and inquiries all indicated that there was an enormous reservoir of interest in the subject.

Farber believes this talk provided a forum for expression of interest and librarians suddenly realized that many others were also interested in and working on library use instruction. Within three short years after this talk, the Ad Hoc Committee on Bibliographic Instruction was formed within the Association of College and Research Libraries, Eastern Michigan held its first annual Conference on Library Orientation and, at the same university, Project LOEX (library orientation exchange) began. In Farber's words, "the movement mushroomed."

•   •   •

Every college reference librarian has, at one time or other, found himself repeatedly answering the same reference question. Perhaps 50 students in a week come asking for interpretations of Falstaff. Or 100 students in two days want the names and addresses of their congressmen. Not only is this a downright waste of a reference librarian's time, but it is even beyond the patience of a saint or a mother to deal creatively with the same question a hundred times. The first few times the librarian will probably interview the student and ask why the information is needed, and find out that the students are all writing their congressmen about an issue raised in a political science course. To encourage the spirit of inquiry, he may introduce the first students not only to the Congressional Directory, but to other sources of biographical and political information, such as the Congressional Quarterly Weekly Report and Biography Index. But it takes five or ten minutes multiplied by 100 to take this creative approach with all the students and by the time the fourth, eighth, or 98th student appears, the reference librarian has probably reached his capacity for creative response, and his attitude is one of resigned endurance. He has now marked the pages in the Congressional Directory and simply hands it out--much as books are

handed out at the Reserve Desk or ice cream in the lunch
line.

Experiences like this, repeated again and again, may
suggest to some that the librarian merely cultivate the vir-
tues of patience, sensitivity and thoroughness, but others
might well infer that something as mundane as library instruction is needed. How much more effective and efficient
it would be to teach a whole class the basic reference
sources in a systematic and (hopefully) engaging way rather
than to teach them one-by-one, catch-as-catch-can, in the
frenzy of a busy reference area. It was from this obvious
solution to what must be a common problem that Earlham
College's program of library instruction evolved.

The basic principles of this program, which has been
going on now for five years, are integration, demonstration
and gradation. 1) The instruction is integrated, whenever
possible, into the course work in those courses requiring
intensive use of the library. It is regarded by the students, we hope, as an integral part of the course. 2) A
class period (or more) is set aside for one of the library
staff to demonstrate the search for and use of library materials. Each student receives an annotated bibliography
which locates and describes the most important reference
tools for that course and watches the librarian demonstrate
the use of these sources by working through a library
search similar to what the student himself is facing. 3) The
instruction is gradated--it builds on previous instruction.
For example, when a librarian talks to a class in which there
are mostly juniors who are beginning their majors, he assumes they have already learned to use the reference materials shown to freshmen and sophomores. He therefore need
mention only in passing the Social Sciences & Humanities
Index, for example, and can spend the time on talking about
the more specialized subject bibliographies and indexes.

Preparation for each term is relatively straightforward.
Before the beginning of the term we talk to faculty members
whose courses, we think, might require extensive library use.
If a particular course does, and the faculty member agrees
that the students need some initiation into the body of reference tools for that subject, we ask for an outline of the
course and for a description of the library project and establish a tentative date for the demonstration. Then we

compile a bibliography of the reference sources most relevant to the assignment, each source annotated as to scope,
use and special features. These are usually arranged by
form in the order that students might use them: if there
are guides to the literature or handbooks on the subject,
these come first; then encyclopedias, bibliographies and
indexes; next, biographical and statistical sources; finally,
comments on special materials or a list of suggested subject
headings. The bibliography is duplicated and handed out
at the lecture-demonstration, which is given at a regular
class hour, but in the library. (Our library has a projec-
tion room which can seat up to 60 students, more than
enough for practically all courses.)

The lecture-demonstration has two primary purposes:
to describe search strategies and to demonstrate the use
of reference sources which, like the New York Times, are
difficult to explain without going into some detail. These
explanations are greatly assisted by the use of transparencies
which can be made quickly and easily on a Xerox. In addition, the lecture emphasizes the difficulties of using the library effectively--most students need to be disenchanted of
the notion that merely because they received some instruction
in high school and used their public libraries they don't need
to receive any additional instruction. We point out that there
are probably more differences than similarities between their
previous library experience and what they should be doing in
college libraries, and that the program of library instruction
to which they'll be subjected during their four years is
aimed to help them to use the library effectively and effi-
ciently--to save them time and permit them to find materials
they otherwise would not have known about.

The entire program is gradated into four levels of instruction, according to students' needs. Briefly, these four
levels may be identified as: pre-freshmen coming from high
school with varying library knowledge, freshmen writing their
first "research" paper, juniors beginning their majors, and
seniors trying to integrate their four years.

The first level of library instruction is related to freshman orientation. In the summer the librarians send a letter
and sample test to entering freshmen stating that during New
Student Week they will be given a library knowledge test.
The test, which simulates a library search for a paper on

Vietnam, covers 12 basic reference sources, which many
students will have used in high school. They are encouraged
to buy Kate L. Turabian's Student's Guide for Writing College
Papers (1963), which is used in a required freshman English
course, and to study it so that they can pass the library
knowledge test given shortly after they arrive on campus.
This test is a relatively simple one and is used to point out
those students whose knowledge of library use is so poor
they need some special instruction. While this first level is
important--it calls the attention of the students to the fact
that use of the library is taken seriously--it is also weak.
Success on the test is partly based on skills in taking tests,
and there may be a real gap between passing the test and
actually being able to use the sources.

Despite its inadequacies, this level of instruction does
seem to be more helpful to students than the usual library
tour offered by colleges during freshman orientation week.
Tours tend to introduce students to the obvious--"This is
the card catalog"--and cannot teach what students need to
know. Even a sound and filmstrip session on the card catalog, Readers' Guide and other sources will not have lasting
benefit, because of the frantic pace of New Student Week and
the lack of motivation to use the sources.

The second level of library instruction is related to a
long paper assigned in a required two-term freshman Humanities course. The first term of this course involves reading,
discussing and writing a short, personal reaction paper on
one book a week. The small classes of about 20 students
also divide into tutorial groups of about five students. This
structure continues in the second term, except that the long
paper replaces several of the short papers. In the second
term, the librarians have one hour in which to instruct students in library search strategy as well as in basic reference
sources common to the humanities and social sciences, but
little known to high school students. These include the following: Subject Headings Used in the Dictionary Catalog of
the Library of Congress, Social Sciences & Humanities Index,
Public Affairs Information Service Bulletin, Essay and General Literature Index, Biography Index, and the New York
Times Index. Students will use these sources throughout
their college careers. Earlham's reference librarian, by the
way, considers Subject Headings Used in the Dictionary Catalog of the Library of Congress to be the most important single

reference book in Earlham's library, because it has no substitute as a guide to the library's most important reference
source, the card catalog. (There are no "see" or "see also"
references in the card catalog; users must consult the subject
heading book.)

   One year, when all the Humanities II students were
writing papers on George Orwell, the library instruction in
the above mentioned sources was illustrated with sample
pages related to an aspect of 1984. In addition, a separately published, comprehensive bibliography by and about
Orwell was brought to students' attention. As a further
service to Humanities II students, the Reference Librarian
prepared individual, short, unannotated lists of specialized
reference sources for certain topics chosen by the students.
For example, a student writing on Such, Such Were the
Joys might want to compare Orwell's memories of his school
days with materials found in Education Index, Short Story
Index, or Fiction Catalog.

   After the Humanities II students had begun their library search, a librarian met with tutorial groups of four
to six students, in order to speak to any specific library
difficulties they were having. After class these students
often came with the librarian to the Reference Collection for
individual guidance. An important fringe benefit of the librarians' meetings with classes was the recognition by students that librarians were not only human but were eager
and able to help them.

   To summarize the library instruction for Humanities II,
librarians first meet all freshmen in groups of about 20 to
introduce them to basic reference sources beyond the high
school level and useful during the college years. Second,
the librarians meet with groups of about five students each,
giving them individual help in locating and using special
sources they would otherwise have missed. Just as important
is that the librarians have a chance to meet the students and
the students a chance to know them and their services.

   The third level of library instruction is related to
courses in the different disciplines that serve, more or less,
as foundation courses for students beginning their majors.
For some disciplines the choice of the course to have library
instruction is obvious, but for others the choice is difficult,

because no single course is expected of beginning majors, or
else the course involves no library research.

The sources covered in the third level are those basic
to a discipline. For example, English majors would learn to
use such sources as PMLA, Annual Bibliography of English
Language and Literature, the Cambridge Bibliography of
English Literature, the OED, and Thrall and Hibbard's A
Handbook of Literary Terms. Psychology students would be
introduced to such sources as Psychological Abstracts, Annual
Review of Psychology, Mental Health Book Review Index,
Buros, Mental Measurements Yearbook, and English and
English, A Comprehensive Dictionary of Psychological and
Psychoanalytical Terms: A Guide to Usage. This instruction
has lasted from one to ten hours, but is generally from one
to four hours.

Library instruction also supports an important component of the popular General Biology course, a course elected
by about half the freshman class and taken ultimately by almost two-thirds of the student body to fulfill their science
requirement. Instead of taking hour-long recall examinations,
students are asked to write a paper in answer to questions
related to the area they have been studying. These questions (e.g., "Several insecticides are known to act by interfering with a normal physiological function or functions of
the target organisms. For each of two insecticides having
different means of so interfering, document from the primary
literature evidence regarding the way in which the insecticides interfere with normal physiological function.") require
library research to locate information and experimental data.
Furthermore, the student must use the basic knowledge of
the subject which he has been studying over several weeks.
This assignment requires extensive use of the scientific
literature--students are taught how and why to locate information through the card catalog, Science Citation Index, and
Biological Abstracts. (A discussion of this fuller instruction
is available in the following unpublished master's thesis by
Earlham's Science Librarian: Kirk, Thomas G. "A Comparison
of Two Methods of Library Instruction for Students in Introductory Biology." Master's Thesis, Division of Library
Science, Indiana University, 1969.) Thus we've seen after
this course the anomalous situation of freshmen knowing how
to use such sophisticated tools as Biological Abstracts and the
Science Citation Index, without ever really having learned

how to use the much more basic tools, such as Social Sciences
& Humanities Index or PAIS. But even this anomaly has its
happy results. By learning and using these, they realize
what the function of abstracting services is and how one can
use footnote citations in tracing the history of ideas, concepts
which are important to know in using many other kinds of
reference tools.

       An interesting method was tried this past term in the
second half of General Biology. The term focussed on the
ecology of the environment and students were asked to use
government documents--bills, hearings, Congressional debates, reports, etc.--in their investigations. To obviate the
problem of introducing 12 biology classes to the intricacies
of government documents without wearing out the Science Librarian, sample pages from each of the document's reference
sources (prepared by lithographing xerographic copies) were
given to each student, and a videotape was made by the
Science Librarian tracing a problem through the materials.
The tape was then shown on an announced schedule over
several days, so that any of the 150 students could use it
on his own time. It's too early to evaluate this procedure,
but the preliminary reports are good.

       The fourth level of library instruction is related to ad-
vanced courses in a discipline. Students in senior seminars,
for example, need to learn about some of the specialized
reference sources not covered in the third level. This level
of instruction is more individualized, because seniors choose
a range of topics for their long papers, many of which are
inter-disciplinary and therefore require a knowledge of
reference sources basic to other disciplines.

       Earlham librarians also give library instruction which
does not fit into any of the levels described above. This is
one-shot library instruction which does not build on any
previous instruction nor lead to future instruction. An example would be the elective in Introduction to Art, which ad-
mits all students, from freshmen to seniors. A freshman
seminar on Black Studies would be another example.

       But it is not enough to have a suitable teaching method
geared to the various levels of students' needs. There are
other factors, over some of which the librarians have no
control. One important factor in our favor, for example, is

the educational climate which encourages, even demands, library use. The size of most classes is small, and the faculty, who are concerned more with good teaching than research and publication, have built a curriculum that includes a variety of seminars, tutorials and independent study programs. A second factor permitting the program's development is the unusual rapport between librarians and teaching faculty. Such cooperation is essential for several reasons--the instructor must be willing to give at least one hour of his lecture time and to build the instruction into the course. Some faculty members may be jealous of their class time or feel that the offer implies that they are not doing their job. In talking with such teachers, the librarian needs to be forceful but not threatening. He should stress the wide range of reference sources helpful for the course and the impossibility of the student getting this information anywhere else.

A program of library instruction will flounder if evaluation shows that it is ineffective. If students cannot use the library any more effectively after library instruction than before, then why should the teacher give up his class time for it? Earlham's program began with a woefully inadequate presentation. The librarians simply brought the reference books to class, discussed them, and passed them around. It was apparent that the students retained very little of the instruction. The preparation of unannotated bibliographies was some help, but not enough. Even the use of transparencies of sample pages did not accomplish the purpose until we selected them to focus on a sample problem. Then the view from the Reference Desk was gratifying indeed. We saw students carrying their bibliographies from source to source and using a wide range of sources with relatively little help from the Reference Librarian.

Another crucial factor for successful library instruction is student motivation. If students feel that the assignment can be done with just the card catalog and Readers' Guide, they may not pay close attention, but if they know that their teacher has higher expectations and will be checking over their bibliographies--preferably two or more weeks before the paper is due--they will be listening and watching carefully.

Timing also affects motivation. The optimal time for

library instruction is within a week of the time that students start the assignment. If the instruction is offered too early or too late, students tend to be indifferent to it. Occasionally, faculty have requested instruction for a course simply because they thought it was "a good thing," but it was not related to any assignment. Then students tended toward somnolence. It is doubtful if even an alert student would learn much in this situation, because real learning takes place when students actually use the sources, not just when they see them used.

Another hindrance to student motivation is too much library instruction. Learning about the Social Sciences & Humanities Index four times a year may immunize the student to other sources. A solution to this problem is to avoid repetition between the levels of instruction, to excuse all but freshmen from the one-shot presentation, and to shorten or omit the class presentations to juniors and seniors.

But these caveats do not adequately account for the fact that a program of library instruction beyond the freshman orientation level is still a rarity in undergraduate education. Perhaps the lack is best explained by several negative views which librarians have expressed toward library instruction.

All college librarians feel that the library function is, of course, to support the educational program, but many feel that this is done by building an appropriate collection and by organizing it for use and offering assistance when asked. We feel that this is only part of the job--that no matter how good the collection, no matter how spacious or comfortable the facilities, if the collection is not used effectively, the librarians are not doing their job.

A second negative point of view is that it is not the librarian's function to teach, that library skills should be taught in the school system, and that specific reference sources should be introduced by the instructors as part of their courses. Unfortunately, the skills are not being taught in all high schools and even where they are, a college or university library is so much more complex that further instruction is imperative. As for the faculty doing the job, most teaching faculty are neither willing nor able to explain how to use the variety of specific sources important to their

disciplines. The library-college dream of a bibliographically
skilled faculty has never been achieved.

A third objection is that instruction detracts from the
reference function. Students introduced to a few sources
will stop with those and not ask for reference assistance,
which could often be more important. This objection may be
answered by the fact that instruction reaches some students
who would never ask for help, and, in addition, our experience has shown that students receiving library instruction are more, rather than less, willing to ask for reference
assistance. They know the reference staff and know its
members are interested in their problems.

A fourth objection commonly expressed regarding library instruction is that there is insufficient time and talent to
do it. The only answer to this objection is that library instruction is as important as any other academic library function, that unless students learn to use the library well, the
validity of the other functions--building a collection and
making it available for use--is largely vitiated. Besides, it
may save time in the long run. Lack of talent, however, is a
more difficult objection to refute. Perhaps it is enough to say
that even librarians who shy away from the idea of teaching
may find that they come to enjoy telling groups about reference sources that will serve their needs.

The cost in staff time needs to be compared with the
benefits expected from library instruction. During the last
five years, Earlham's four librarians who give instruction have
prepared and updated some 130 annotated bibliographies and
met more than 200 classes. (A list of most of these bibliographies is available from the author, Earlham College Library,
Richmond, Indiana, 47374. Please enclose a self-addressed
long envelope.) This undertaking has required perhaps a
third of the staff's time for the first half of each term. Is
the program worth all the effort that goes into it? The answer
is yes, if we may judge from the increasingly favorable response from faculty and students. Students receiving library
instruction do use the library more effectively, and increasing
numbers of faculty are accepting the librarians' offers to meet
their classes. Several faculty have commented that library instruction has produced a notable improvement in term papers,
and a number of students who have gone on to graduate
school have expressed their appreciation for the instruction.

A program of library instruction also appears to be worth the effort when the absence of any such program is considered. Conventional reference service has too many built-in handicaps to be fully satisfying to students, faculty, librarians, or administrators. On the one hand, administrators and librarians should regard it as wasteful in time and money for the Reference Librarian to help many individual students with the same basic needs. On the other hand, there are many students who need help, but who would never ask a reference question, either out of shyness, overconfidence, time pressure, or ignorance as to the function of the Reference Librarian. The Reference Librarian should, of course, approach students who appear to be in a quandary. However, it may well be that the student who spends 30 seconds at the card catalog, jots down a number, and hastens to the stacks, needs far more help than the student who pleads total incompetence at the Reference Desk. Then, of course, there are the legions of students who ask reference questions, but whose questions disguise their real needs. Finally, the faculty get discouraged from reading papers that betray an ignorance of the basic reference sources in their disciplines.

College librarians have a great longing for the library to serve as "the heart of the college." For a few students this is the case, but the sad fact is that for most students the library is little more than a study hall. The greatest benefit of an effective program of library instruction is that it can bring the library into its rightful position as an essential element in a college education.

College Librarians and the University-Library Syndrome

Evan Ira Farber

Evan Farber has emerged from his long-time position as head
librarian at Earlham College to become one of the most influential and respected of contemporary librarians, thus his
influence extends beyond college librarianship and library
use instruction. In addition to his election as the chairman
of the College Libraries Section and his involvement in the
Bibliographic Instruction Section of the Association of College
and Research Libraries, he served as president of the Association in 1979-1980 and the following year received its
Academic/Research Librarian of the Year Award. Farber is
the author of numerous articles and the editor of several
books and sets of reference works. He continues to serve
on the Council of the Association of College and Research
Libraries and is much in demand as a speaker and consultant.

In this selection, Farber hypothesizes that the influence
of university libraries on teaching faculty and librarians has
caused both groups to overlook the teaching function of the
undergraduate library. Teaching faculty, he concludes, do
not consider the teaching role of the undergraduate library
because of the attitudes they formed toward the university
library during their own graduate educations. In addition,
many librarians also suffer from what he describes as the
"University-Library Syndrome" because of their contacts with
the university library and the dominance of university librarians in the literature and in professional associations.
Farber comes down solidly on the side of the teaching function of librarians, as opposed to the information provision
function supported by Schiller in an earlier selection.

While empirically untooted, Farber's hypothesis provides

a compelling explanation for many of the attitudes and beha-
viors of teaching faculty that Knapp observed in the Monteith
Library Project. Farber's notion is further verified by the
experience of many librarians involved in user instruction.
Finally, it also partially explains the hesitation of many librarians to accept the underlying ideas that support library use
instruction.

Reprinted by permission of the author and publisher from
The Academic Library: Essays in Honor of Guy Lyle, edited
by Evan Ira Farber and Ruth Walling, pp. 12-23. Metuchen,
N.J.: Scarecrow Press, 1974.

•   •   •

Of the various types of academic libraries, college libraries
should find it easier to achieve their purposes. Their
manageable size should permit a focus on the kind and level
of materials they acquire and distribute, and the relative
clarity of institutional goals should point out more or less
precisely the services they perform. Their personnel is
almost always deeply dedicated, not merely to the profession
and to the needs of their immediate clientele groups, but to
the academic and social objectives of the parent institutions.
Their students and faculty comprise a clientele who are, for
the most part, captive, and with whom the library can
establish almost any relationship--in kind and in depth--it
wants. And yet ... is there any knowledgeable observer
who can say that college libraries are really doing the job
they should?

That the undergraduate library in the large university
has shortchanged the university undergraduate is fairly common knowledge. For those unaware of the situation, it has
been documented in Billy Wilkinson's Reference Services for
Undergraduate Students. He studied two of the more
prestigious undergraduate libraries, those of Cornell University and the University of Michigan, and compared them
with libraries in two liberal arts colleges.

The basic conclusion ... is that full advantage has
not been taken of the opportunities afforded by the

creation of undergraduate libraries. The librarians
in the Cornell and Michigan undergraduate libraries
have not closed the 'gap between class instruction
and library service.' Reference services are of
low calibre. Too often the assistance given students is superficial and too brief. Although the
reference services in both undergraduate libraries
have been in a state of decline for several years,
there have been almost no attempts to discover why
or to make changes from traditional practices.[1]

One might infer from the comparisons made in this
study that college libraries are doing a much superior job.
And, indeed, if one were to assume that the services afforded by the two college libraries (Earlham and Swarthmore)
which Dr. Wilkinson studied as a contrast to the universities'
examples were typical of college libraries, the inference
would be more than justified. But the services given in those
two college libraries are not typical--far from it--and undergraduates in even the smallest colleges are also being shortchanged.

For what reasons? Is it a lack of funds? To be
sure, most college libraries have not been well supported,
but one could respond that the lack of support results--in
part, anyway--from libraries not doing an effective job. Even
more to the point, however, is the fact that many college libraries that have been relatively affluent have not done as
well or as much with their material resources as have other,
poorer, libraries. Is it conservatism, inertia, smugness?
Lack of faculty cooperation or administrative support?
There's not much question that all of these factors have contributed, in one way or another, in one institution or another,
and at one time or another, to inadequate college library
service, and in many books and articles they have been duly
recognized and inveighed against. And while I do not dis-
count their effects, I think another factor has been at work
here which has been just as detrimental. Just as detrimental,
but even more deplorable because its impact--if it were recog-
nized--could have been prevented or at least reduced. This
factor is what I call the "university-library syndrome." It
is a pattern of attitudes which cause college faculty, administrators and librarians to think of their libraries in terms of
university libraries--and thus to imitate their practices, attitudes and objectives.

The Teaching Faculty

It is neither unfair nor inaccurate, I think, to point out
that so many college faculty members suffer from this syndrome, and it is especially true of newer, younger faculty.
Time after time prospective faculty members--many of whom
turn out to be excellent teachers--ask me about our library,
but these questions almost invariably are about reserve book
procedures, how one orders materials, the size of the collection, facilities for interlibrary loan, or borrowing privileges for faculty wives and children. Rarely are the questions in terms of how students use the library, and certainly
never in terms of what the library staff is doing to contribute
to the teaching program--other, of course, than supplying
materials. The assumption such faculty members make is
that all the teaching takes place in the classroom, and the
library is there if the students are sent to it.

What else can one expect? These faculty are in many
cases "junior members" of their disciplines, often only recently out of graduate school, and they view the college library's relationship to their teaching much as they viewed
their university library's relationship to their graduate
studies. That the graduate schools have been most responsible for the poor quality of undergraduate teaching is no
secret. Their emphasis on research, in particular, has
caused university faculty members to slight the teaching of
undergraduates, not only by turning over such teaching to
graduate assistants so that the senior faculty can focus on
their research and their graduate courses, but also by
training graduate students for research rather than teaching.

> The assumed unimportance of preparation for in-
> structional responsibilities reflects the academic
> value hierarchy of the graduate school. American
> graduate study was modeled after the nineteenth
> century German university, an institution estab-
> lished to produce the scholar-researcher rather
> than the scholar-teacher.... This system forces
> the embryonic professor to read prodigiously in
> order to gain a command of his special brand of
> knowledge, and disciplines him to analyze, synthe-
> size, and hypothesize as his professors do.
> Inevitably, he learns to judge his own accomplish-
> ments by the values his graduate professors honor.

It is when this modeling has occurred that the
trainee is judged ready to strike out on his own.
Meanwhile, the novice professor has been
graduated without teaching preparation, and im-
bued with the values of a system which deempha-
size its importance.[2]

The attitude of members of the teaching faculty toward
the staff of the college library is also affected adversely by
their experience in the university library. University graduate students and faculty have had their closest library relationships with those members of university library staffs who
work in the same subject areas, who have the same academic
interests; these have increasingly been the subject specialists
on whom the research scholar could depend for information
and for maintaining the usefulness of the subject collection.
As subject specialists have become increasingly prevalent in
university libraries they have been replacing the general
reference librarians as the handmaidens of the researcher.[3]
For the purpose of research, and for building collections in
depth, such subject specialists are important, but their particular competencies have meant that the scholar has perforce
become less dependent on the general reference librarian and
has put a lower value on his services and worth. Such an
attitude carries over to the college library, though the need
for the subject specialist isn't there. As a matter of fact,
his approach isn't even desirable in working with undergraduates, but the college professor, because he assumes that
the college library's purposes are similar to the university's,
while also noting that the college library staff doesn't know
as much about his field as did the university library's subject specialist whom he'd always depended upon, takes upon
himself the library responsibilities for his students and for
the collection even though the college librarian is much more
suited for this than the specialist would be. Thus, many
college faculty reject the reference librarian's offer of bibliographic instruction to their students and also insist that
the purchasing of materials in their areas be left up to the
departments.

The faculty member's academic background and training
work against an understanding of the proper role of the college library. He has been trained as a scholar-researcher
and is not really interested in how his students use the library; he, after all, learned to use it in his discipline and

he assumes students can also. Moreover, if students need
help, they can either come to him and he'll recommend
titles they should use, or they can of course ask the reference librarian. Rarely does it occur to him that learning
how to use the library intelligently and independently is not
only a desirable part of the educational process but will
also permit students to do better work for him, and certainly
the idea that anyone else can lead his students through the
intricacies of his discipline's material is foreign to him.
Similarly, his selection of library materials is based primarily
on the scholarly reviews, and so he requests specialized
monographs, sets of primary sources, and foreign language
commentaries which the scholarly journals emphasize.[4] No
one who is serious about higher education would deny the
importance of many of these for college libraries, but too
often they are purchased at the expense of materials that
are less highly regarded by specialists but are more appropriate for undergraduates.

The teaching faculty's lack of confidence in their librarians as colleagues in the educational process has another
unfortunate consequence: the librarian's role is viewed as a
passive one, one devoted to housekeeping, to getting materials quickly and making them accessible with dispatch and
efficiency, and to being available when needed for answering
questions, compiling bibliographies, or putting materials on
reserve. Deans and presidents, most of whom have come
from faculty ranks and are prone to the same attitudes, want
their librarians to "run a tight ship"--to keep their accounts
balanced, to make sure all student assistants and clerical
help are working hard, and to answer the needs of the academic departments. Whether the college's students are really
deriving much benefit from the library is rarely questioned.
Lip service is paid to the library's being "the heart of the
college" but as long as faculty members don't complain, as
long as the size of the collection and other standards meet a
level acceptable to accrediting agencies, the administration is
happy to let the library alone.

And, unfortunately, too many librarians like it this
way.

The Librarians

Why are so many college librarians caught in the university-library syndrome? Why have not more of them been able to focus on the special mission of the undergraduate library, just as many college teachers (though still not enough, certainly) have been able to focus on their mission--teaching-- rather than on research? Is it simply a response to what librarians think faculty and administrators think of them? Partly, but there are also reasons which derive from within the profession itself.

The outlook of university librarians is constantly impressed upon college librarians through the fact that university librarians are the spokesmen for academic libraries. They are the ones who edit the journals, write most of the books and articles, hold the positions of eminence not only in library organizations but in councils of higher education which bring together administrators, teaching faculty and librarians. It is quite understandable: most university library administrators are more articulate, travel more widely, have a greater breadth of experience, possess more academic credentials, and have more time because of their larger staffs, and so they do tend to dominate the academic library scene and set its tone. Hopefully, this is changing: better salaries in colleges, disenchantment with the bureaucracy that is necessarily a part of large library systems, and the appeal of smaller, more personal situations for many younger librarians should mean more able college librarians who can establish their own patterns of objectives. But in the meantime, the university librarian is dominant.

Another influence is the fact that so many college librarians either began or spent an earlier portion of their careers in university libraries. They were, to begin with, trained in library schools which were associated with, if not located in, university libraries, and many of them worked in these same libraries while they were going to library school; also, a sizeable number of each year's library school graduates go into university library work. Now, it would be ridiculous to assert that experience in a university library should be regarded negatively when, say, one is interviewing candidates for a college library position, and I hope I have not implied that: surely the desirability of having staff members who have had contact with the expertise, the approach to scholarship, the breadth and depth of materials that only experience in a good research library can provide, is too apparent to need more than simple mention. The point, however,

is that desirable as this experience is, the mind-set that
too often accompanies it, a mind-set resulting in not really
understanding the difference between the purposes of a
research library and those of an undergraduate library,
should be recognized and must be deplored.

Perhaps the most egregious and widespread indication
of college librarians ignoring this difference is the handling
of government documents, especially in those libraries that
are selective depositories. I've seen too many college library documents collections that are in basements or out-of-
the-way corners of the library and are seldom used. The
location of documents collections in many university libraries
is, to be sure, not very much better, but in those libraries
one assumes that the location is not that crucial since their
clientele--faculty and graduate students--must use them,
wherever they are located. But undergraduates are rarely
required to use documents and if the collections are relatively hidden, these superb resource materials are virtually
unused. While some of the blame can be attributed to
teaching faculty who don't direct students to documents,
college librarians must accept much of it for taking the attitude that all that need be done is acquire and organize the
material, and for doing nothing to insure or even encourage
its use.

Just as graduate study in the disciplines has done
little to prepare Ph.D.'s for teaching undergraduates, so
have the library schools done little to train reference librarians to work in college libraries. Reference courses have
taught that the function of the reference librarian is to
provide answers or information--quantitative data, biographical identification, bibliographical citations, comprehensive or
selective bibliographies, or whatever; to become experts in
information retrieval; accuracy and expedition are of the essence. To be sure, one should not off-handedly denigrate
these objectives--that function is an extremely important
one--but when it displaces the educational function of the
reference librarian, then its appropriateness for the undergraduate library must be examined. The role of the information expert is a tempting one, indeed. What reference
librarian doesn't glow under the admiration and gratitude of
a college student for whom he has found that elusive information in a matter of minutes or even seconds after the student
had spent precious hours and had finally, in desperation,

asked for help? But what has the student learned--other
than to ask for help the next time? He has his information,
of course, and can proceed with his work. True also, that
if he needs similar information again, he will know where to
look for it. But how much more the reference librarian
could have done! At that moment the student was interested
in finding out about something and was open to instruction,
so that not only could he have been given the information he
needed, but he could have been taught something about how
one goes about finding information on one's own and he
might perhaps have begun to understand something about
search strategy. This is the process of education, and this
is what college librarians should be engaged in.[5]

Not too long ago Guy Lyle, in preparing for a new
edition of his Administration of the College Library, asked
me for the names of some college libraries that were doing
exciting, innovative things for their students. It was hard
to think of any, and it occurred to me that how far ahead
of college libraries the public libraries are in imaginative
programs which reach out to their publics, even though the
college library's clientele is so handy and so much more
identifiable. Why don't college libraries serve their commu-
nities--their administrators, the staff and their families as
well as students and faculty? Compare, just for example,
the browsing areas of a sampling of college libraries with a
sampling of public libraries. Why isn't the encouragement
and enjoyment of reading part of the college library's responsibility to its community just as a public library's is?
Limited funds, shortage of personnel? Perhaps. But more
important, I think, is the attitude that the library exists
only to support the academic program--and that in a most
traditional way, reflecting the university-library syndrome.

The result of this syndrome is so dismaying because
it so effectively vitiates the potential role of the library in
undergraduate education. Most universities are by their
very nature--their size, their bureaucratic patterns of
operation and governance, their political accountability--
unwieldy and educationally hidebound: educational reform
and innovation is slow and sporadic and so often as not
retreats after a brief flurry of change. Colleges, on the
other hand, by virtue of their variety, independence and
size, are much more capable of innovation in the teaching
and learning process. Sad to say, however, they have not

taken advantage of these attributes nearly enough, and most colleges don't live up to their potential or even to the statements in their catalogs. Nor have their libraries.

Undoubtedly some of the reasons for each falling short are different; there is no question, on the other hand, that the same factor--the emphasis of the university on research and on graduate study rather than on teaching undergraduates--has had sufficient impact on the university's products so that even when they shift to a different educational context that single influence has worked to the disservice of both the classroom and the library.

Insofar as college teaching is concerned, this detrimental effect has been recognized and a variety of corrective approaches have been suggested and are being tried to ameliorate the situation. But the university's impact on college libraries has not been recognized. College libraries are quite different from university libraries, not only in quantitative terms but in their educaitonal roles. They have their own goals and purposes and unique opportunities to achieve them. Only if the differences are kept in mind can college librarians begin to work successfully toward these goals.

NOTES

1. Wilkinson, Billy R. Reference Services for Undergraduate Students; Four Case Studies (Metuchen, N.J.: Scarecrow Press, 1972), p. 347.
2. Raymond P. Whitfield and Lawrence M. Brammer, "The Ills of College Teaching: Diagnosis and Prescription," Journal of Higher Education 44 (1973), 5.
3. Reference service to undergraduates, which, as has been pointed out earlier, has not been good in university libraries, is being handicapped even more by this development since such reference service receives, when its needs are weighed against those of the subject specialists, a lower priority. Eldred Smith, in his essay in this volume on the "Impact of the Subject Specialist Librarian on the Organization and Structure of the Academic Library," asks: "Should general reference stations be staffed by a few reference specialists, supplemented by subject specialists, by new library school graduates who stay only a year or two, or by non-professionals?" A few years ago the suggestion of using

non-professionals for any reference work would have been
considered unthinkable. With the increasing demands of the
subject specialties and the decreasing financial ability to
meet them, the undergraduate libraries, which have no one
speaking strongly for them in the rarefied atmosphere of
the upper echelon university administrator, are being caught
in the squeeze, and services for them will be kept at their
present minimal level.

  4. Fortunately, the growing practice of distributing
Choice cards to faculty members is reducing their independence on reviews by specialists for other specialists.

  5. I've been struck by how quickly students, when
they're shown how, learn to use subject tracings to go from
one subject to another in the card catalog. Yet I know that
for students in most libraries they mean nothing; in one college library I was appalled to see that subject tracings were
omitted from all but the main entry card, even though,
since the cards were computer-produced, tracings on the
subject cards would have entailed no additional expense.

Organizing the Academic Library for Instruction

Howard W. Dillon

In the early issues of The Journal of Academic Librarianship
appeared two articles that reveal the growing sophistication
and institutionalization of library use instruction. This
first selection by Howard Dillon, then university librarian
at Sangamon State University and later Associate Director of
Public Services at the University of Chicago, outlines the
efforts at one institution to reorganize the library specifically to encourage library use instruction.

This contribution is significant on several points.
First, Dillon describes an obvious attempt to remove some of
the traditional clerical functions from librarians so they
could devote more time to library use instruction, collection
development, and other collegial activities with classroom
teaching faculty. Second, it reveals the influence of
Patricia Knapp's ideas on a university president who, in
turn, sought to enhance the role of the academic library in
the educational process.

Sangamon State's new organizational structure met
with considerable excitement among librarians at the time,
and some observers predicted that it would become the organizational pattern of academic libraries in the future.
While this prediction has yet to occur, the change in job
descriptions described in this selection has had considerable
influence on the responsibilities involved in library use instruction. Several changes in both the university administration and the library administration at Sangamon State
have tempered the original enthusiasm and success of this
arrangement, but its essential structure remains intact.

254

•   •   •

For five years at Sangamon State University, there has been
developing a new approach to library organization in which
librarians are viewed as teachers and are freed from administrative duties by non-professional department heads familiar with library work.[1] The experiment has been successful. The report of the evaluation team for the North Central
Association of Colleges and Schools notes: "The library must
definitely be counted as one of the institution's strengths,"
and continues, "...the university has been able to create a
'library faculty' of professionals who are essentially free of
administrative library duties and devote the majority of their
time to the initiation of students into the effective use of
library resources."[2] It is the purpose of this essay to describe how this new form of library organization has developed.

In 1970, shortly after his appointment as Sangamon
State's first president, Robert C. Spencer emphasized that
the new institution would restore teaching to its rightful
pre-eminence in the university. President Spencer was familiar with the writings of Patricia Knapp concerning the
Knox and Monteith College studies[3] and sought to establish
a climate at Sangamon State in which library faculty would
join with their classroom colleagues in making the use of library resources an integral part of the educational process.
With the support of the President and the example of
Patricia Knapp's studies, the interlacing of library and
teaching philosophies became the aim of the library.

The university accepted three basic premises concerning
library learning:

1. That library resources are a vital component in the
educational process and, as such, adequate collections are
necessary as curricular programs are initiated;
2. That library resources should reflect a multi-media
approach to learning and, therefore, include both print and

non-print materials; and,

    3. That library competence is a valid objective of
liberal education and, as such, the library has a responsibility to teach this competence.

    As a result of this third premise, the primary instruc-
tional goal of the library became the commitment to teach
library literacy and the independent use of the library. A
teaching program was designed to supplement formal classroom instruction with the following competencies:

    1. Knowledge of the basic kinds of print and non-
print materials available and how they are arranged;

    2. Knowledge of basic bibliographic tools and how to
use them;

    3. Knowledge of specific bibliographic tools in a par-
ticular area of interest and how to use them;

    4. Knowledge of other subject areas related to the
primary area of interest and how to find reference to them;
and,

    5. Ability to define a problem or an aspect of a prob-
lem within a particular area of interest and to limit and
select materials most relevant to it.

    Writing in Drexel Library Quarterly two years later,
John G. Williamson reviewed the "teaching library" proposals
of Swarthmore College, which sought to augment the role of
the library in instruction.[4] The Swarthmore proposals were
consistent with the library instructional program being developed at Sangamon State. As a result, the phrase "teaching library" was adopted in the library's second annual
report to describe and characterize the activities underway.
The preface to that report quotes the Williamson definition
of the teaching library:

> The teaching library not only concedes to the
> faculty its traditions but accepts the obligation of
> helping the faculty fulfill these functions in the
> most efficient manner possible. At the same time,
> however, it aims at providing the student with the
> library skills and bibliographic sophistication for
> life-long independent work.... The goal of the
> teaching library is merely to extend faculty-
> centered, discipline-oriented studies to include de-
> velopment of research ability and bibliographic

sophistication to levels not normally achieved by undergraduates ... The aim of the teaching library is to make a "conscious effort to train the student in the proper use of the resources of the library as an organized body of information."[5]

Although these goals were clearly in mind during the early months of the university's development, there were overriding concerns related to acquiring resources, facilities, and staff, and to the development of operating procedures.[6] These immediate concerns had to take priority. The initial library faculty consisted of seven professionals and one professional in instructional media. They were recruited with the understanding that each individual would carry administrative responsibility for the development of some aspect of the organization. Each librarian also agreed to share in the reference function as a means of insuring that there would be an awareness of user needs in all operations. It was agreed that developing the library would be a participatory process in which no one would take unilateral action. Rather, each would be responsible for developing suggested policies and procedures to be discussed and decided upon collectively. The library faculty accepted these temporary administrative responsibilities with the understanding that, as it became feasible, non-professionals would assume the day-to-day supervisory responsibility for library operations and at that time new opportunities for library faculty to address the problems of library literacy would be created.

Within a year and a half, responsibility for the ordering function was transferred to a former member of the support staff. This administrative appointment was the first of four to be made from the support staff over the next six months. The introduction of this new type of position, without faculty status, became the fourth category of employment within the organization. The other three were student assistants, civil service support staff, and library faculty.

Fall Semester, 1972, opened with non-librarian administrators in charge of the departments of acquisitions, cataloging, media operations and production, and utilization.[7] Each had shown the ability to supervise employees, to manage budget and schedules, and to relate well to student and faculty users. Each had also mastered the skills necessary

to provide leadership in the functions of the department to
be administered.

The first step in developing a new organizational structure had succeeded. It now remained to express the library
faculty role in the teaching library in more concrete terms.

The library faculty turned its attention to the description of duties that could be included in the work of what
came to be called an Instructional Services Librarian (see
Exhibit I). Each member of the library faculty was to continue to work as a reference librarian and to share in the
responsibilities of developing the collections. An obligation
to prepare guides to resources and to offer research workshops emphasized the faculty member's contribution as a
teacher of library skills and as a compiler of materials to
assist in that process. Liaison with individual classes would
take the library faculty member into the classroom and bring
the classroom into the library. This would give identity to
the librarian as a faculty member with skills to teach and
demonstrate an interest in meeting students and fellow faculty
at the point where learning and information needs come into
conjunction. Liaison responsibilities to the academic programs
promote a mutual understanding of the departmental and library contributions to the educational program.

Liaison to academic programs has proven very effective
in developing collegiality between librarians and other faculty
and is reflected in the strength and appropriateness of the
collections being developed, the services the library provides
for students, and changes in faculty expectations and behavior toward the library. It is a more effective bond than can
be accomplished by having the director of the library sit on
the curriculum committee or the council of deans, although
those vehicles for communication are also valuable and occur
at Sangamon State.

In the position description for Instructional Services
Librarians, it is also indicated that library faculty should
continue to play a role in the development and improvement
of the library's basic operations. As a professional, each is
to be available to the departments and administrators as a
consultant and advisor when needed. While the department
administrators are expected to manage current operations and
to plan for future needs, it is expected that they will wish

EXHIBIT I--JOB DESCRIPTION

Title: Instructional Services Librarian

Qualifications: Master's Degree in Library Science or equivalent. Appropriate perception of the goals of the University and the Library's role in implementing these goals.

Basic Function and Responsibility: To serve the University community by building and maintaining adequate library resources, and to teach and to assist in the effective use of these resources.

Duties and Responsibility:
1. Serves as a reference librarian. This involves:
    a. Assistance in formulation and interpretation of questions.
    b. Outlining steps in the library search.
    c. Helping the user evaluate information found.
    d. Helping the user plan for effective further self-instruction.
2. Assumes responsibility for development of the collection, print and non-print. This involves:
    a. Research into current publications for the purpose of active selection of materials.
    b. Continuous evaluation of the existing collection to determine areas of strength and weakness.
    c. Evaluation of other collections within the area regarding their strengths and weaknesses.
3. Prepares bibliographic guides and offers research workshops in his or her area of expertise. This may occur:
    a. In response to illustrated needs.
    b. In response to specific requests from faculty colleagues.
    c. In response to our public affairs mandate to inform the larger community of our available resources.
4. Assumes liaison responsibilities with one or more academic programs. This involves participation in Program Committee meetings to:
    a. Help relate stated program objectives to existing library resources.
    b. To solicit and/or recommend additions to the library collection in support of the program.
    c. To assist the Program Committee members in the incorporation of library literacy objectives into their courses.
5. Participates in library liaison with individual classes. This involves working with a classroom colleague to relate the problems addressed in that classroom to resources available in our library and other information sources within the community.
6. Serves as a member of the Library Cabinet. This involves application of professional knowledge and skills to:
    a. The planning and development of new library programs.
    b. The evaluation of existing library services and instruction.
    c. The formulation of library policies and procedures.
7. Performs other faculty responsibilities as stated in the memorandum, Considerations in Appointing New Faculty.

to take advantage of the education and experience of the
library faculty. Therefore, individual library faculty may
be asked, or may volunteer, to study a problem area and to
present a proposed plan for its solution to the appropriate
administrator. It is understood that the library faculty member does not interfere with the administrative line from the
University Librarian to the department head and from there
to the supporting staff. The consulting librarian is, in effect, an employee of the department head and the solution
posed is accepted, rejected, or modified by the administrator.
Policy and procedural proposals that result from such studies
are presented at the Library Cabinet for discussion and approval as a means of insuring that individual departments do
not implement changes that would inadvertently hinder the
operations of another unit.[8] Library Cabinet discussions
also have the benefit of building consensus for policies and
procedures. As a result, the library is able to avoid the
unfortunate criticism sometimes expressed to the public when
one department disagrees with, but is helpless to change,
the policies of another.

Given the new description of the role of a library faculty member, the Vice President for Academic Affairs accepted the University Librarian's suggestion to revise the
titles used on contracts in the library. Phrases descriptive
of former administrative roles, such as Serials Librarian,
were removed, leaving only academic ranks and titles reflecting the new organization. The words "Library Science" were
replaced by "Library Instructional Services." As an example,
the new contract title for the person who had been Assistant
Professor of Library Science and Documents Librarian became
Assistant Professor of Library Instructional Services.

The significance of this revision is that it provides a
contractual relationship fully analogous to other faculties.
The individual faculty member's work load plan from semester
to semester is negotiated within the library faculty and approved by the University Librarian as other teachers nego-
tiate duties in a department and with a dean. As the faculty
member's responsibilities shift with the needs of the library
program, it is not necessary to revise the title on the contract document.

Second, this change shifted the basis for compensation
and promotion from one which focuses on relative administra-

tive responsibility to one which reflects an individual's growth as a librarian and the development of skills in teaching the use of libraries. Third, the recruitment and evaluation of library faculty shifted from one primarily based on internal criteria relating to the perceived needs of the professional and support staff to a balanced set of criteria which also emphasized the individual's role vis-a-vis faculty colleagues and students.

Instructional activities at SSU are organized into "program committees" rather than traditional departments in order that the disciplines will not turn inward upon themselves. Each consists of the faculty teaching in the program, some faculty from other program committees, and students. A coordinator is elected, usually for a one-year term. The guidelines for program committees describe them as "the primary units of faculty and student participation in Sangamon State University."[9]

Significantly for the library, the function and responsibility statements for program committees included the following language at the suggestion of the Vice President for Academic Affairs:

> Program Committees shall provide measures that
> will enhance relations between the program com-
> mittees and the library holdings, broadening the
> understanding of the philosophy of the library,
> and increasing the use of the library facilities by
> program committee members, faculty and students.[10]

This responsibility underscored the liaison role that library faculty were to assume as members of other program committees and placed an obligation on those committees to find their own ways to relate to the library.

The Library Program Committee was formed in early 1973 and, in addition to the ten library faculty, had the volunteer membership of eight faculty representing seven program committees and, unfortunately, only two students. A member of the library faculty was elected Coordinator and the committee assumed responsibility for determining needs and recommending priorities for the instructional programs of the library. Within this context, the committee would select and recommend candidates for appointment to the library

faculty, evaluate performance for promotion, and initiate
tenure decisions.[11]

The relationship between the Library Program Committee and the University Librarian is that of a faculty to a
dean. The committee's decisions and recommendations are
passed up through governance lines to the university committees on personnel and tenure decisions. Simultaneously,
they are forwarded to the University Librarian, who passes
them on to the Vice President for Academic Affairs with con-
currence, comments or disagreement. Interaction between
the governance and administrative lines is built into the process at each level before the recommendations are finally
transmitted to the President.

Evaluation

Sangamon State's ability to define new roles for library staff
and the responsiveness of the university faculty and students
to this experiment can largely be attributed to the environment for innovation that surrounded this new, upper-division
university in its early years. The library began with eight
faculty positions in a university faculty of fifty-four. The
President provided leadership and support for a library with
active involvement in the educational process. The faculty
were open to interdisciplinary representation on academic
program committees and willing to shed traditional biases
about teaching and the use of libraries. Our students helped
most of all by responding immediately and enthusiastically to
the concern for learning, which they recognized in the library. Their expressions of satisfaction reinforced the sympathetic views of their classroom teachers and gave encouragement to the library faculty and staff to continue with the new
program.

Evaluation of many aspects of the university was part
of the institution's self-study for accreditation. Reaction to
questions concerning the library's efforts to provide students
with library skills for life-long independent work prompted
the self-study committee to write: "Student response to this
aspect of the library's teaching role has been largely positive,
with over half of the students who completed the NCA Self-
Study Questionnaire reporting that their library skills had
improved since their enrollment at SSU." The report con-

tinues: "Given the emphasis SSU places on restoring teaching to preeminence in the educational process, the library's
second teaching function--that of assisting faculty to up-
grade their own teaching theories and skills--is of at least
equal importance. Significantly, over two-thirds of the faculty have credited the library with helping them to be
better teachers."[12]

Implications

Although the organization described has been developed under special circumstances surrounding the creation of a new
university, its philosophical and theoretical roots are im-
planted in a rich literature concerning the role of the academic librarian. It is hoped that this example will encourage
others to experiment with new models of organization and
new roles for staff that will enable their libraries to become
stronger as "teaching libraries."

The implications of this experiment are intriguing.
What will it mean for library education if more libraries
adopt similar models of organization? What if libraries move
toward a clearer distinction between the technical-vocational
aspects of library operations and the professional roles in
which librarians can engage? Is not the model that has been
described consistent with the technological changes occurring
with respect to the availability of cataloging data through
computerized data bases? Will we not see a decreasing need
for the professional staff of libraries to be engaged in the
bibliographic description and classification of materials?
Does the emergence of open-access library services among
consortia and cooperative library networks require that we
place more emphasis on instructing library users in the
skills for finding information in order that they may use many
libraries effectively? Do the "new students" in our colleges
and universities require more from their libraries than their
predecessors did? Does the reemergence of the concept of
the library as every person's "university" call for more of
our professional energies to be directed to the user and,
through our new technology, less time absorbed in internal
processing and administrative details?

Librarians and library educators must ask such questions. The viability of the library within an academic

community depends on our willingness to face these questions and to experiment with the alternatives the answers suggest.

NOTES

1. Located in the state capital, Springfield, Illinois, Sangamon State University opened in 1970 as an upper-division university emphasizing public affairs. Sangamon State and its sister institution, Governors State University, located near Chicago, serve a capstone role for an alternative system of public higher education built on the state's community colleges.

2. North Central Association of Colleges and Schools, Commission on Institutions of Higher Education, Report of a Visit to Sangamon State University, Springfield, Illinois, December 8-11, 1974, p. 4.

3. Knapp, Patricia B., College Teaching and the College Library, (ACRL Monograph no. 23), Chicago: ALA, 1959.

   Knapp, Patricia B., The Monteith College Library Experiment. Metuchen, N.J.: Scarecrow, 1966.

4. Williamson, John G., "Swarthmore College's 'Teaching Library' Proposals," Drexel Library Quarterly 7, nos. 3 and 4 (July and October, 1971).

5. Ibid., p. 204.

6. The SSU Library has added an average of 30,000 volumes each year. Holdings as of January 31, 1975 were 155,818 volumes, 39,180 government publications, 189,720 microforms, 5,891 non-print items, and 3,220 current periodical subscriptions. There are fifty-two staff, including 9.5 positions in the Media Department.

7. Professional librarians are not employed in any of the departments on a regular basis, although there are appropriate roles for persons trained in many professions in a multi-media library. The SSU library employs a photographer, a commercial artist, an electronics technician, an accountant and a specialist in personnel.

8. The Library Cabinet consists of all library faculty, department heads, one representative each from the supporting staff and student employees, the University Librarian and the library administrative assistant.

9. Sangamon State University, Office of the President, Administrative Bulletin 3, no. 2 (October 12, 1972): p. 5.

10. Ibid., p. 7.

11. Since the formation of the Library Program Committee, one instructor has been promoted to Assistant Professor, two Assistant Professors have been promoted to Associate Professors, and two library faculty have been granted tenure.

12. Sangamon State University, University in Process: Self-Study Report of Sangamon State University (Springfield, Ill., The University, 1974) p. 61.

Information Structure and Bibliographic Instruction

Elizabeth Frick

The second influential article from an early issue of The
Journal of Academic Librarianship, this selection demonstrates
both the influence of the Earlham College program and the
growing sophistication of librarians involved in user instruction. At the time of the writing, Elizabeth Frick served as
reference librarian at Earlham College; she later moved to
the University of Colorado at Colorado Springs where she
served as project librarian for a Library Service Enhancement
Program grant sponsored by the Council on Library Resources
in 1977-1978. She currently teaches at the School of Library
Service, Dalhousie University.

Many, if not most, of the instructional programs of the
1940s, 1950s, and early 1960s made little distinction between
library orientation and library instruction. Only slowly has
library use instruction evolved beyond the basic level of
teaching students how to locate library resources. With this
article, however, Frick points out the need for a higher level
of instruction involving an understanding of the different
types of information sources as they vary from one discipline
to another.

For related discussions, the reader is referred to the
following articles: John MacGregor and Raymond G. McInnis,
"Integrated Classroom Instruction and Library Research,"
Journal of Higher Education 48 (January/February 1977):
17-38; Topsy N. Smalley, "Bibliographic Instruction in Aca-
demic Libraries: Questioning Some Assumptions," The
Journal of Academic Librarianship 3 (November 1977): 280-
283; and Pamela Kobelski and Mary Reichel, "Conceptual
Frameworks for Bibliographic Instruction," The Journal of
Academic Librarianship 7 (May 1981): 73-77.

Reprinted by permission of the author and publisher from
the Journal of Academic Librarianship 1 (September 1975):
12-14.   Copyright © 1975 by the Journal of Academic Librarianship.

•   •   •

The literature concerning library instruction has emphasized
the functional aspects of establishing a program. Only recently has it begun to focus upon the goals of instruction,
in spite of the fact that consideration of the nature of the
competencies we hope to develop in students should be of
prime concern in designing an instructional program.[1] Furthermore, before we try to convince educators that library
instruction should be an important part of any curriculum,
we must develop a convincing rationale for such a claim.
This paper is an attempt to describe the important role
bibliographic instruction at the undergraduate level can play
in educating the student and the ways in which the structure
of information can contribute to the nature of instruction.

Bibliographic instruction at its most basic level aims at
helping a student locate material for a particular project.
However, the goal can be broadened to include developing
the student's ability to manipulate library resources for whatever need. Psychologist Douglas Heath believes that the
produce of education ought to be what he calls an "educable
person."[2] If this is not to mean simply an "impressionable"
person, then somewhere in each student's course of study
there must be a component which involves the rigorous
assessment and understanding of information sources. Ultimately, we should aim at developing intelligent persons who,
independently, can locate and assess the sources of information needed for a wide variety of intellectual, social and personal concerns.

Some writers on reference theory and practice clearly
believe that the primary function of a reference librarian is
to supply requested information.[3] I could not disagree more.
I would assert that society does not need more people who
are content simply to accept information handed to them by
an expert. We need to educate students who are able to
discriminate among the various sources of information in order

to locate pertinent data and to discover countervailing opinions to those which are first presented to them. We want to
help students develop a sense that they receive data from a
variety of sources: libraries, mass media, community agencies, politicians, experts and friends. Some of these sources
will prove to be reliable, some will need always to be carefully checked.

Were this rationale for bibliographic instruction to be
adopted, it would, I think, lead to the creation of a program in which the student is taught the appropriate skills
in information location and selection, as well as helped to
acquire an appreciation of the interconnections between information structure, reference source structure and retrieval method.

To achieve these purposes, we need courses that explore the retrieval of literature at a level more sophisticated
than the usual list of sources appropriate for a particular
paper. In these courses, four distinct levels of bibliographic
awareness need to be developed: 1) awareness of particular
reference sources, 2) awareness of types of sources, 3) a-
wareness of the ways in which reference sources reflect the
nature of the disciplines they serve, and 4) awareness of the
information structure in the society.

Particular Sources

The first level, dealing with particular titles, includes instruction in the use of particular encyclopedias, bibliographies
and indexes, card catalog, and so forth. For freshmen, the
sources will tend to be fairly elementary ones like the Readers'
Guide, while for upperclass students, the sources will include
more sophisticated or specialized material, such as the Journal
of Economic Literature.

Classes/Types of Sources

The second level evolves from the first: the awareness of
reference sources as being separable into distinct groups (indexes, bibliographies). The ability to recognize categories
in reference sources enables the student to transfer what he
has learned about information gathering in one discipline to a

different discipline. As an obvious example, the existence
of Psychological Abstracts might suggest to a student a similar service for sociology.

Relationship: Source Structure/Disciplinary Literature

The third level is more sophisticated than either of the first
two. At this point we can attempt to show the student that
he is able to learn a great deal about the nature of his particular discipline just from looking at the types of reference
sources which are available and useful to the discipline. For
example, what does it mean about a discipline when a really
current periodical abstracting service is not available? What
does it mean about the type of sociology being done if it
uses primarily statistical sources? Why are history bibliographies generally better developed than periodical indexes in
the same field?

Information Structure in the Society

The fourth level of bibliographic awareness is still more sophisticated. It is concerned with the ways in which information within a discipline is generated by specialists and disseminated to other specialists within the field and to the
general public. Harold Lasswell has posited a succinct "five
W's" to formulate the questions that should be asked: Who?
says what? in which channel? to whom? with what effect?[4]
This is a broader reflection of the same questions attempted
in the third level where we consider the relationship between
reference sources and the disciplines. Here we study the
relationship between information sources and the society.

Some of us, considering the implications of this fourth
level, may balk. Is it an activity more appropriate to the
training of graduate students, reference librarians, or even
"information specialists?" I think not, at least not at the
level of intensity which I would suggest. My concern is to
discover the proper mode of undergraduate instruction, whose
end is the development of a self-educable person who can
continue to find and use information intelligently long after
graduating from college.

Having defined the goals of the different levels of

bibliographic awareness, it will be useful to review each of
them in order to discuss some of the methods by which each
may be achieved.

     In teaching particular sources for particular needs,
we generally find it convenient to use a fairly conventional
form of teaching, which may involve individual instruction,
a seminar or a lecture. Whatever the form, the instructor
generally concentrates on the advantages and disadvantages
of each reference item. Even here the librarian should try
to emphasize to the student the need for clarity and
reasoned order in searching. To pull a bibliography magi-
cally from the shelf is to underscore what many students
already feel, rightly or wrongly, about library "mystique."
While this approach may emphasize the librarian's expertise,
it does not enlighten the student concerning why we are
going from one set of references to another (e.g., "We've
listed the books the library has, now we want to see what
periodical articles are available."). The opportunity to emphasize the habit of discrimination in the use of reference
material ought not to be wasted.

     The ability to discriminate shades into the next level
of the student's bibliographic development, namely, an appreciation of the different types of sources. The student
who learns to recognize a useful bibliography in the first
stage has recognized certain characteristics of bibliographies
in general. The student who has been encouraged to be
lucid and orderly in searching is already predisposed to
understand the logic of the suitability of different types of
sources for answering different types of questions. We can
discuss this latter problem with students as we help them
at the reference desk. We can also underscore it in instructional programs which include a prepared bibliography, provided that we order the bibliography so that it reflects
search procedure. For example, a model bibliography might
begin by describing the encyclopedias in the field, proceed
to bibliographies, and then to the use of the card catalog,
periodical indexes, pamphlet file, etc. When we are dealing
with more advanced students, particularly those who are
majoring in the discipline in which they are seeking assistance, we might encourage them to suggest what sector of
the information network could best answer their question.
For example, students in economics and sociology might be
made aware that government documents probably offer the

most comprehensive nation-wide labor statistics, whereas a
private research report might offer the best study of interpersonal dynamics in a given factory.

An awareness of the relationship between the reference
sources in a discipline and the structure of information in
that discipline is our third goal. It involves the ability to
recognize the ways in which the needs of certain disciplines
determine the form and content of the information sources
upon which they rely. The emergence of the Social Sciences
Citation Index (SSCI) offers a fine example. Here, for the
first time, is an index which assumes that the social sciences
are "scientific" enough to be building extensively on previous research, that every researcher is not, as one of our
Earlham sociologists put it, "Robinson Crusoe on his own,
beginning afresh."[5] Furthermore, the computerized Permuterm index, based exclusively on title words, assumes the
precision and universality of the language used by the social
scientist. Instructive contrasts can be made for students
who are working in the humanities, pointing out what
Permuterm or KWIC indexes would do to a search in that
area. In looking for material on "college students" in the
Social Sciences & Humanities Index, I found an article entitled "Sun, Surf and Sex." Such allusively titled material
would be lost in the Permuterm or KWIC systems.

The correlation between the structure of the literature
in a discipline and the reference sources in that discipline
can be illustrated by tracing the progress of a piece of
research from the time of its inception to its appearance in
specialized texts. In the field of psychology, for example,
the same information may appear in several successive
guises. Depending upon his purposes, the student may find
it relevant to consult the research report (in which case
Psychological Abstracts will be the appropriate reference
tool) or a generalized description of that work (for which
Annual Review of Psychology might be germane). Different
sources are designed to plug the researcher in at various
points along the information line, and the different intentions
of the information sources are often an exact mirror of the
research/publication process within the discipline.

The influence of disciplinary structure on reference
source structure is analogous to the influence of the overall
pool of information in a society upon that society's communi-

cation structure. Or, put another way, just as the kind of
reference source used has a great deal of bearing on the
kind of information received (as implied in the paragraph on
the Social Sciences Citation Index above), so the nature of
the source of information in a society will play an important
role in determining the type of information the members of
a society receive. In the process of arranging a library
instruction component for a senior class in Political Science
which was discussing alternative models for the future, I
had an opportunity to explore this aspect of information
structure with undergraduates. They conjectured that much
future decision-making might take place in the councils of
"technocratic experts." The questions then became what
kind of information structure that situation might imply.
What kind of information would be fed to these technocrats,
through what channels, and what kind of information would
they then relay, to whom, and through what channels?
These questions can lead to the technical analysis of information structure or to social and ethical questions concerning
access to information. In either case, the answers are relevant to an understanding of the decision-making process
within a society and of the quality of the individual lives of
the members of that society.

     For anyone who follows the media closely, it will be
clear that examples abound. When Richard Nixon said, on
nationwide television, "I am not a crook," he had the innate
prestige of the American Presidency compounded by the most
persuasive mass media available. Viewers could not take his
statement lightly. It was an example of the channels of information weighting the information given. The resulting
decision on the part of the citizenry speaks only for the
weight of the information coming through other channels.
The crucial importance of the control of information channels
has been noted by Servan-Schreiber, and virtually every
political sociologist and futurologist would agree with his
comment:

> The power to inform ... is not only essential to
> the media, but to citizens. It is central to sorting
> out the conflicts and issues in our post-industrial
> societies. [6]

     In our academic libraries, it is well that we look care-
fully at our tools of communication and examine the way in

which they direct our search for information, by setting the
parameters within which the facts of a given situation will
be discovered.

> The old belief that bibliography is a value-free,
> innocuous tool has been shaken by those who have
> become aware of hidden biases in bibliographic
> rules and codes.[7]

There has already been at least one study done of the
biases in the Subject Headings Used in the Dictionary Catalogs of the Library of Congress, and the class bias of libraries in the past has been well-documented, most recently
in a Library Journal article by Michael Harris.[8] As early
as 1964, another librarian asked, "What communication channels for recorded information in our society are of particular
significance to decision-making processes?"[9] Such queries
eventually lead to the McLuhanesque question, "What significance does the structure of those channels have for our
society?"

I believe that it is essential that we carry this line of
thought into library instruction, making it clear to students
that reference structures both open and close certain information channels, that (as one instance of this phenomenon)
the rigidity of certain periodical indexes in regard to subject
headings perpetuates certain views of the discipline. Further,
bibliographic instruction can help the student recognize that
by understanding who generates information, who publishes it,
who disseminates and classifies it, how, and for whom, he
will develop a more subtle grasp of the value and limitations
of that information.

Summary

The ways in which students conceive of information gathering
in the context of library resources will have a bearing on the
manner in which they set about acquiring information in the
larger context. Information gathering is a process which librarians are uniquely suited to discuss with students, but
only occasionally does material appear which links information
structure with methods of library instruction.[10] These
linkages should be of primary concern in discussing the retrieval of information. Faculty show students how to analyze

and develop concepts. Librarians can show them how to
locate and document these concepts and how to assess their
sources. Library instruction can best enrich the educational process when the librarian is able to link bibliographic
skills to an awareness of the implications of the information
function in society, developing in the student a sense of the
library as a flexible, subtle instrument for the gathering of
information.

NOTES

1. For a systematized effort to outline goals, see
"Academic Bibliographic Instruction: Model Statement of
Objectives (1st complete draft 4/74)." LOEX News 1, no. 2
(May 1, 1974): 3-7. These goals focus only on the two
lowest levels of what this paper outlines as the four levels
of bibliographic awareness.
2. "Priorities should reflect the core goal of a
liberal education which is to further the growth of an
individual. A person should be educated to be educable,
that is, more adaptable." Douglas H. Heath, Growing Up
in College (San Francisco: Jossey-Bass, 1968), p. 256.
3. For late examples see Charles R. McClure, "A
Reference Theory of Specific Information Retrieval," RQ 13,
no. 3 (Spring, 1974): p. 207-212, and Jack B. King, The
Hamline Project: An Educational Information System for the
Small College Campus (St. Paul, Minn.: Hamline University,
1974).
4. Harold Lasswell, "Structure and Function of Communication in Society," in The Communication of Ideas.
Lyman Bryson, ed. (N.Y.: Harper, 1948), p. 37-51.
5. The SSCI offers an alternative search method to
undergraduates, one that may be more suited to their needs.
Even mature researchers find this a fruitful search strategy.
Melvin Weinstock, Director of Marketing for ISI, which publishes SSCI, argues this in his "ISI's Social Sciences and
Humanities Citation Index," in Conference on Access to
Knowledge and Information in the Social Sciences and Humanities, New York, 1972, Access to the Literature of the Social
Sciences and Humanities (Flushing, N.Y.: Queens College
Press, 1974), p. 120-130. "In general, user studies confirm
that scanning journals is the most frequently used technique
to keep up, and in the scanning process, more is learned of
the previous literature by the references to it. Abstracting

and index publications and reviews are also important, but
do not rate as high and are not used as frequently as journals." (p. 122).

6. Jean Louis Servan-Schreiber, The Power of Inform;
Media: The Information Business (N.Y.: McGraw-Hill, 1974),
p. x.

7. Ilse Bry, "The Emerging Field of Sociobibliography:
Reassessment and Reorientation of Access to Knowledge in the
Social Sciences" in Conference on Access to Knowledge and
Information in the Social Sciences and Humanities, N.Y.,
1972, Access to the Literature of the Social Sciences and Humanities (Flushing, N.Y.: Queens College Press, 1974), p.
11.

8. S. Berman, Prejudices and Antipathies: A Tract
on the LC Subject Heads Concerning People (Metuchen, N.J.:
Scarecrow, 1971); M. H. Harris, "Purpose of the American
Public Library: A Revisionist Interpretation of History,"
Library Journal 98 (Sept. 15, 1973), p. 2509-2514.

9. Don R. Swanson, "The Intellectual Foundations of
Library Education: Introduction," The Library Quarterly
34, no. 4 (Oct. 1964), p. 290.

10. A stimulating book by Thelma K. Freides,
Literature and Bibliography of the Social Sciences (Los
Angeles: Melville, 1973) makes the connection between
reference sources and the literature in the field quite explicit. Papers presented at the 1972 Conference on Access
to Knowledge and Information in the Social Sciences and
Humanities have been cited above. Several of the papers
provoke serious thought concerning research methods,
source structure and sociobibliography, although none make
the connection with bibliographic instruction.

Academic Libraries and Undergraduate Education:
The CLR Experience

Nancy E. Gwinn

The Council on Library Resources provided a major impetus
to the development of library instruction programs during
the 1970s. Both through its own resources and in joint
sponsorship with the National Endowment for the Humanities,
it provided approximately three million dollars to more than
fifty academic institutions in support of library use instruction. In this selection, Nancy Gwinn, information and publications officer and later program officer with the Council
during much of the 1970s, offers her analysis of the results.

Gwinn concludes that despite efforts to institutionalize
the various programs the Council funded, few continued beyond the initial grant period. Turnover of faculty, administrators, and librarians, lack of cooperation from faculty, and
indifference on the part of administrators are common factors
among those programs that failed. She recommends effective
working relations with the teaching faculty as the key to
successful library use instruction programs.

Not all critics shared Gwinn's pessimism. Edward G.
Holley, then dean of the University of North Carolina School
of Library Science, noted that the Council had a major impact
in focusing the attention of librarians on the service approach
to library users in his paper "Library Instruction: Some Observations from the Past and Some Questions about the Future," in Improving Library Instruction, edited by Carolyn
Kirkendall (Ann Arbor, Michigan: Pierian Press, 1979), pp.
89-96. Still, Gwinn rightly concludes that the Council's
efforts did not create a revolution among the American teaching faculty and that its expectations for change were un-
realistically high.

Given the history of the adoption of innovation in higher education, one decade and a few million dollars are insufficient to alter attitudes and practices developed over numerous decades regarding the role of the academic library in higher education. However the Council on Library Resources, through its grant program, played a major role in institutionalizing library use instruction in academic librarianship. Grant recipients are well-represented in the literature, in leadership positions of the Association of College and Research Libraries, and in positions of responsibility in academic libraries. This is not an insignificant accomplishment and it serves as a solid springboard for the future of library use instruction.

•   •   •

Is it possible for an academic library to find happiness as an active, committed partner in the education of college and university undergraduates? In true soap-opera style, for some ten years the Council on Library Resources, Inc., (CLR) has been preparing episodes in a continuing narrative whose climax, one might think, would resolve that question. Through a series of grant programs, each project has carried along the story line, with that question always pushing us to turn the page, to listen in again tomorrow, to keep searching for the answer. There have been subplots and side excursions along the way. It is time, now, to stop and see how far we've come.

As a foundation, the council awards grants to other organizations and individuals for projects that fall within its program objectives; as an operating foundation, it also develops and administers programs of its own. CLR's program goals have shifted over the years as some problems were solved and new ones emerged. Its current interests include bibliographic services (particularly efforts toward developing a nationwide computerized service), library resources and their preservation, professional education and

training, research and analysis, and, last but certainly not
least, library operations and services.

CLR and Library Instruction

The council's interest in user education in academic libraries
began in 1964 when CLR supplied funds for a project at
Mt. San Antonio College in Walnut, California, to develop a
slide-tape program for use with a then-new "teaching
machine." The purpose of the machine was to provide
general information to students on the use of the library.
Even the language used to describe the grant sounds a little
antiquated to our more technologically sophisticated ears. It
was reported that the machines were effective in teaching
about the use of the library and in reducing demands on
library staff, but the equipment had severe mechanical limitations. [1]

In 1968, because the council was then interested in
developing prototype equipment, it made a small supplemental
grant for an improved design of a machine for use in academic libraries and suitable for commercial manufacture. Apparently it never reached the marketplace.

In 1970 the Model Engineering Library within the
Massachusetts Institute of Technology's Barker Engineering
Library received the first of two grants as one component
of Project Intrex.

Project Intrex (Information Transfer Experiments) was
a program of research that attempted to establish the bases
upon which the technical library of the future would be laid.
The project involved the adaptation of technology to improve
access to information through a full-text retrieval system
coupled with a computer-based catalog. But through the
Model Engineering Library, attention also turned to the instruction of library users. It was through this program that
the well-known Library Pathfinders emerged, and successful
experiments with point-of-use instruction using audiovisual
equipment were made. [2]

In 1969, however, the council initiated two programs,
under the umbrellas of which most of its projects involving
user education have gathered; the CLR Fellowship Program

and the College Library Program. The latter was jointly
sponsored by the council and the National Endowment for
the Humanities (NEH).

In 1975 a third program, the Library Service Enhancement Program, added another mechanism through which to
explore the possibilities of establishing an effective union of
academic libraries and teaching programs. None of these
programs had user education as its specific goal.

The CLR Fellowship Program

Under its Fellowship Program, the council offered support
to midcareer librarians who developed projects that would
occupy a minimum of three months. The projects had to be
designed to advance the individual's technical, administrative, or substantive skills in librarianship and could involve
research, travel, or internship experiences--anything, that
is, short of work toward a degree. Over the years, 215
fellowships were awarded, and thirteen of them focused, in
whole or in part, on user education.[3]

The CLR Fellows approached the topic from a variety
of angles, from an enumeration of strengths and weaknesses
of various teaching strategies to methods of program evaluation, from a synthesis that would form a model program to
a view of library instruction as part of a broader study,
such as the role of the specialist librarian or interpersonal
communication. Most of the research was keyed to the librarian's own work situation. The CLR Fellows most often
were either attempting to start a library instruction program
or to improve one already in existence.

The methods used were similar: visits to a number of
libraries, usually preceded by a questionnaire (although we
tried to discourage this) and followed up with interviews
either in person or by telephone.

Thus CLR helped Allan Dyson look at how undergraduate library instruction was organized in ten U.S. and
about a dozen British libraries, and the council assisted
John Lubans' examination of instructional programs in twelve
libraries and his conduct of a detailed user survey at the
University of Colorado.

Many of the fellows' conclusions are consistent with the last ten years' history of interest and enthusiasm for the topic and would come as no surprise to persons familiar with the basic literature. In the early 1970s, for example, a fellow concluded that there "seems to be emerging an awareness of a need for a new breed of teaching librarian for academic libraries."[4]

By mid-decade many programs with dedicated staff had emerged, and the conclusions drawn by visiting fellows focused on obstacles as well as successes. Dyson, for example, concluded that "the overriding factor determining the success of an instructional program is the extent of commitment to it by the library administration."[5] Johnnie Givens' "clearest understanding" from her study was that "the development of skills in the use of the library by any instructional method is likely to be sterile and void of general acceptance and success if it is separate from the other processes of educational experiences the learner is offered."[6]

By 1978 Hannelore Rader used her personal experiences and a fellowship study of ten academic library instruction programs in the U.S. and Canada in a classic nuts-and-bolts article on how to set up a program in a college library.[7]

The CLR-NEH College Library Program

The fellows generated useful information, but the program was supplemental to the council's main efforts of the past decade, which were embodied in two programs that supported experimental endeavors to improve the relationships of academic libraries with faculty, students, and the college or university as a whole.

Based on concepts generated by Patricia Knapp's Monteith College library experiment,[8] the CLR-NEH College Library Program provided thirty-six institutions with grants to explore innovative ways of enhancing the library's participation in the education process, of making faculty and administrators more aware of the collections and human resources at hand, and of imparting to students a clearer notion of the enriching cultural and educational role libraries can play throughout their lives.[9] The NEH participation brought with it the added focus of enhancing the role of academic libraries in respect to humanistic scholarship.

The thirty-six institutions had enrollments ranging from a few hundred students to more than 20,000. There was an emphasis in the early years of the program on helping historically black academic institutions; as the years passed the program grew more competitive and the proposals became more sophisticated. Thus, while at one end of the spectrum institutions such as Miles College in Alabama established very traditional orientation programs, at the other end, Northwestern University hired librarians with Ph.D.'s to carry on research and instructional activities (including developing a course on the history of written and printed communication), and Lake Forest College in Illinois built a program around on-line bibliographic services.

Those thirty-six institutions displayed (and continue to display, since the last institutions to be funded will not finish their programs until the early 1980s) a variety of activities in their search for the key that would unlock the door of library-faculty cooperation on their respective campuses.

Some of them brought faculty members into the library to staff the reference desk, keep regular office hours, survey the collection, redesign their courses to include library components, etc. Some used graduate or undergraduate student assistants and gave them special training so that they might help other students. Some brought speakers to campus and arranged exhibits, lectures, films, and other cultural events, around which were built seminars, special classes, workshops, and other educational scaffolding--all of which brought new people into the library. Some held workshops for faculty-- one small college library even going so far as to hold two-week summer sessions, or refresher courses for faculty.

Collectively they have filled to overflowing a cornucopia of workbooks, handbooks, bibliographies, pre- and posttests, flyers, brochures, and a few audiovisual materials. New librarian positions were created with titles such as "Librarian at Large," "Humanities Librarian," "Scholar Librarian," "Coordinator of Instructional Services," "Orientation-Instruction Librarian," etc. Librarians have been appointed to curriculum committees and worked part-time in departments--

in one case even holding half-time departmental appointments.
All were committed to working closely with faculty (a requirement of the program), and most engaged in some form
of bibliographic instruction, whether it meant developing a
separate course, team teaching in the classroom, assisting
faculty and students on an individual basis, or a combination
of these.[10]

The College Library Programs were funded for three-
to five-year periods. CLR and NEH invested more than
$2,341,000, but each institution was also required to match
its grant with funds above and beyond the library's regular
budget. These stipulations were consciously inserted to
help the library "institutionalize" the program and to bring
extra money to the library that, it was hoped, would
continue after the grant period. In both cases, the results
have been quite varied.

The CLR Library Service Enhancement Program

In 1975 the council decided that it would accelerate the
demonstration process started in the College Library Program
on a more modest basis by providing small planning grants
to a variety of institutions.

CLR invested nearly $400,000 for the resulting Library
Service Enhancement Program, which provided each of
twenty-five institutions with the equivalent of one librarian's
salary in order to relieve that person of normal duties and
allow him or her to work full time for one year with faculty,
administrators, students, and staff.[11]

The goal, again, was to find ways of integrating the
library more fully into the teaching and learning process and
to expand the library's role in the academic life of the college
or university. Unlike the College Library Program, the
science curriculum could be included. Again, nothing was
said that would limit the design of the program to any particular form of bibliographic instruction. But, of course, that
method continues to be a most attractive way of working with
faculty and of developing a more tangible campus role for
librarians as instructors.

The Enhancement Program had a particularly beneficial

effect on the project librarians. They were required to be
senior staff members who presumably were familiar with the
institution and faculty. Their release time provided them
with an opportunity to leave behind the established routine
for a year and work with faculty and administrators outside
of the library. Furthermore, many took the opportunity to
travel and gather ideas from other programs in the vicinity.
Some were invited to give conference presentations or workshops. Their year of intense professional growth perhaps
can best be summed up by the concluding comment of one
Enhancement Program librarian's final report. "Thank you,
Council," she wrote, "for the most demanding, fun-filled,
frustrating, impossible, rewarding, fast year of my life."

Accomplishments

In ten years of involvement, then, what has been accomplished in these programs? There have been two attempts
on the part of the council to evaluate program activity.

In the summer of 1975, a team of CLR and NEH
evaluators visited twelve of the College Library Program libraries. Despite the fact that nearly all of the participants had to make major modifications in their plans at the
end of either the first or second year, the evaluators found
that the effort had provided many benefits.

At a minimum, the team learned that the joint program
focused the attention of the college and university administration on the importance of the library in the total teaching
effort. At the most, the learning process was greatly
strengthened, since the program brought faculty and librarians together (for the first time on some campuses) in
efforts to enlarge the educational perspectives of students
and to improve their investigative skills.

Clearly more students were using the libraries than
had formerly been the case. And the participants were ex-
changing a great deal of information with nearby institutions,
producing the well-known "ripple effect." After measuring
these results against their necessarily flexible yardstick, the
team members were convinced that the program should
continue.

Last spring I conducted a rather unscientific evaluation by telephoning project and library directors. I called all of the College Library Program grantees who had finished the grant period and a selected number of Enhancement Program recipients--a total of twenty-two institutions.

In two cases it appeared that the program had been dropped in its entirely at the end of the grant period. In neither of these cases, I might add, was bibliographic instruction by librarians the focus of the program. In all of the others it was apparent that while most required adjustments, what had been started was continuing to develop, at least in part, often to expand, and that there was still enthusiasm for the activity.

At Cornell, former project director Joan Ormondroyd, an Enhancement Program grantee, credited some of the successful growth of their program to changes in teaching style, a return to the basics of rhetoric, composition, and research papers. "The farther we get from the sixties," she said, "the closer we get to the fifties."[12]

It is impossible to measure quantitatively the effect that these grant programs have had, but it is clear that in many institutions, administrators and faculty are now more aware of the possibilities for productive integration of library and teaching programs.

The ripple effect observed in 1975 has increased, partly due to Project LOEX, the clearinghouse located at Eastern Michigan University (EMU), which grew out of EMU's College Library Program grant and was itself supported for several years by the council.[13]

Several institutions that prepared Enhancement Program proposals but were not funded wrote to say that the mere activity of putting together the document forced them to reevaluate their philosophies, missions, and service goals and encouraged them to find ways of carrying out their plans on their own, at least in part.

The council was not attempting to develop a single model program; one result of our experience that has been quite evident is the need for a variety of approaches on each campus that suit each institution's unique environment and

personality. But many of the funded programs have become
models, frequently cited in the literature and recognized for
their innovative ideas and leadership in the field.

At the same time, a number of them have lacked a pur-
poseful plan of evaluation that would objectively measure
progress. Too often evaluation was not considered until the
final year, when it was too late to gather statistics, to
measure growth in skills, or to conduct more than a per-
functory survey. And despite the council's encouragement,
with some outstanding exceptions (Earlham being one), few
have disseminated their results widely, although many proposals and reports are available through the Educational Resources Information Center (ERIC) System and Project
LOEX.[14]

Lewis and Clark College, a small institution in Portland,
Oregon, provides an example of what a little seed money can
accomplish if it happens to land on particularly fertile soil.
Lewis and Clark received an Enhancement Program grant for
the 1976-77 academic year. Reference librarian Louise Gerity
was released for the year to begin planning a coordinated
program of orientation and instruction. Based on the sound-
ness of her work, and in recognition of the fact that a new
program of this sort needs time to grow, the college on its
own extended the program for an additional two years,
naming Gerity as bibliographic instruction librarian and continuing to give her the freedom to build on her past efforts.
This past summer a college committee was appointed to
evaluate the three-year effort and determine if it should be
continued. The committee endorsed the activities that had
been carried out and supported those planned for the next
two years. The report emphasized the need for close working relationships and coordinated activity between faculty
and library staff. It is clear that, through the grant process, the library was able to garner strong support for its
activities, support that, it is to be hoped, will be continued.

In the telephone interviews I conducted, I asked such
questions as "What were the greatest problems you had in
establishing the program?" and, "If you had to do it all over,
would you do the same thing?" The responses became a
repetitive litany: poor cooperation from faculty; faculty and
administrative turnover; library staff turnover; library

director turnover; lack of adequate planning with faculty
input, etc.

Turnover directly relates to commitment, of course,
and it quickly became clear that the most progressive, well-
organized programs had been blessed with stable staff and
faculty from the beginning. This is one reason, of course,
why the Earlham College program has been so successful.

Lack of support or, perhaps more accurately, indifference on the part of university officials remains a problem
on several campuses. Although in the College Library Program the council required a personal letter of commitment
and pledge of continuance from the college or university
president, with some outstanding exceptions this seems to
have made little difference when the grant period ended
and competition for internal funds increased.

And where libraries were able to maintain new positions funded under the grant, the funds for the position
were more often the result of adjustments or changes of
priorities within the library rather than of an increase in
the budget.

It is my impression from the telephone interviews,
from reading the reports, and from a few site visits, that:

1. In those institutions that, in addition to developing an instructional program, tried such innovative ideas as
bringing faculty into the library or training graduate stu-
dents--ideas that depended on paying some sort of stipend
or honorarium--only the instructional program has survived.
Even the University of Richmond, which had the most
promising program of incorporating grant activity into the
campus' faculty development program, failed in the end to
win approval of the effort as a recognized activity for
tenure purposes.

2. Even the strongest programs will wax and wane
depending on staff energies and faculty turnover. Turnover
is endemic, a problem incapable of solution. It will continue
to affect programs both positively and negatively. One must
simply learn to live with it and work around it.

3. Nevertheless, building faculty relations--getting

out of the library and into campus affairs--is still the key
to building support for the library's instructional program
and other services.

4. Finally, our sights may be too high. Perhaps we
should not try to reach every student on campus but only
those who are most interested or whose needs for research
skills are clear. We should not be afraid to enlist faculty
and, in some cases, turn instruction over to them. We
should be realistic about our capacities and constraints.
Perhaps more attention should be given to instructing the
instructors, i.e., the teaching faculty.

Looking Ahead

The council had enough funds to support only two years of
the Library Service Enhancement Program. Last year NEH
and the council arrived at a mutual decision to discontinue
the College Library Program, and recently the council has
suspended its Fellowship Program, although it still will fund
research projects on an individual basis.

The reasons for these decisions are complex. True,
in both the College Library Program and the Fellowship
Program, fewer and fewer applications were appearing on
the horizon. But perhaps more to the point, most foundations and funding agents--and CLR is no exception--see
themselves as catalysts. It is not possible, with the
limited funding at our disposal, for the council to help
every library that exists or help any one library over an
extended period of time. As a funding agent that in turn
is supported by other foundations, CLR has itself no assurance of immortality. In fact, if programs are not seen
as desirable and worthy of local support, few foundations
will continue funding them just to keep them from dying.

The idea behind CLR's library services program was
to provide to the academic library world examples of things
that could be done to integrate the library more fully into
campus life so that other libraries would be able to learn
and perhaps engage in similar activities.

This has happened and has contributed to the momentum of the last ten years. CLR's library programs, and

bibliographic instruction programs in general, have not
caused a major revolution among the American teaching
faculty. They are not, for the most part, crowding into
the library to enlist the aid of eager librarians. It will
take much longer than ten years for a feeling of general
acceptance of this activity to develop--and even then the
idea may never catch fire in some institutions or in certain
disciplines.

Nevertheless, it is clear that instructional programs
are slowly having a positive impact on the educational process and on the image of academic libraries and librarians.
The council would underscore the fact that it has not lost
interest in the subject of enhancing academic library services and helping libraries improve their abilities to serve
the causes of scholarship and teaching. It is time, however, for a new approach.

It is no secret that libraries have entered into a
world of financial constraint and limited growth. We have
left behind those expansionist years when, to add a new
service, it was a simple matter to ask for and receive newly
budgeted positions. Dyson has found that where instructional programs have flourished, they are an expensive addition to, rather than a replacement for, traditional undergraduate library activities.[15]

Somehow, instructional activities have to become
meshed with other library services; they must cease to be
isolated or added on and instead must be viewed as part
of the total operation, as one of a number of library functions that must be managed wisely.

The Academic Library Program

Earlier discussion focused on the council's feeling that if it
gave its College Library Programs enough time to evolve,
they would become institutionalized. Perhaps given more
time, they will. But perhaps the problem needs to be approached from another perspective, that of management and
institutional planning, in order for instructional services to
attain their rightful place among the library's priorities and
goals. To this end, the council sees library services as one
of the principal components of the Academic Library Program,

a new program announced last year that is cooperatively
funded by CLR, the Andrew W. Mellon Foundation, the Lilly
Endowment, and the Association of Research Libraries (ARL).

The Academic Library Program is operated by the ARL
Office of Management Studies, which has applied a kind of
self-help methodology to library operations in such programs
as the Management Review and Analysis Program, the
Academic Library Development Program, or the Collection
Analysis Project. These programs provide guidance in the
form of manuals, procedures, and personal consultation to
academic libraries to help them examine themselves, analyze
their operations, identify strengths and weaknesses, and
outline areas and methods for change.

A high priority for development is a program that will
emphasize services. Scheduled to be available in spring
1980, the Services Department Program will help academic
libraries examine such services as reference, circulation,
interlibrary loan, reserve book, and bibliographic instruction. It will draw in its design on both the College Library
Program and the Library Service Enhancement Program.

In preliminary discussions on the design of the program, Office of Management Studies director Duane Webster
listed six objectives of the new effort:

1. To provide tools and techniques to enable libraries to determine and analyze use patterns, user needs, and
user satisfaction levels;
2. To provide assistance in relating use of the library to current operating policies and services;
3. To design measures of performance that can be
applied in evaluating the success of current service programs and in planning future improvements;
4. To provide guidelines for a library to use in designing new service activities or remodeling current ones;
5. To suggest improved methods for promoting the
use of library services and enhancing the image of the library on the campus; and
6. To develop and apply principles of effective library service.

All academic libraries in the United States are eligible
for the Academic Library Program. It requires a modest

fiscal commitment of \$4,000-\$7,000 for a library to participate.
Such modest amounts, we hope, can be found among local
sources of support and will result in an enormous pay-off in
providing libraries with a capacity for change.

Conclusion

It is my view from working with CLR's services programs
that service activities must be seen as an integral part of
library operations and must be integrated into the local
library environment. The objectives of this new program
encompass that perspective and also a very important function that has still to be adequately addressed: measures of
performance.

Libraries cannot depend on outside funding for continuing operations but must find ways to provide services
within current budget constraints and priorities. It is
hoped that the Academic Library Program and its services
development module will help with this process.

Most of the previous discussion has emphasized what
librarians are doing to instruct users in response to the
users' documented (through surveys) or perceived needs.
Other than the use of pre- and posttests, little has been
done to really measure how much library instruction is
retained by users and whether it truly contributes to
academic performance.

In their review of research trends in library instruction, Young and Brennan point to the fact that "for nearly
50 years, librarians have attempted to document a positive
correlation between library use and/or proficiency and
academic performance."[16] In those studies that have been
done, they say, statistically significant relationships have
not emerged. Lubans has called for "a long-range program
of evaluation ... that would study groups of students
through four or five years of college and [determine] what
library use instruction or the lack of it means."[17]

Until a way of evaluating learning is found, library-
use educators will have to find their motivation in the comments and reactions of faculty and of students, such as the
undergraduate who, in response to a query of the University

of New Hampshire Enhancement Program director, said that the library instruction program "made me see the library as a tool, rather than as a pain in the neck."

NOTES

1. Harriett Genung, "Can Machines Teach the Use of the Library?" College & Research Libraries 28:25-30 (Jan. 1967).
2. Charles H. Stevens, Marie P. Canfield, and Jeffrey J. Gardner, "Library Pathfinders: A New Possibility for Cooperative Reference Service," College & Research Libraries 34:40-46 (Jan. 1973); Charles H. Stevens and Jeffrey J. Gardner, "Point-of-Use Library Instruction," in John Lubans, Jr., ed., Educating the Library User (New York: Bowker, 1974) p. 269-78.
3. For a list of these and resulting publications see appendix 1.
4. James Riddles, "Final Report to Council on Library Resources," mimeographed (Stockton, Calif., 1971), p. 14.
5. Allan J. Dyson, "Organizing Undergraduate Library Instruction: The English and American Experience," Journal of Academic Librarianship 1:9-13 (March 1975).
6. Johnnie E. Givens, "A Study of Selected Academic Institutions within the Small and Medium Size Range to Determine What Has Been Done or Is Being Planned to Integrate the Library Service Program with the Instructional Program of the Institution," mimeographed (Clarksville, Tenn.: Austin Peay State University, 1974), p. 44.
7. Hannelore B. Rader, "The Humanizing Function of the College Library, or Providing Students with Library Know-How," Catholic Library World 49:278-81 (Feb. 1978).
8. The U.S. Office of Education entered into a contract with Wayne State University in 1960 to conduct at Monteith College a research project concerned with exploring methods of developing a more vital relationship between the library and college teaching. As quoted in Patricia B. Knapp's Monteith College Library Experiment (New York: Scarecrow, 1966), p. 11, the purpose of the project was "to stimulate and guide students in developing sophisticated understanding of the library and increasing competence in its use," by providing students with "experiences which are functionally related to their course work."
9. For a list of institutions that received College

Library Program grants see appendix 2.

    10.   For details of individual programs see the bib-
liography in appendix 4.

    11.   For a list of institutions that received Library
Service Enhancement Program grants see appendix 3.

    12.   At the end of Cornell's Library Service Enhance-
ment Program grant, three professional librarians were assigned to support the program.   In the last academic year,
the group worked with 133 faculty and reached more than
2,800 students.

    13.   Project LOEX (Library Orientation-Instruction
Exchange) was funded from 1975 to 1978, when Eastern
Michigan University assumed full responsibility.   As of
June 30, 1978, more than 360 libraries had become fee-
paying members of the clearinghouse.   Over the years, members have contributed more than 12,000 items to the project's
circulating collection.

    14.   ERIC is a national system that makes available
unpublished, hard-to-find documents on all phases, levels,
and subject areas of education.   Information as to the
availability of reports can be obtained from the ERIC Clearinghouse on Information Resources, School of Education,
Syracuse University, Syracuse, NY 13210.   Project LOEX is
located at Eastern Michigan University, Ypsilanti, MI 48197.

    15.   Allan J. Dyson, "Library Instruction in Universi-
ty Undergraduate Libraries," in John Lubans, Jr., ed.,
Progress in Educating the Library User (New York: Bowker,
1978), p. 101.

    16.   Arthur P. Young and Exir B. Brennan, "Bib-
liographic Instruction: A Review of Research and Application," in John Lubans, Jr. ed., Progress in Educating the
Library User, p. 15.

    17.   John Lubans, Jr., "Report to the Council on Li-
brary Resources on a Fellowship Awarded for 1971-72,"
mimeographed (Boulder, Colo.: University of Colorado
Libraries, 1972), p. 6.

Appendix 1
                    CLR Fellowship Reports

The reports listed below are not available from the Council
on Library Resources.   They are the property of the individual Fellows.   Where articles or books resulting from the
research have been published, they are also listed.

Dale, Doris Cruger. "Current Trends in Community College Libraries." Paper read at Illinois Association of College and Research Libraries, 9 April 1976, at William Rainey Harper College, Mimeographed.

_____. "The Community College Library in the Mid-1970s," College & Research Libraries 38:404-10 (Sept. 1977).

_____. "A Question of Concern: How to Inform Community College Students about Library Services." Paper read at eleventh Annual Community College Learning Resources Conference, 20 April 1976, at Belleville Area College, Belleville, Illinois. Mimeographed.

_____. "Questions of Concern: Library Services to Community College Students," Journal of Academic Librarianship 3:81-84 (May 1977).

Dyson, Allan J. "Organizing Undergraduate Library Instruction: The English and American Experience." Mimeographed. Berkeley, Calif.: University of California, 1974. (Available as ERIC document ED 152 309.)

_____. "Organizing Undergraduate Library Instruction: The English and American Experience," Journal of Academic Librarianship 1:9-13 (March 1975).

Givens, Johnnie E. "A Study of Selected Academic Instructions within the Small and Medium Size Range to Determine What Has Been Done or Is Being Planned to Integrate the Library Service Program with the Instructional Program of the Institution." Mimeographed. Clarksville, Tenn.: Austin Peay State University, 1974.

Fretwell, Gordon. "Programs of User Support That a Typical Group of Fifteen U.S. Colleges and Universities Provides Graduate Students in the Social Sciences and Humanities through Libraries and Library-related Services." Mimeographed. Amherst, Mass.: University of Massachusetts Library, 1973.

Lubans, John, Jr. "Report to the Council on Library Resources on a Fellowship Awarded for 1971-72." (To study patterns of academic library use and nonuse and the effect library orientation and library use presentations could have.) Mimeographed. Boulder, Colo.: University of Colorado Libraries, 1972. (Available as ERIC document ED 093 311.)

_____, ed. Educating the Library User. New York: Bowker, 1974.

_____. "Evaluating Library User Education Programs," Drexel Library Quarterly 9:325-43 (July 1972).

Milby, T. H. "A Study of Instructional Programs in the Use of Biological Literature at Selected U.S. Universities." Mimeographed. Norman, Okla.: University of Oklahoma, 1972.

_____. "Teaching Biological Literature," BioScience 23:663-65 (Nov. 1973).

Nelson, Jerold. "A Search for Power: Librarian/Faculty Communication in Academe." Mimeographed. Mercer Island, Wash., 1977.

Rader, Hannelore B. "An Assessment of Ten Academic Library Instruction Programs in the United States and Canada." Mimeographed. Ypsilanti, Mich.: Eastern Michigan University, 1976. (Available as ERIC document ED 171 276.)

_____. "The Humanizing Function of the College Library; or, Providing Students with Library Know-How," Catholic Library World 49:278-81 (Feb. 1978).

Riddles, James. "Final Report to the Council on Library Resources." (To investigate administrative techniques that have been successful on the medium-size college campus in redirecting teaching objectives and techniques to utilize more fully the resources and services of the library.) Mimeographed. Stockton, Calif., 1971.

Roberts, Anne. "A Study of Ten SUNY Campuses Offering an Undergraduate Credit Course in Library Instruction." Mimeographed. Albany, N.Y.: SUNY Albany, 1978. (Available as ERIC document ED 157 529.)

Rottsolk, Katherine. "Council on Library Resources Fellowship Final Report." (To examine orientation and instruction programs at several colleges for the purpose of designing a comprehensive program for students at St. Olaf College.) Mimeographed. Northfield, Minn.: St. Olaf College, 1977.

Schwass, Earl R. "Library Orientation and Instruction in Military Graduate Professional Schools." Mimeographed. Newport, R.I.: Naval War College, 1976.

Smith, Eldred R. "The Specialist Librarian in the Academic Research Library." Mimeographed. Berkeley, Calif.: University of California, 1971.

Appendix 2
            CLR-NEH College Library Programs
            (July 31, 1979)

Institution (State) and Termination Date of Project

Ball State University (Ind.): August 31, 1980
Brown University (R.I.): June 30, 1975
Clark College (Ga.): June 30, 1980
Colorado, University of: August 31, 1978
Davidson College (N.C.): January 31, 1978
DePauw University (Ind.): August 31, 1982
Dillard University (La.): June 30, 1975
Eastern Michigan University: September 1, 1975
Evansville, University of (Ind.): June 30, 1982
Franklin and Marshall College (Pa.): December 31, 1982
Hampden-Sydney College (Va.): August 31, 1978
Hampshire College (Mass.): September 1, 1975
Howard University (D.C.): August 31, 1976
Jackson State University (Miss.): December 29, 1978
Jamestown College (N. Dak.): August 31, 1978
Johnson C. Smith University (N.C.): December 31, 1981
Kearney State College (Nebr.): July 1, 1980
Kentucky, University of: July 1, 1979
Lake Forest College (Ill.): December 31, 1983
Manhattanville College (N.Y.): October 31, 1978
Miles College (Ala.): August 31, 1978
Mills College (Calif.): July 31, 1979
North Carolina Central University: January 31, 1977
Northwestern University (Ill.): June 30, 1982
Occidental College (Calif.): December 31, 1978
Pacific University (Oreg.): July 1, 1980
Richmond, University of (Va.): July 31, 1978
St. Olaf College (Minn.): June 30, 1982
Salem College (Mass.): June 30, 1981
Swarthmore College (Pa.): August 31, 1977
Toledo University of (Ohio): September 30, 1980
Tusculum College (Tenn.): June 30, 1982
Utah, University of: June 30, 1980
Wabash College (Ind.) (CLR funding only): December 31,
      1976
Washington & Lee University (Va.): June 30, 1976
Wisconsin-Parkside, University of: December 31, 1980

Appendix 3
       CLR Library Service Enhancement Programs

1976-1977

Cornell University (N.Y.)
DePauw University (Ind.)
Earlham College (Ind.)
Lawrence University (Wis.)
Lewis and Clark College (Oreg.)
University of New Hampshire
North Carolina Agricultural and Technical University
Oregon State University
Presbyterian College (S.C.)
University of South Carolina
State University College at Potsdam (N.Y.)
West Georgia College

1977-1978

Beloit College (Wis.)
Colorado College
Georgia Southern College
Georgia State University
Glenville State College (W. Va.)
Guilford College (N.C.)
Hampton Institute (Va.)
Joint University Libraries (Tenn.)
Lake Forest College (Ill.)
Tusculum College (Tenn.)
University of Colorado at Colorado Springs
University of Missouri at Kansas City
Wayne State University (Mich.)

Appendix 4
       Publications about CLR-Supported Programs
    Involving Academic Libraries and Their Users, 1970-79

General

       Association of Research Libraries. Office of Manage-
ment Studies. "Library Use Instruction in Academic and
Research Libraries," ARL Management Supplement, vol. 5,
no. 1. Washington, D.C., 1977.

Gwinn, Nancy E. "The Faculty-Library Connection,"
Change 10:19-21 (Sept. 1978).
CLR Annual Reports, starting with the 14th . Washing-
ton, D.C.: Council on Library Resources, 1970-   .
Marshall, A. P. "This Teaching/Learning Thing:
Librarians as Educators," in Herbert Poole, ed., Academic
Libraries by the Year 2000; Essays Honoring Jerold Orne,
p. 50-63. New York: Bowker, 1977.

College Library Program*

Andrew, Ann, and Rader, Hannelore B. "Library
Orientation Is Reaching Out to People," in Sul Lee, ed.,
Library Orientation; Papers Presented at the First Annual
Conference on Library Orientation Held at Eastern Michigan
University, May 7, 1971, p. 36-45. Ann Arbor, Mich.:
Pierian Pr., 1972. (Eastern Michigan University).
Bodner, Deborah. "CLR-NEH Library Programs,"
North Carolina Libraries 36:3-10 (Summer 1978).
Brittain, Michael, and Irving, Ann. "The Work of
the Council on Library Resources (CLR)," in Trends in the
Education of Users of Libraries and Information Services in
the USA, p. 6-10. Loughborough, England: Loughborough
University, 1976.
Brown, Barbara. "The Consciousness IV Library Pro-
gram at Howard University," in Hannelore B. Rader, ed.,
Academic Library Instruction; Objectives, Programs, and
Faculty Involvement, p. 23-25. Ann Arbor, Mich.: Pierian
Pr. 1975.
"Clark, Kearney State Colleges, Pacific University, U.
of Utah Receive Grants," CLR Recent Developments 3:3
(July 1975).
"Course-related Library Instruction Program: A Three-
Way Involvement of Librarians, Faculty and Students,"
Featuring Faculty at Ball State University 2:1-2 (Oct. 1978).
Dusenbury, Carolyn. "University of Utah Receives
CLR/NEH Grant for Humanistic Approach to Library Orienta-
tion," MPLA Newsletter 20:12 (1975-76).
Edwards, Susan E. "Faculty Involvement in the Uni-
versity of Colorado Program," in Hannelore B. Rader, ed.,

*The College Library Program is jointly supported with
the National Endowment for the Humanities.

Faculty Involvement in Library Instruction, p. 7-22. Ann
Arbor, Mich.: Pierian Pr., 1976.
_____. "Library Use Studies and the University
of Colorado," in Hannelore B. Rader, ed., Library Instruction in the Seventies, p. 105-7. Ann Arbor, Mich.: Pierian
Pr., 1977.
    Evrard, Connie F.; Schumann, Elizabeth S.; and Swift,
Janet M. "Graduate Reference Assistants at Brown University," in John Lubans, Jr., ed., Educating the Library
User, p. 368-75. New York: Bowker, 1974.
    _____, and Waddington, Charles C. "The Under-
graduate Survey: Its Role in Changing Patterns of Reference Use," Drexel Library Quarterly, 7:351-56 (July & Oct.
1971). (Brown University)
    "Final CLP Grants Go to Lake Forest, Tusculum,
Franklin and Marshall," CLR Recent Developments 6:3 (Nov.
1978).
    "Four Win College Library Program Grants." CLR Re-
cent Developments 5:3 (Dec. 1977). (Ball State University,
DePauw University, University of Toledo, University of
Wisconsin-Parkside)
    Henning, Patricia A. "Council on Library Resources
Activities," Drexel Library Quarterly 7:343-45 (July & Oct.
1971).
    "Jamestown, University of Colorado Get CLR-NEH Joint
College Library Grants," CLR Recent Developments 1:3 (May
1973).
    LaBue, Ben. "Evaluating Faculty Involvement in Libra-
ry Instruction," in Hannelore B. Rader, ed., Library Instruction in the Seventies, p. 109-11. Ann Arbor, Mich.:
Pierian Pr., 1977. (University of Colorado)
    Marshall, A. P. "Library Outreach: The Program
at Eastern Michigan University," Drexel Library Quarterly
7:347-50 (July & Oct. 1971).
    Millis, Charlotte Hickman. "Developing Awareness: A
Behavioral Approach," in John Lubans, Jr., ed., Educating
the Library User, p. 350-63. New York: Bowker, 1974.
(Wabash College)
    _____. "Involving Students in Library Orientation
Projects; A Commitment To Help," in Sul Lee, ed., A Challenge for Academic Libraries: How to Motivate Students to
Use the Library, p. 63-85. Ann Arbor, Mich.: Pierian Pr.,
1973.
    _____. "The Wabash Project: A Centrifugal Pro-
gram," Drexel Library Quarterly 7:365-74 (July & Oct. 1971).

_____, and Thompson, Donald E. "Wabash College Library Project," Library Occurrent 23:311-16 (Feb. 1971).

"Mills College, University of Kentucky Receive CLR-NEH Grants; LOEX Funded," CLR Recent Developments 2:3 (Dec. 1974).

"Occidental and Manhattanville Colleges Receive Grants under CLR-NEH Program," CLR Recent Developments 2:4 (Jan. 1974).

Rader, Hannelore B. "EMU's Library Instruction Experiences in the 70's," in her Library Instruction in the Seventies, p. 85-98. Ann Arbor, Mich.: Pierian Pr., 1977.

Taylor, Robert S. "Orienting the Library to the User at Hampshire College," Drexel Library Quarterly 7:357-64 (July & Oct. 1971).

"Three-Year-Old, NEH-Assisted Program Is Broadening Library Role on 16 Campuses," CLR Recent Developments 1:1-2 (July 1973).

Tucker, John Mark. "An Experiment in Bibliographic Instruction at Wabash College," College & Research Libraries 38:203-9 (May 1977).

"University of Evansville, Northwestern, St. Olaf Receive College Library Program Awards," CLR Recent Developments 5:1 (July 1977).

Library Service Enhancement Program

Collins, John W., and Gillespie, David M. "Library Services in Colleges," in "Bibliograhic Instruction; West Virginia Library Association Working Conference of the College and University Section, Bethany College, April 21, 1977," compiled by Barbara Mertins, p. 4-11. Mimeographed. (Available as ERIC document ED 144 582) (Glenville State College)

Farber, Evan I. "Bibliographic Instruction and Library Organization: Problems and Prospects," in Sul H. Lee, ed., Emerging Trends in Library Organization: What Influences Change, p. 49-59. Ann Arbor, Mich.: Pierian Pr., 1978.

_____. "Library-Faculty Communications Techniques," in Cerise Oberman-Soroka, ed., Proceedings from Southeastern Conference on Approaches to Bibliographic Instruction, p. 71-80. Charleston, S.C., 1978.

Frick, Elizabeth. "Some of My Best Friends are Faculty," Colorado Libraries 4:7-9 (June 1978).

Hardesty, Larry; Lovrich, Nicholas P., Jr.; and Mannon, James. "Evaluating Library-Use Instruction," College & Research Libraries 40:309-17 (July 1979). (DePauw University)

Kirkendall, Carolyn, ed. "Library Instruciton; A Column of Opinion," Journal of Academic Librarianship 3:344-45 (Jan. 1978). Question posed: In your opinion, what will be the permanent effects of the past year's Library Service Enhancement Program (LSEP) activity on your library's instruction program?

"Library Service Enhancement Program Leaders Work to Improve Library Services," CLR Recent Developments 6:3-4 (April 1978).

Werking, Richard Hume. "Library Service Enhancement," Wisconsin Library Bulletin 73:279 (Nov.-Dec. 1977). (Lawrence University)

Project LOEX

Bolner, Mary. "Project LOEX: The First Year," in her Planning and Developing a Library Orientation Program, p. 53-59. Ann Arbor, Mich.: Pierian Pr., 1975.

Butterfield, Mary Bolner. "Project LOEX and Continuing Education," Michigan Libraries 41:11-12 (Fall 1974).

_____. "Project LOEX Means Library Orientation Exchange," RQ 12:39-42 (Fall 1973).

Kirkendall, Carolyn. "Project LOEX--The Third Year," in Hannelore B. Rader, ed., Faculty Involvement in Library Instruction, p. 41-42. Ann Arbor, Mich.: Pierian Pr., 1976.

_____. "The Status of Project LOEX," in Hannelore B. Rader, ed., Library Instruction in the Seventies, p. 25-30. Ann Arbor, Pierian Pr., 1977.

Project INTREX--Model Library Project

Canfield, Marie P. "Library Pathfinders," Drexel Library Quarterly 8:287-300 (July 1972).

Gardner, Jeffrey J. "Point-of-Use Library Instruction," Drexel Library Quarterly 8:281-85 (July 1972).

Stevens, Charles H.; Canfield, Marie P.; and Gardner, Jeffrey J. "Library Pathfinders: A New Possibility for Cooperative Reference Service," College & Research Libraries 34: 40-46 (Jan. 1973).

_____, and Gardner, Jeffrey J. "Point-of-Use Library Instruction," in John Lubans, Jr., ed., Educating the Library User, p. 269-78. New York: Bowker, 1974.

Yagello, Virginia E. "Model Library Program of Project Intrex," American Journal of Pharmaceutical Education 36: 752-57 (Dec. 1972).

Larry L. Hardesty is Director of Library Services at Eckerd
College in St. Petersburg, Florida. He has a Ph.D.
in library and information science from Indiana University, an M.L.S. from the University of Wisconsin, and
additional graduate degrees in history and instructional
development. He directed two library use instruction
projects funded by the Council on Library Resources
and served as a consultant for the Association of Research Libraries, Office of Management Studies. His
publications include Use of Slide/Tape Presentations in
Academic Libraries (Jeffrey Norton, 1978) and papers
in College and Research Libraries, Drexel Library Quarterly, The Journal of Academic Librarianship, Library
Research: An International Journal, and Library
Scene.

John P. Schmitt is Head of Reference Services at the College
of Charleston in Charleston, South Carolina. He has a
B.A. and an M.L.S. from the University of Wisconsin.
From 1979 to 1984 he served in the Purdue University
Libraries, most recently as Undergraduate Reference
Librarian in which capacity he established reference
and bibliographic instruction programs in the newly
constructed Undergraduate Library. He has published
papers on collection development and library use in
College and Research Libraries and he reviews books
in literature and bibliography for American Reference
Books Annual.

John Mark Tucker is Senior Reference Librarian in the Humanities, Social Science, and Education Library at
Purdue University. He has a Ph.D. in library and
information science from the University of Illinois and
M.L.S. and Ed.S degrees from George Peabody College

for Teachers. From 1973 to 1976 he worked with the Wabash College Library Project funded by the Council on Library Resources. He has published papers in College and Research Libraries, Journal of Education for Librarianship, Journal of Library History, and Library Trends and was co-editor of Reference Services and Library Education: Essays in Honor of Frances Neel Cheney (Lexington Books, 1983).